Volpone's Bastards

Theorising Jonson's City Comedy

Isaac Hui

EDINBURGH
University Press

Edinburgh University Press is one of the leading university presses
in the UK. We publish academic books and journals in our selected
subject areas across the humanities and social sciences, combining
cutting-edge scholarship with high editorial and production values
to produce academic works of lasting importance. For more
information visit our website: edinburghuniversitypress.com

Edinburgh University Press Ltd
The Tun – Holyrood Road
12(2f) Jackson's Entry
Edinburgh EH8 8PJ

Typeset in Sabon and Futura by
Servis Filmsetting Ltd, Stockport, Cheshire,
and printed and bound in Great Britain.

A CIP record for this book is available from the British Library

ISBN 978 1 4744 2347 2 (hardback)
ISBN 978 1 4744 2348 9 (webready PDF)
ISBN 978 1 4744 2349 6 (epub)

Contents

Acknowledgements

An earlier version of Chapter 2 and portions of Chapter 3 were published in *Comedy Studies* as 'On Comedy and Death: The Anamorphic Ape in *Volpone*' (5:2 (2014), pp. 137–47) and 'The Dis-orienting Orients – A Lacanian Reading of Philip Massinger's Tragicomedy *The Renegado*' (8:1 (2017), pp. 22–35). A small section of Chapter 4 appeared in 'Re-negotiating Domesticating and Foreignizing: Bridging *The Symposium* and *Niezi* through the Imagery of Emptiness' in *Asia Pacific Translation and Intercultural Studies* (3:1 (2016), pp. 33–46). A version of Chapter 5 was published as 'The Comedy of the "Para-site": *Duck Soup*, *Volpone*, and *Hamlet*' in *The Comparatist* (40 (2016), pp. 170–89). I am grateful to the publishers for their permission to reproduce these materials. My thanks to the editors for their interest in my work and to the readers for their comments.

Parts of this research have benefited from the financial support of the Research Committee of Lingnan University, to which I am grateful. The funding gave me an opportunity to conduct research trips to the British Library, during which I was able to watch many live theatre performances of Jonson and Shakespeare, including *Volpone* and *The Alchemist* at Stratford-upon-Avon. I want to thank my teachers and friends at the University of Hong Kong; my colleagues at Lingnan University: they give me a wonderful platform to develop this project; and the students, especially those who sat through my classes on Jonson, Shakespeare, the Marx Brothers, and Lacan, Žižek and Zupančič.

I am grateful to Edinburgh University Press, especially Michelle Houston, Adela Rauchova, James Dale and Ersev Ersoy, for their interest in this project and assistance. Many people have offered me their support and advice throughout the course of writing this book and my career; among them I want to specifically acknowledge Alfie Bown, Andrew Cutrofello, Richard Dutton, Roger Holdsworth, Zoe Ross, James Smith, Joel Swann and Eliza Wright. Finally, this book would not have appeared were it not for Jeremy Tambling, who introduced me to Jonson when he learned about my interest in comedy. For many of his students in Hong Kong, who are far away from the Anglo-American academic world, he provides us with a role model for how a scholar should and would conduct himself. Without his teaching and encouragement, I would never have imagined myself becoming a fan of Jonson, let alone writing a book on him.

For my wife, Jennifer

Chapter 1

Introduction: Jonson and Comedy

NANO   Now room for fresh gamesters, who do will you to know
        They do bring you neither play nor university show;
     And therefore do entreat you that whatsoever they rehearse
        May not fare a whit the worse for the false pace of the verse.
     If you wonder at this, you will wonder more ere we pass [...]
                                 (*Volpone* I.ii.1–5)[1]

Not only is *Volpone* (1606) Ben Jonson's most well-known work, it also, according to some critics, marks the turning point of his career. The play is about how Volpone, the Venetian *Magnifico*, tricks the old fortune-hunters Voltore (the vulture), Corbaccio (the raven) and Corvino (the crow) into believing that they will get his inheritance when he dies. With the help of Mosca (the fly, the parasite), Volpone pretends to be sick and lies in a huge bed onstage, weaving one plot with another, making 'so rare a music out of discords' (V.ii.18). This makes the old Corbaccio think that he can outlive Volpone, so that he disinherits his son Bonario; while Corvino, who gets jealous because his wife Celia throws down a handkerchief to the mountebank (who is actually Volpone), makes himself a virtual cuckold. However, since the fox 'glories more in the cunning purchase of wealth than in the glad possession' (I.i.30–2), he does not know when to stop and is sold out by the fly and has to expose everything in the end, preferring to ruin their scheme rather than allow the latter to outwit him. The play has been widely discussed and studied, and often performed, and remains Jonson's most popular piece, but it still poses many problems.[2] I want to concentrate on one, which has not been successfully solved, and has usually been ignored.

I refer to the interlude in Act I scene ii acted by what Mosca calls Volpone's bastard children, namely, Nano the dwarf, Androgyno the hermaphrodite and Castrone the eunuch. Why these characters? The incident is usually brushed aside by critics who claim it to be comparatively insignificant.[3] These arguments and this treatment of the interlude, for me, seem to be too easy, as if Jonson, who is famous for being knowledgeable and an 'author', would devote a scene to a minor extravaganza.[4] Indeed, the scene is really puzzling. For instance, what are the implications of being a 'gamester' in Jonson's comedies? What can be read from the metempsychosis of Apollo, Aethalides, Euphorbus, Hermotimus, Pyrrhus of Delos, Pythagoras, Aspasia, Crates the Cynic, the kings, knights, beggars, knaves, lords, fools, ox, ass, camel, mule, goat, and brock (I.ii.6–24)? And why does the interlude end with the song praising 'Fools' as 'the only nation / Worth men's envy or admiration' (I.ii.66–7)? How are these questions relevant to our understanding of *Volpone* and other Jonsonian comedies? This book argues for the significance of the interlude and the three bastards, answering these questions, and more.

This book has another purpose: to read Jonson through the theory of comedy. T. S. Eliot writes:

> Of all the dramatists of his time, Jonson is probably the one whom the present age would find the most sympathetic, if it knew him. There is a brutality, a lack of sentiment, a polished surface, a handling of large gold designs in brilliant colours, which ought to attract about three thousand people in London and elsewhere.[5]

Eliot's comment on Jonson is still as relevant as ever. In the 2015 production of *Volpone* by the Royal Shakespeare Company at Stratford-upon-Avon, the play's background is moved from seventeenth-century Venice to the current world, which is struggling with the aftermath of the financial tsunami of 2008. Eliot's words and the RSC production both suggest a point: *Volpone* is still a play that resonates with us, the twenty-first-century readers and audiences. They raise another question: can we understand the play and its comedy from a twentieth- and twenty-first-century perspective? For example, can we interpret the play on the basis of the more recent theories of comedy, or critical and cultural theory, so that it would be even more relevant to current audiences and readers? Drawing on references to many contextual materials of Jonson and *Volpone*, this book gives the dramatist a more contemporary reading by discussing Jonson's texts with many critical and comedy theories, and some examples of modern film comedies. I want to understand Jonson, first and foremost, as a comedy writer, and to discuss how his work is still instrumental to our understanding of the current world and comedy.

My aim, in essence, is to demonstrate how the interlude matters through arguing for the importance of the bastards, and this helps us to read Jonson's comedies differently. Through the use of modern theories of comedy, such as those of Freud and Alenka Zupančič, I want to show how *Volpone* and other Jonsonian and early modern city comedies comment on the nascent early modern capitalism through concepts such as death, castration and nothingness. Each of Jonson's bastards provides us with an angle to interpret his comedy. However, they also signify the construction and the powerful presence of the city subjects, as they embody a multiplication of identities that is linked with the transformative power of gold, performance and signifiers. Reading these bastards together, we can say that Jonson's city comedy is built upon a series of comic misrecognitions. These bastards are significant because of their slippages of identity and their refusal to be categorised. The dwarf is the Vice, the hunchback, the ape and the zany; the androgyne is simultaneously the fool, the hermaphrodite and the epicene, who is related to the eunuch. Nano, Androgyno and Castrone are interrelated, while Mosca, the parasite, does not differ much from them. In other words, while the early modern city comedies relate to the 'bastardised' nature of a city subject, they celebrate new forms of identities emerging in the city. Responding to disability studies, this book agrees that 'one of the tasks for a developing consciousness of disability issues is the attempt . . . to reverse the hegemony of the normal and to institute alternative ways of thinking about the abnormal'.[6] Studying Jonson's comedies through the bastards allows us to see that while his comedies laugh at the city and its subject, there is something slipping away from the control of the author, the text and the audience. This book reverses the concept of proper and improper: while the seemingly 'normal' subjects are indeed 'deformed', the recognition and the acknowledgement of the 'deformity' within us represent an affirmation of life and comedy. Jonson's city comedy relates to the anxiety of being 'improper', or the ambiguity between proper and improper. If money de-legitimates, corrupts, destroys paternity, and paternity destroys the future, comedy is a matter of begetting an improper issue. Jokes can be seen as the affirmation of the improper, because they lift the barrier on repressed or censored material, as Freud argued in *Jokes and Their Relation to the Unconscious*. For Freud, the purpose of jokes is either to be hostile, which serves 'the purpose of aggressiveness, satire, or defence'; or to be obscene, which serves 'the purpose of exposure'.[7] Much in the interlude contains double entendres, of which a good example is Nano ending with the 'cobbler's cock'. While this is a reference to Lucian, as suggested by Dutton, there is a sexual connotation in the word 'cock', raising the question of whether the origin of the transmigration is related to the phallus, yet at the same time ridiculing it.[8]

Bastardy

CORVINO   Has he children?
MOSCA   Bastards,
Some dozen, or more, that he begot on beggars,
Gypsies, and Jews, and blackmoors, when he was drunk.
Knew you not that, sir? 'Tis the common fable.
The dwarf, the fool, the eunuch are all his;
He's the true father of his family
In all save me; but he has giv'n 'em nothing.

(I.v.43–9)

First of all, before discussing the representations of the dwarf, the androgyne and the eunuch, I want to underline the point that all the characters in the interlude are called bastards. Mosca's response to Corvino links the three of them with beggars, gypsies, Jews and black-moors, showing that the first important characteristic of Volpone's bas-tards is their heterogeneity. Reading the play in parallel with *King Lear* (1605), the three bastards can be seen as three brothers. However, we should question the parasite's position, because the meaning of the line 'He's the true father of his family / in all save me' is ambiguous as it is not clear whether the word 'save' really implies that Mosca is outside the family, or part of it.[9] Presenting himself as an outsider, Mosca sounds like another Vice figure, Richard III, who tells Buckingham to 'infer the bastardy of Edward's children' (*King Richard III* (1592–3) III.v.73).[10] Using Volpone's bastards as an example, Michael Neill suggests that 'being unholy, the bastard can never be "whole"', and he links them with the deformed.[11] Following John Danby's argu-ment, he associates bastardy with being an outsider.[12] If Mosca says Volpone does not give them anything, is he hinting to Corvino that he, Mosca, will get all the inheritance because he is Volpone's son? Or, does the line foretell that he is going to get the inheritance because, compared with them, he is the *real* bastard? Indeed, the possibility of seeing Mosca as one of Volpone's bastards should not be undermined. His suggestion that 'I fear I shall begin to grow in love with my dear self and my most prosp'rous parts' (III.i.1–2) reminds us of Edmund's words in *King Lear*, in which he says, 'I grow; I prosper. / Now, gods, stand up for bastards!' (I.ii.21–2). Edmund's question, 'Why brand they us / With base? With baseness? Bastardy? Base, base?' (I.ii.9–10) allows readers to link bastardy with baseness. Baseness is the image that Hamlet abhors when he says, 'To what base uses we may return, Horatio!' (V.i.187). While bastards represent the power of baseness, the prince is traumatised by it.[13] The difference indicates the distinction between comedy and tragedy, a subject which I will return to in Chapter 5.

Volpone shows how bastardy originates from the desire of wanting to be 'proper', but which turns the subject into being 'improper'. Gulling Corbaccio into thinking he is Volpone's sole heir, Mosca tells him to disinherit Bonario:

> And, last, produce your will – where, without thought
> Or least regard unto your proper issue,
> A son so brave and highly meriting,
> The stream of your diverted love hath thrown you
> Upon my master, and made him your heir.
>
> (I.iv.102–6)

To disinherit a son is to show no regard to the proper issue, which links bastardy with the concept of property and city comedy.[14] In *Volpone*, while Corbaccio wants Volpone's inheritance, he turns his son into a bastard, making both of them 'improper'. Bastardy associates with the idea of (un)naturalness. Bonario says that Corbaccio becomes unnatural by disinheriting him: 'it is impossible. / I know not how to lend it any thought, / My father should be so unnatural' (III.ii.52–4). His words uncover his anxiety since they imply that he will become unnatural as he will be turned into a bastard. In response, Mosca tells Bonario, 'It is a confidence that well becomes / Your piety, and formed (no doubt) it is / From your own simple innocence, which makes / Your wrong more monstrous and abhorred' (III.ii.55–8). He insults Bonario through the word 'simple' and through making him monstrous. He further suggests that Bonario wants to kill his father. The result of this is for Corbaccio to proclaim Bonario as 'The mere portent of nature. / He is an utter stranger to my loins' (IV.v.108–9), and the old man turns himself into a cuckold.

Comparing Jonson with Shakespeare, we can see another example of bastardy and comedy in *The Merchant of Venice* (1596–7), in which Lancelot Gobbo, whose name means 'the hunchback' in Italian, 'tries confusion' with Old Gobbo, who is the 'true-begotten father' and yet 'more than sand-blind – high-gravel-blind' (II.ii.28–30).[15] Lancelot is the servant of two masters, first Shylock and later Bassanio. When disclosing he is Gobbo's son, he says:

> LANCELOT   Do you not know me, father?
> GOBBO   Alack, sir, I am sand-blind, I know you not.
> LANCELOT   Nay, indeed, if you had your eyes you might fail of
> the knowing me. It is a wise father that knows his own child.
>
> (II.ii.63–6)

Comedy builds on the fear of bastardy, and the paternity of Lancelot is questioned. He risks becoming a bastard, since Old Gobbo fails to recognise him. However, it would not make any difference even if Gobbo had his eyes, because it takes a wise father to know his own child, and, perhaps, the threat of being turned into a bastard is within all of us. This scene is a parody of the Genesis story when Jacob pretends to be his brother Esau to get the blessing from his blind father Isaac.[16] Lancelot's words recall what Telemachus says in *The Odyssey*. When Pallas Athena asks him whether he is Odysseus's son, he replies, 'My mother says that I am his child; but I do not know this, for never yet did any man know his parentage of his own knowledge', which indicates the impossibility of proving paternity.[17] As Philip the bastard says to King John (in response to the latter's words 'You came not of one mother then, it seems'), 'Most certain of one mother, mighty King – / That is well known – and, as I think, one father. / But for the certain knowledge of that truth / I put you o'er to heaven, and to my mother. / Of that I doubt as all men's children may' (*King John* I.i.58–63).

In *Much Ado about Nothing* (1598), also a play about vision and deception, Don John, the bastard, tricks Claudio into believing that Hero is unfaithful to him before she marries him. His plot to prevent Hero and Claudio marrying is revealed as his followers Borachio and Conrad discuss how the latter is 'planted, placed, and possessed' (III.iii.130–1), without realising the watchman is overhearing their conversation:

> BORACHIO   That shows thou art unconfirmed. Thou knowest
>   that the fashion of a doublet, or a hat, or a cloak is nothing to
>   a man.
> CONRAD   Yes, it is apparel.
> BORACHIO   I mean the fashion.
> CONRAD   Yes, the fashion is the fashion.
> BORACHIO   Tush, I may as well say the fool's the fool, but seest
>   thou not what a deformed thief this fashion is?
> A WATCHMAN   [*aside*] I know that Deformed. A has been a vile
>   thief this seven year. A goes up and down like a gentleman. I
>   remember his name.
>
> (III.iii.102–12)

Alison Findlay argues that Don John exposes 'an implicit, perhaps even unconscious, antagonism to marriage in Don Pedro and Claudio', demonstrating 'a lack of faith in female fidelity amongst the male characters'; he 'represents a withdrawal of consent from these social structures and thus de-legitimises them', only to be used as a scapegoat in the end.[18] While Shakespeare's plays portray homosociality with re-codification of marriage, Jonson cuts out the pretence altogether, as in examples such as *Epicoene* (1609). It would be interesting to question if there is a little bit of Don John within Jonson, which means that the unsettling force of bastardy is always within his plays. Adding to this, the conversation between Borachio and Conrad exhibits a relation between bastardy, deformity and fashioning. Fashion as a deformed thief means that, first of all, fashioning is a kind of deformity. Clerimont, in *Epicoene*, links fashioning with a 'de-formed' beauty, saying, 'A pox of her autumnal face, her pieced beauty!' (I.i.67). The conversation shows the fashioning power of the 'deformed', and the de-forming power of fashioning. Moreover, the 'deformed' could uncover the point that we all depend on fashioning, as bastardising and deforming. Conrad asks Borachio, 'but art not thou thyself giddy with the fashion, too, that thou hast shifted out of thy tale into telling me of the fashion?' (III.iii.123–5). The person who talks about fashioning as a deformed thief should not think that he can exclude himself from it. More importantly, their conversation is interrupted and displaced by the watchman, who suggests that deep inside the play, there is a thief called Deformed, who is Don John the bastard who manipulates fashioning.

While Don John is a bastard, Volpone has his deformed bastards, which implies his heterogeneity. These examples suggest that the anxiety of being turned into a bastard lies within the comedies of Shakespeare and Jonson. However, what does being a bastard mean in Jonson apart from the issues of paternity, deception and cuckoldry? As suggested above, bastardy in *Volpone* is associated with the issue of property and what is proper, which allows us to link the theme with the context of the city. The dwarf, the androgyne, the eunuch and the parasite can be read as a troupe of bastards, each carrying his own significations and implications, referring to and commenting on each other simultaneously. These bastards represent an unsettling force that is at the same time liberating. In the context of the city, no subjectivity is stable, which may be troubling for some but liberating for others. As an 'issue' of the 'improper', they may be a product of the city, which suggests how they are essentially different from other similar figures in Shakespeare.[19]

The Interlude

Before discussing the representations of these Jonsonian bastards, I want to give a preliminary reading of the interlude in Act I scene ii, suggesting how the scene indicates to us that we can read it and the play from a more theoretical and critical perspective. Even though the interlude is sometimes cut from production, it would be wrong to say that it has never captured critics' attention.[20] These readings mainly have two characteristics. The first is that most of them read it from a moral perspective; and the second is that they read Jonson from the perspective of Shakespeare. For instance, John W. Creaser writes that the presence of the dwarf, the androgyne and the eunuch is not essential to the play. They are the 'appalling caricatures of a family'; their function is 'to make perversion visible'.[21] The interlude

> takes a series of ambiguous, complex, or controversial figures such as Pythagoras and treats them all as straightforwardly stupid or corrupt, and it carefully blends Jonsonian satire (as in the lines on lawyers and Puritans) with corrosive cynicism, so that words like 'beautiful', 'divine', and 'Reformation' are contaminated by their context.[22]

Creaser argues:

> But characteristically, even the fool is desecrated. There is nothing 'numinous' about Nano, Androgyno and Castrone, nor do they share anything with the king's railing truth-teller, 'scoffing his state, and grinning at his pomp' . . . Volpone's delight in the doggerel verse of the interlude parallels a modern taste for *Kitsch* – it flatters the sophisticate's feeling of superiority . . . Enacted by mundane and self-possessed grotesques, and complacently enjoyed by Volpone, the interlude – like caricature – gives visible form to the narcissism and perversion of humanity which make the atmosphere of this buoyant and resilient play so unsettling.[23]

Creaser views the interlude and the play from a moral perspective. His comments can be re-examined from different levels. First of all, the idea that Volpone's bastards are perverse, stupid and corrupt downplays the importance of the grotesque, the deformed and their bastard nature. Moreover, the sexual implications of being a dwarf, or a hermaphrodite or a eunuch are neglected. His statement that 'the fool is desecrated' suggests that Shakespeare's fools are sacred while Jonson's are secular, which is partially true since, for instance, metempsychosis is a religious concept, and the whole passage can be seen as commenting on the degradation of religion. Jonson brings in the idea of metempsychosis in his grotesque figures. The binary opposite between the Shakespearean/sacred fool and the Jonsonian/secular fool is questionable. The quotation that the bastards are not 'scoffing [Volpone's] state, and grinning at his pomp' comes from Act III scene ii of *Richard II* (1595). The line, which refers to the antic or the jester, recalls the gravedigger in *Hamlet* Act V scene i. Both scenes point to the relation between the king/prince and fool/death. Again, such a suggestion can be re-examined because while Shakespearean fools criticise the state, or its pompous representatives, Jonsonian bastards respond to the middle class; and the power of folly is making fun of Volpone as well as other city subjects.

Moreover, perhaps we need to consider the differences between Jonson and Shakespeare. Gabriele Bernhard Jackson suggests that Jonson's comedy is 'the comedy of non-interaction', while in Shakespeare's plays, the 'subplot and main plot meet, they merge into one another, each clarifying the other: the moment of meeting is the moment of resolution'.[24] The mechanical quality of Jonson's characters recalls Henri Bergson's discussion of laughter.[25] While Shakespeare's plays emphasise organic unity, Jonson's plays do not. The suggestion that these bastards give 'visible form to the narcissism and perversion of humanity' has overlooked the importance of their deformity. While they may help to construct Volpone's identity, they are simultaneously breaking it. There is nothing 'self-possessed' about them. In fact, they may be the only characters in the play who have a sense of self-awareness. If they make the atmosphere of the play unsettling, it is only because their heterogeneity challenges order, making disorder and gaming the centre of Jonson's world. Therefore, although this book also makes constant references to Shakespeare's works, it will attempt to bring out the differences between the two playwrights, a topic that I will address in Chapter 4.

Even though many critics diminish the interlude's significance, Harry Levin sees it differently and relates it to John Donne's poem 'Metempsychosis, or the Progress of the Soul'.[26] Metempsychosis is associated with the Greek philosopher Pythagoras, who believed in the transmigration of souls, especially from human to animals. Levin traces the influence of Lucian, the Greek satirist of the second century, on Jonson, suggesting that the latter may have learnt from *The Dream* the 'object-lesson in the blessings of poverty and the corruptions of wealth'. The transmigration is 'a series of Cynic jibes against the other philosophers'. Such a theme is common among various works, one example being Ovid's *Metamorphoses*, which Levin says works 'as a far-fetched proof of the immortality of the soul'. Jonson takes the theme of disinheritance and turns it into 'a comic distortion'.[27] According to Levin, Donne's poem was written during the poet's 'feverish crisis of intellectual pride' as he had lost his Catholic faith at the time but still had not found a haven in the Anglican Church; hence he uses Lucian's work as a 'point of departure for his own explorations into the problem of evil'.[28] Referring to the ending of the poem, 'There's nothing simply good, nor ill alone, / Of every quality comparison, / The only measure is, and judge, opinion', Levin argues that Donne finds his solution in 'ethical relativism', which 'accept[s] the Reformation as a necessary evil and regard[s] the aging queen as neither good nor bad but great'.[29] As his essay continues, Levin switches his argument from the metempsychosis in Donne to the one he said was happening in Jonson: while the former chooses the idealistic extreme through his choice in religion, the latter prefers realism.[30] *Volpone* marks the turning point of the playwright's career, because Jonson undergoes his own metempsychosis after the play: from a 'stern satirist' to a 'genial observer'.[31]

Also comparing the interlude with Donne's poem, Richard Dutton argues how the play targets Robert Cecil (1563–1612), who was the chief minister to both Elizabeth I and James I, and the man who some thought was behind the Gunpowder Plot. Based on various references, he shows that the poem aims at Cecil. Pointing to the Epistle, which says 'this time when she is he', he suggests that 'the great soul' may not necessarily inhabit and animate the Queen, but be 'a separate force, manipulating that which manipulates us – literally, the power behind the throne, which in the wake of Essex's demise could only be Robert Cecil'. Such a description illustrates 'the perverse exploitation of religion by Cecil in pursuit of wealth and power'.[32] For Dutton, the fact that Pythagoras's soul rests on the hermaphrodite at the end of the interlude echoes the play on gender in the Epistle to Donne's poem. Therefore, the use of what Dutton calls the 'metempsychosis show' in *Volpone* is an allusion to it. However, apart from suggesting the physical resemblance between Nano and Cecil, Dutton argues that none of the interlude has 'any bearing on the wider plot, but it signals a wide range of thematic issues', such as degeneration.[33] The importance of these bastards, not only Nano, but also Androgyno and Castrone, is what I want to add to the discussion.

Emphasising the importance of the interlude opens up two significant perspectives on the reading of Jonson. First, even though many critics discuss the interlude in comparison with Donne's poem, we have seen that Jonson based it on *The Dream* or *Dialogue of the Cobbler and the Cock*. Therefore, this Lucianic influence on him is important. In the story, Micyllus, the cobbler, is angry at the cock, who is Pythagoras reincarnated, because the latter wakes him from his dream of gold and wealth, and praises poverty. In addition to the transmigration of souls, many references to *The Dream* can be found in *Volpone*, for example the emphasis on gold, the suggestion of Pythagoras's golden thigh, and the cobbler's remark that gold 'transforms ugly people and renders them lovely', which recalls Mosca's words that gold 'transforms / The most deformèd, and restores 'em lovely' (V.ii.100–1).

Lucian's importance is stressed by the Russian theorist Mikhail Bakhtin in his study of Rabelais. He writes that 'the third source of the Renaissance philosophy of laughter is Lucian, especially his image of Menippus laughing in the kingdom of the dead'.[34] Menippus was a Greek philosopher of the third century BCE. The Menippean satire is distinguished by its use of parody or burlesque, and its mixture of different styles or genres. Such laughter relates 'to the underworld and to death, to the freedom of the spirit, and to the freedom of speech'.[35] Lucian shares many similarities with Rabelais. For instance, 'Lucian describes the underworld as a gay picture. He stresses the element of travesty and exchange of roles.'[36] However, Bakhtin argues for a crucial difference between Lucian and Rabelais:

> Lucian's laughter is always abstract, ironical, devoid of true gaiety. Scarcely anything remains of the ambivalence of the saturnalian symbols . . . Lucian's banquet presents the same commonplace, superficial aspect; the inmates of Lucian's underworld also eat, but eating has nothing in common with Rabelaisian feasting. Former kings may not enjoy it, but neither can the former slaves and beggars . . . Lucian's material bodily principle merely serves to debase the higher images, to render them commonplace, with almost no ambivalence. It does not renew or regenerate. Hence the crucial difference between Lucian and Rabelais is in tone and style.[37]

According to Bakhtin, Lucian's writings do not have the true carnival spirit of Rabelais. He remains stoic and his writing serves a moral purpose, lacking the regenerative power of the comic. If Jonson was influenced by Lucian, it would be interesting to examine if his writings are similar to, yet different from, the carnival spirit, meaning that he cannot be read as purely moral or carnivalesque.[38] When Jonson portrays his version of metempsychosis, does he simply 'debase the higher images, to render them commonplace, with almost no ambivalence'? Perhaps there is a new form of renewal and generation in the context of the city, and Jonson is celebrating and criticising it simultaneously.

Second, since the interlude ends with the song praising folly, it is instrumental for us to examine the relationship between Jonson's comedies and the notion of folly, and, possibly, madness. We should consider the argument made by Michel Foucault in *Madness and Civilization*, who writes that by the end of the Middle Ages,

> a long series of 'follies' which, stigmatizing vices and faults as in the past, no longer attribute them all to pride, to lack of charity, to neglect of Christian virtues, but to a sort of great unreason for which nothing, in fact, is exactly responsible, but which involves everyone in a kind of secret complicity. The denunciation of madness (*la folie*) becomes the general form of criticism.[39]

Such change in the nature of folly and madness has its significant meaning:

Paradoxically, this liberation derives from a proliferation of meaning, from a self-multiplication of significance, weaving relationships so numerous, so intertwined, so rich, that they can no longer be deciphered except in the esoterism of knowledge. Things themselves become so burdened with attributes, signs, allusions that they finally lose their own form. Meaning is no longer read in an immediate perception, the figure no longer speaks for itself; between the knowledge which animates it and the form into which it is transposed, a gap widens. It is free for the dream.[40]

Folly, madness and dream have the power to fascinate people; they associate with the loss of form. Such de-forming relates to the excess and the multiplication of meanings, it distorts figures, yet tempts us to continue reading them. Borrowing the notion of 'waking dreams' from Lucian, Jonson writes about it many times. For example, Volpone says, 'Thou being the best of things, and far transcending / All style of joy in children, parents, friends, / Or any other waking dream on earth' (I.i.16–18); and in *Epicoene*, while Truewit wants to make Otter and Cutbeard 'the deepest divine and gravest lawyer', Dauphine says, 'Thou canst not, man; these are waking dreams' (IV.vii.36–8). The notion in Jonson relates to theatricality and fashioning, and it can be related to 'de-forming' and the multiplication of meanings, especially if we consider Foucault's comments:

At the beginning of the Renaissance, the relations with animality are reversed; the beast is set free; it escapes the world of legend and moral illustration to acquire a fantastic nature of its own. And by an astonishing reversal, it is now the animal that will stalk man, capture him, and reveal him to his own truth.[41]

The beast and animality recall the different images in *Volpone*, which allows us to decipher their plural meanings. Foucault further illustrates that:

In this delusive attachment to himself, man generates his madness like a mirage. The symbol of madness will henceforth be that mirror which, without reflecting anything real, will secretly offer the man who observes himself in it the dream of his own presumption. Madness deals not so much with truth and the world, as with man and whatever truth about himself he is able to perceive.[42]

The interlude can be seen as a mirage that Volpone generates, reflecting his 'madness'. Not only do the bastards act in the interlude, they are his next 'generation', thus becoming the allegory of madness. The world of the early seventeenth century, Foucault concludes, is 'strangely hospitable' to madness, even though things begin to change soon afterwards.[43] At such a dawn of changes, folly and madness relate to the multiplication of meanings and the unveiling of hidden truth. Therefore, the

deformity, monstrosity and bestiality that we find in Volpone's bastards should not just be understood as a condemnation of moral fail-
ings; they tempt the audience to read more from it, asking them to
reach for the excess. Starting with the next chapter, I will examine how
these marginal figures in *Volpone* represent the different 'generations'
of Volpone. They are not only Volpone's bastards, but also his crea-
tions, signifying his imaginings and perceptions. In other words, they
are the 'excess' of Volpone, multiplying his presence in various parts of
the play. They are the 'bastards' whom Volpone will leave behind, as
represented by the fact that the three of them are the characters who
escape without suffering any consequences. By the end of the play,
their presence will be everywhere, which means that their signification
will become part of the city, and nobody can prevent themselves from
having contact with them.

Theorising Jonson's City Comedies

In the next chapter, I will discuss the importance of the dwarf. In *The
Order of Things*, Foucault argues how Velázquez's *Las Meninas* (*The
Maids of Honour*) (1656/7) challenges our ordinary vision, questioning
the belief that there is a clear distinction between inside and outside,
confusing the boundary between subjects and objects. Within the painting are two dwarfs, standing next to a child heiress, creating an ambiguity between young and old, and, therefore, becoming part of a complex
network of a distortion in display. The dwarfs in Velázquez relate to
concepts such as imitation and death, embodying the presence of both
comic and tragic. In his analysis of Holbein's *The Ambassadors* (1533),
Lacan draws our attention to the anamorphic skull in the middle of
the painting. I argue that the dwarf, with his image of distortion and
compression, can be described as a figure of anamorphosis. Through
a detailed rereading of different parts of the play, I will demonstrate
how Nano challenges us to understand it from an anamorphic perspective, and the dwarf should not simply be understood as a comic figure
who is there (along with other bastards) to bring forth some sports to
his master and 'make the wretched time more sweet' (III.iii.1–2). If
we understand the importance of reading the dwarf as an anamorphic
figure, we will see how the 'shadow' of the dwarf is embedded everywhere. Many images within the play, such as Volpone lying on the bed
onstage, and pretending to be sick and near death, will appear to us in
a different light.

Chapter 3 discusses how the theme of castration is central to our understanding of *Volpone*, arguing for the possibility that Volpone can perhaps really be 'castrated', especially if we analyse this from a Lacanian perspective. My analysis focuses on Act III scene vii, in which Volpone has a chance to force a sexual encounter on Celia. However, instead of imposing his action immediately, he jumps into a long speech on transformation. My chapter rereads the scene in detail, examining the relationship between sexuality and theatricality. I will discuss different literary materials ranging from Boccaccio and Chaucer to Philip Massinger. Lacan says that 'there is no chance for a man to have jouissance of a woman's body, otherwise stated, for him to make love, without castration, in other words, without something that says no to the phallic function'.[44] His statement 'There is no such thing as a sexual relationship'[45] means that there is always a certain Other situated between man and woman,[46] which suggests that human relationship is caught within the symbolic order, and human contact is barred from the excess and being transgressive. Given the importance of performance in *Volpone*, I would say that in the play, being a castrated subject means that a person cannot have sex without the 'screening' of the theatre. The word 'screening' is used in two senses: first, it is a form of censorship, because it seems that Volpone cannot perform without the 'scripts', and this need signifies that there is always a gap between him and Celia. Second, human beings can only encounter each other on this 'screen', meaning that human contact can only be possible when we are in a certain role. Therefore, one may wonder if following the logic of the theatre, or the texts, as in the case of Volpone, is the only chance for him to be transgressive. Jonson plays with the theme of castration in his comedy: while Volpone takes pleasure in taking away the possessions of his suitors, he fears the presence of Lady Would-be, indulges in his theatrical performance instead of having a sexual encounter when he is with Celia, and is not immune to being cut from his act by none other than his parasite. The concept of castration should be understood together with Volpone's transformations, hinting that behind each city subject is the presence of a void, driving the subject towards having more possessions. While it is common to see Bonario as the agent who stops Volpone's action, this book argues that the presence of Castrone in Volpone's house is an equally, if not more, important issue.

The androgyne is a complicated figure: he is portrayed by Jonson as being a fool, who is 'free from care or sorrow-taking' (I.ii.68); however, he takes delight in varying between sexes, even though that pleasure has become 'stale and forsaken' (I.ii.54–5). It is a complex issue because Jonson's attitude towards the hermaphrodite is ambiguous. If every character in *Epicoene* raises the notion of gender ambiguity – as

Edward B. Partridge notes, 'nearly everyone in the play is epicene in some way'[47] – Jonson seems to be celebrating the wit of Dauphine, Truewit and Clerimont, while ridiculing others such as La Foole, John Daw, Thomas Otter and the collegiate ladies in equal measure. The same can be said in *Volpone* as the dramatist is creating comedy based on gender ambiguity in the subplot of Politic Would-be, and making fun of another collegiate ladies-like figure in Lady Would-be. Suffering from the 'strange fury' (III.iv.41) of Lady Would-be, Volpone says, 'Before, I feigned diseases; now I have one' (III.iv.62): while Volpone, in earlier parts of the play, emphasises the importance of pretending and performing, Lady Would-be really takes Peregrine as 'a female devil in a male outside' (IV.ii.56). Such distinction may signify the difference between folly and madness: the former concept embraces the liberation of identities, but the latter implies a subjectivity who is labelled and categorised. Mosca's interlude ends with the song 'Fools, they are the only nation / Worth men's envy, or admiration' (I.ii.66–7), as if being a fool surpasses every type of enjoyment.

In Chapter 4, I will compare Jonson's androgyne with two important literary references on this subject, namely, the androgyne, as raised by Aristophanes in Plato's *The Symposium*, and the hermaphrodite in Ovid's *Metamorphoses*. The androgynes in Plato are described as having eight limbs, and 'went like our acrobats' when they started running fast, 'whirling over and over with legs stuck out straight; only then they had eight limbs to support and speed them swiftly round and round'.[48] In his discussion, Samuel Weber argues how Aristophanes's story does not concern 'abstract or incorporeal beings, a "self" or an "ego", but *bodies*'.[49] Their bodies highlight the importance of double-ness, with an emphasis on plurality, or even multiplicity. Such bodies and their movement as cartwheels allow us to understand the andro-gyne through Bakhtin, who stresses the importance of grotesque bodies in the Middle Ages carnival, which 'offered a completely different, nonofficial, extraecclesiastical and extrapolitical aspect of the world, of man, and of human relations'.[50] These double bodies and the liberation of gender identities and relationships they entail become a symbol of subversion, challenging the norms of 'heterosexual' society.

The hermaphrodite in Ovid is a different creature: he has a body that combines both sexes because of the sexual threat of Salmacis. His identity as a boy highlights one aspect of his gender ambiguity as if he possesses both masculine and feminine qualities even before his encounter with Salmacis, and he has been fixed in that state because of her. The story of Hermaphroditus shows the hidden anxiety within a man when he is in the face of 'excessive' femininity and female sexuality, as it is suggested that he was becoming 'impure' at the end.[51] Becoming 'impure' brings in the concept of being bastardised, and the story implies a fear of transgression and the idea that sexual encounter should remain within given normative standards. The subject and object relation between the two genders is reversed: not only does Salmacis take an active role in their encounter, but the 'gaze' belongs to the woman instead of the man, thus bringing in the idea of castration anxiety.[52] The story raises the notion of death, because female power is constantly linked with the pool and water, meaning that to surrender oneself to the feminine power is to be 'liquidated'. At the end of the story, Hermaphroditus cries, 'Oh, grant this boon, my father and my mother, to your son who bears the names of both: whoever comes into this pool as man may he go forth half-man, and may he weaken at touch of the water.'[53] The notion of gender fluidity is not celebrated in the story. Instead, it is more like a prison and a curse, highlighting the threat of castration that comes from an 'excessive' femininity.

Reading and watching Jonson and Shakespeare at a time of increased and often fraught visibility for intersex and trans issues, a rereading of the portrayals of the hermaphrodite may be more permanent than ever.[54] According to *OED*, the earliest reference to 'epicene' comes in 1450, and it was more commonly used in the early seventeenth century. The word was still a comparatively new concept in Jonson's time, and it seems that he was the person who constantly used the word in different senses. *OED* suggests three entries that are related to Jonson: not only does he write a play called *Epicoene* in 1609, he uses the word in his masque *Neptune's Triumph* ('And of the epicene gender, hes and shes: Amphibian Archy is the chief' (183–4)) and his poem *An Epigram on the Court Pucelle* ('What though with tribade lust she force a muse, / And in an epicene fury can write news / Equal with that which for the best news goes / As airy, light, and as like wit as those?' (*The Underwood* 49, 7–10)). Judging from this evidence, one might wonder if Jonson was deeply interested in this concept. Jonson's epicene is a combination of the androgyne and the eunuch, which, in other words, means the presence of both Androgyno and Castrone, because the notion of gender ambiguity in Jonson is connected with the theme of castration in many different ways. In *Epicoene*, 'castration' can be represented by the taking away of the rapiers of La Foole and John Daw. After this symbolic act, Clerimont says to Daw, 'you carry the feminine gender afore you' (V.i.25), meaning that the latter possesses more feminine than masculine quality within him. Castration can be signified thematically, such as being cut away from inheritance in the case of Dauphine, which may explain why Jonson gives his male character a female name.

Morose's act takes away Dauphine's family status, rendering the latter effeminate. For Jonson, the epicene is a city creature, meaning that the fluidity of gender identities is inseparable from the city's transactions and exchanges. Because of the monetary, material and sexual transactions, no person or relationship can remain stable and unchanged, and the city and the exchanges within it allow the emergence of different forms of new identities. It is something to be ridiculed. However, it is also a cause to celebrate because it is where the comedy comes from. Jonson's attitude towards this creature is ambivalent.

Jonson's attitude towards the androgyne will be compared with that of Shakespeare. Discussing the 1609 play with *Twelfth Night* (1601), I suggest how Jonson's comedy celebrates the wit of the epicene, disagreeing with those critics who accuse the dramatist of upholding gender distinctions.[55] In Shakespeare, the confusion of gender identity and relationship is expressed through different images of doubleness. The first of these images can be seen in the parallel between Olivia and Viola. Their names are near anagrams of each other, and one can see the word Viola within Olivia, and vice versa. The anagram makes them 'mirror images' of each other, which seems to suggest their similarities and differences simultaneously. While Orsino was first in love with Olivia, he matches with Viola at the end when her 'true' gender is revealed. As suggested by the reversal of their names, their roles seem to be interchangeable. This resolution allows the audience to question if Orsino was already in love with Cesario (Viola) when he first met him, and was only barred from it because he refused to recognise his own same-sex desire. This importance of doubleness is also suggested through the identical appearances of Viola and Sebastian: even though Olivia's love towards Viola is more like a dream (II.ii.24), the tension of this ambiguous gender relationship is resolved because of the appearance of the twin brother, as if the latter is a substitute for his sister. Therefore, even though the play ends with these 'heterosexual' marriages, it leaves us wondering if Olivia's love towards Viola is somewhat 'fulfilled' in the end, because, after all, the twins should look identical to each other.

In Chapter 5, the representation of Mosca the parasite will be examined. While the parasite might think that he is different from the three bastards, a detailed analysis of his speech in Act III scene i shows that he is, to use a Lacanian psychoanalytic phrase, in the 'mirror stage', which refers to 'the transformation that takes place in the subject when he assumes an image'.[56] From a Freudian perspective, Mosca can be described as someone who has shown the characteristics of 'megalomania and diversion of [their] interest from the external world – from people and things'.[57] Extending the concept to Lacan, the parasite is a figure that is in his 'Imaginary' state, who mistakenly believes that he can possess a 'complete' subjectivity: as he praises himself onstage, he fails to realise the fragmented nature of his speech and his body. Through a comparison with the Marx Brothers' *Duck Soup* (1933), Chapter 5 will discuss how the mirror is essential to the understanding of a comic subject and his comedy, as the joke is built on the gap between the subject and the mirror object, and their interchangeability. In other words, the parasite's comedy is a manifestation of the 'mirror image' at work. The parasite might not be that different from the dwarf, the androgyne and the eunuch. Moreover, this chapter will compare the logic of comedy with that of tragedy through a discussion of *Hamlet* (1600), showing how a comic figure and a tragic figure may react differently when they face the question of 'To be, or not to be'.

In Chapter 6, I will discuss how the theme of bastardy can be seen in Jonson's other plays, such as *The Alchemist* (1610) and *Bartholomew Fair* (1614). Comparing *Volpone* with *The Alchemist*, the fact that Lovewit is absent from the house most of the time is interesting because it suggests that Jonson is doing away with the master figure in the latter play. If we could substitute the characters of *Volpone* for those in *The Alchemist*, it would mean that Mosca, or Nano, Androgyno and Castrone have taken centre stage in 1610. Therefore, even though Lovewit comes back at the end, the play is about how the three bastards 'slip away' from the master's control. Indeed, it is possible for us to read Face as another version of Mosca. Moreover, we could read the confrontation between Face and Subtle at the beginning of the play as the split between Androgyno and Castrone, because while Face represents the celebration of folly and the embodiment of multiple identities, Subtle may signify the lack within. In the discussion of *Volpone*, I suggest that Nano the dwarf is an allegory of both the gold and the skull. Such a combination of 'omnipotence' and 'impotence', to use a phrase from *Epicoene* (V.iii.147–8), is more obvious in *The Alchemist*. An alchemist claims he can transform a base metal into gold or silver, and Jonson makes reference to this in several parts of the play. For instance, Epicure Mammon says:

> This night I'll change
> All that is metal in thy house to gold,
> And early in the morning will I send
> To all the plumbers and the pewterers
> And buy their tin and lead up, and to Lothbury
> For all the copper.

(II.i.29–34)

By 1610, Jonson has found the art of alchemy as a metaphor to capture the logic of capitalism in his city comedy. In this new capitalist logic, while it is full of possibilities as almost everything can be transformed into gold, Jonson is reminding his audience that they are still, after all, base metal. In *The Alchemist*, Epicure Mammon often speaks in a way as if he is another Volpone.[58] Responding to Surly's doubts over alchemy, Mammon says, 'But when you see th'effects of the great med'cine, / Of which one part projected on a hundred / Of Mercury, or Venus, or the Moon / Shall turn it to as many of the Sun, / Nay, to a thousand, so *ad infinitum*, / You will believe me' (II.i.37–42). The comparison of the gold with the sun reminds the audience of the first scene in *Volpone*. Moreover, the metaphor of medicine makes him sound like another Scoto of Mantua. In the same speech, Mammon says:

> Do you think I fable with you? I assure you,
> He that has once the flower of the sun,
> The perfect ruby which we call elixir,
> Not only can do that, but by its virtue
> Can confer honour, love, respect, long life,
> Give safety, valour, yea, and victory
> To whom he will. In eight-and-twenty days
> I'll make an old man of fourscore a child.
>
> (II.i.46–53)

The word 'fable' can be read as a reference to *Volpone* (recalling Mosca's words to Corvino: ''Tis the common fable. / The dwarf, the fool, the eunuch are all his; / He's the true father of his family' (I.v.46–8)). The suggestion of turning an old man into a child reminds the audience of Corbaccio. In many ways, different parts of *The Alchemist* can be seen as an elaboration of Mosca's idea that gold 'transforms / the most deformèd, and restores 'em lovely' (V.ii.100–1). However, I am not suggesting that *The Alchemist* is simply an extension of *Volpone*. For instance, if Mammon sounds like another Volpone, the fact that he is duped has already marked the two plays' differences. In more than one way, *The Alchemist* is really a masterless comedy. Jonson no longer needs a Volpone-like figure to link up all the characteristics of his bastards. Instead, he allows them to control the plots, and the play indulges in the logic of the city more than *Volpone*.

In Act V of *Bartholomew Fair*, Zeal-of-the-Land Busy, the puritan, accuses the puppet Dionysus for its confusion of being both male and female at once, and in response, Dionysus says they have neither male nor female among them. It then takes up its garment, making a 'plain' demonstration (V.v.85), converting the puritan successfully. In 'Jonson's Metempsychosis', Harry Levin writes that 'Possibly Mosca's interlude was written before the rest of the play, like the puppet-show in *Bartholomew Fair*.'⁵⁹ His suggestion hints at the importance of the two scenes. Therefore, by rereading them in detail, we can see that these minor scenes are instrumental for us to understand Jonson and his comedies.

We can take Edgworth's use of the word 'plain' as an instance. The word has two meanings: not only does it suggest that it is a simple demonstration, the word also refers to the genitals of the puppet as a site of nothingness. The 'plain' demonstration can be interpreted from a Freudian perspective: in his discussion of castration, Freud argues that a boy's fear of castration is raised when he realises that the woman does not have penis. While the puppet Dionysius has no gender within it, it shares a similar function with what Freud would think of the genital region of a little girl. They are both a site of nothingness, a sight that reminds the male that the penis, and, therefore, the supposedly patriarchal power that comes with it, does not necessarily exist. The boy's discovery involves more than the threat of a possible loss of something that presently exists, as it suggests that even the presently existing object may be nothing more than an appearance. Therefore, the conversion of Busy might not be something that is so hard to believe, especially if we consider the importance of castration, because what the puppet does, in demonstrating its 'plainness', is to make Busy tongue-tied, which is another image of castration. Moreover, the words are uttered by Edgworth, which by no means is a coincidence, as his being a cutpurse, apart from signifying the rapacity of urban life, links him with the concept of castration. His occupation suggests the act of taking away other people's possessions, and it can be read as a sexual innuendo. However, the two subjects might be interrelated, as within the context of the city, a person's authority is more or less based on his possession of wealth, and the lack of it would render him effeminate (one can recall, for instance, how the feminine name 'Dauphine Eugenie' can be seen as relevant to his being disinherited in *Epicoene*).

Comparing this scene with the ending of *Epicoene*, in which Dauphine shows that Epicene is actually a male within a female body, Jonson takes another approach five years later in *Bartholomew Fair*. In *Volpone*, the representation of the bastards remains subtle. The moral tone is more or less like an appendage, something that is added as an extra to the play. If we read it with the imagery of castration, the moral message is still 'hanging' in there, refusing to go. In *Epicoene*, Jonson shows the triumph of the third gender. Even though some scholars criticise it for its seemingly male-centred treatment, it cannot simply be read as a confirmation of the traditional patriarchal success. The play celebrates the power of the epicene as Dauphine, Clerimont and Truewit possibly render everybody effeminate. In *The Alchemist*, the representations of Volpone's bastards have taken a more important role, and Jonson seems to be able to indulge more in the pleasure of folly. In *Bartholomew Fair*, the dwarf, the androgyne and the eunuch are no longer separate characters as their representations are embodied in the puppet Dionysus. There is no longer any need to divide the concepts of castration and folly. They are combined into one. At the end of the book, I will illustrate how this logic of slippage and multiplication of identities is inherent in the interlude of Act I scene ii. The logic is a comedic metaphor, and the understanding of it is essential for us to appreciate the city comedy of Jonson. Considering the importance of the bastards and the epicenes, I will use Susan Sontag's notion of 'Camp' to rethink Jonson's comedies. Moreover, I will use the reading of Volpone's bastards to rethink some modern theories of comedy and examine some film comedies and other early modern city comedies, such as the works of Thomas Middleton. Perhaps, as the ending of *Volpone* indicates to us, the presence of these bastards is everywhere. They tell us how comedy often plays on the thin line between proper and improper, between insistence and deferral, and between madness and folly.

Notes

1. All the quotations of Jonson in this book are from Jonson, *Cambridge Edition*.
2. For works on Jonson and *Volpone*, see Barish, *Jonson: Volpone*; Barton, *Ben Jonson, Dramatist*; Cave, *Ben Jonson*; Boehrer, *Fury of Men's Gullets*; Donaldson, *Jonson's Magic Houses*; Sanders et al., *Refashioning Ben Jonson*; Dutton (ed.), *Ben Jonson*; Harris, '"I am sailing to my port, uh! uh! uh! uh!"'; Dutton, *Ben Jonson, Volpone and the Gunpowder Plot*; Hennessey, 'Jonson's Joyless Economy'; Cousins and Scott, *Ben Jonson and the Politics of Genre*; Meskill, *Ben Jonson and Envy*; Sanders, *Ben Jonson in Context*; Zucker, *Places of Wit*; Steggle, *Volpone*; Loxley and Robson, *Shakespeare, Jonson*. For works on city or city comedy, see Gibbons, *Jacobean City Comedy*; Leggatt, *Citizen Comedy*; Easterling, *Parsing the City*; Mardock, *Our Scene Is London*.
3. For the critics who argued against the significance of the interlude, see Herford and Simpson (eds), *Ben Jonson*, vol. 2, pp. 57–8; Knights, 'Jonson and the Anti-Acquisitive Attitude'; Welsford, *The Fool*, p. 252.
4. Jonson was the first writer to publish his collected works including plays written for the public stage. See Dutton, *To the First Folio*; see also Brady and Herendeen, *Ben Jonson's 1616 Folio*.
5. Eliot, 'Ben Jonson', p. 121.

6. Davis, 'Constructing Normalcy', p. 17. On disability studies, see Siebers, *Disability Theory*; Siebers, *Disability Aesthetics*.

7. Freud, *Jokes and Their Relation to the Unconscious*, p. 97.

8. Richard Dutton writes that the 'cobbler's cock' refers to 'the cock in Lucian's *Dream*, who tells his story to a cobbler dreaming of riches. Pythagoras's followers were not supposed to touch white cocks.' See Jonson, *Cambridge Edition*, vol. 3, p. 51.

9. Even though Dutton says that 'Mosca dissociates himself from Volpone's paternity', the word 'save' could mean both 'with the exception of' and 'protection and preservation'. See Jonson, *Cambridge Edition*, vol. 3, p. 69.

10. All the quotations of Shakespeare in this book are from Shakespeare, *Norton Shakespeare*.

11. Neill, '"In everything illegitimate"', p. 142. On the subject of bastardy, see also Krell, *Purest of Bastards*.

12. Danby, *Shakespeare's Doctrine of Nature*.

13. See Hui, '"To what base uses we may return, Horatio!"'.

14. There are some traces of Volpone's bastards in Jonson's humour plays. For instance, in the folio version of *Every Man in His Humour* (first performed in 1598 and published in quarto in 1601), as if everyone is bastardised in some way, Knowell says, 'The first words / We form their tongues with are licentious jests. / Can it call "whore"? Cry "bastard"? Oh, then, kiss it; A witty child! Can't swear? The father's darling! / Give it two plums' (II.v.19–23).

15. The play entered in the Stationers' Register on 22 July 1598, and was mentioned by Meres in September 1598; while *Much Ado about Nothing* (the play I am going to discuss next) was mentioned in the Stationers' Register on both 4 and 23 August 1600, and published in an edition dated 1600. See Wells et al., *William Shakespeare*, pp. 119–20.

16. For a discussion of this scene, see Hockey, 'The Patch is Kind Enough'; Fortin, 'Launcelot and the Uses of Allegory'; Danson, *Harmonies of The Merchant of Venice*.

17. Homer, *Odyssey*, Book 1, p. 29.

18. Findlay, *Illegitimate Power*, pp. 103–6.

19. Except, perhaps, *The Merry Wives of Windsor*, a play which I will draw references to in this book.

20. See Noyes, *Ben Jonson on the English Stage*; Hinchliffe, '*Volpone*', pp. 50–84. On the theatre productions of Jonson's plays, see Cave et al., *Ben Jonson and Theatre*; Jensen, *Ben Jonson's Comedies on the Modern Stage*; Jones, *Engagement with Knavery*.

21. Creaser (ed.), *Volpone, or, The Fox*, p. 44.

22. Creaser (ed.), *Volpone, or, The Fox*, p. 23.

23. Creaser (ed.), *Volpone, or, The Fox*, p. 45.

24. Jackson, 'Protesting Imagination', pp. 92–3.

25. Bergson writes: 'The first point to which attention should be called is that the comic does not exist outside the pale of what is strictly *human*.' The function of comedy is to laugh at mechanical inelasticity, and 'the attitudes, gestures, and movements of the human body are laughable in exact proportion as that body reminds us of a mere machine'. See Bergson, *Laughter*, pp. 9, 15, 32.

26. Levin, 'Jonson's Metempsychosis'.
27. Levin, 'Jonson's Metempsychosis', p. 90.
28. Levin, 'Jonson's Metempsychosis', p. 93.
29. Levin, 'Jonson's Metempsychosis', p. 93.
30. Levin, 'Jonson's Metempsychosis', p. 94.
31. Levin, 'Jonson's Metempsychosis', p. 96.
32. Dutton, *Ben Jonson, Volpone and the Gunpowder Plot*, pp. 45–7.
33. Dutton, *Ben Jonson, Volpone and the Gunpowder Plot*, pp. 49–50.
34. The first two sources, according to Bakhtin, are Hippocrates and Aristotle. See Bakhtin, *Rabelais and His World*, pp. 67–9. On Bakhtin and Renaissance theatre, see Stallybrass and White, *Politics and Poetics of Transgression*; Womack, *Ben Jonson*; Knowles, *Shakespeare and Carnival*; Coronato, *Jonson versus Bakhtin*; Vaught, *Carnival and Literature*.
35. Bakhtin, *Rabelais and His World*, p. 70.
36. Bakhtin, *Rabelais and His World*, pp. 386–7.
37. Bakhtin, *Rabelais and His World*, pp. 387–8.
38. Rick Bowers argues that 'the freedom offered through comedy surpasses Freudian conceptions of psychic release, Bergsonian observations about the mechanized and the humane, even Hobbesian senses of overcoming our former inferiority'. See Bowers, *Radical Comedy*, p. 3.
39. Foucault, *Madness and Civilization*, p. 11.
40. Foucault, *Madness and Civilization*, p. 16.
41. Foucault, *Madness and Civilization*, p. 18.
42. Foucault, *Madness and Civilization*, p. 23.
43. Foucault, *Madness and Civilization*, p. 33.
44. Lacan, *On Feminine Sexuality*, pp. 71–2.
45. Lacan, *On Feminine Sexuality*, p. 12.
46. Lacan, *On Feminine Sexuality*, p. 68.
47. Partridge, 'Allusiveness of *Epicoene*', p. 94.
48. Plato, *Lysis; Symposium; Gorgias*, pp. 135–7.
49. Weber, *Legend of Freud*, p. 193.
50. Bakhtin, *Rabelais and His World*, p. 6.
51. A. D. Melville's translation reads: 'Both parents heard; both, moved to gratify / Their bi-sexed son, his purpose to ensure, / Drugged the bright water with that power impure.' See Ovid, *Metamorphoses*, trans. Melville, p. 85.
52. This reading is a bit different from Freud's analysis in 'Medusa's Head'. On the basis of Freud's interpretation, one can argue that it is less the female gaze per se than an unsettling object of the male gaze that signals the threat of castration. See Freud, 'Medusa's Head'.
53. Ovid, *Metamorphoses, Volume I*, trans. Miller, p. 205. Arthur Golding translates this as 'O noble father Mercurie, and Venus mother deere, / This one petition graunt your son which both your names doth beare, / That whoso commes within this Well may so be weakened there, / That of a man but halfe a man he may fro thence retire.' See Ovid, *Ovid's Metamorphoses*, pp. 98–9.
54. For a Lacanian reading on the subject, see, for instance, Gherovici, *Please Select Your Gender*.
55. See, for instance, Howard, 'Crossdressing, the Theatre, and Gender

Struggle'; Tiffany, *Erotic Beasts and Social Monsters*; Rackin, 'Androgyny, Mimesis, and the Marriage of the Boy Heroine'.

56. Lacan, 'Mirror Stage', p. 76.
57. Freud, 'On Narcissism', p. 74.
58. An interesting comparison can be seen in *The Merry Wives of Windsor*, in which Ford, referring to Falstaff, asks, 'What a damned epicurean rascal is this!' (II.ii.253).
59. Levin, 'Jonson's Metempsychosis', p. 94.

Chapter 2

'For pleasing imitation of greater men's action': Nano the Anamorphic Ape

My first focus is the dwarf, or the ape figure, in *Volpone* and elsewhere in Jonson. In *Every Man Out of His Humour* (1599), Asper, the presenter, describes the new parvenus and parasites in London as apes:

> Well, I will scourge those apes,
> And to these courteous eyes [*Indicating the audience*] oppose a mirror
> As large as is the stage whereon we act,
> Where they shall see the time's deformity
> Anatomized in every nerve and sinew,
> With constant courage and contempt of fear.
>
> ('Induction', lines 115–20)

Asper's words characterise Renaissance satire, which used concepts such as the mirror and the anatomy to describe what the comedy was doing in studying such 'apes'. Showing figures of deformity by means of the mirror, Asper emphasises the need to see Jonson's comedies as distorting, creating anamorphic shapes, hence the idea of apes. Asper's characterisation of 'apes' is instrumental for us to think of another of Jonson's apes: Nano in *Volpone*. Critics usually slight the significance of Volpone's three bastards. Herford and Simpson argue that the three of them are there to 'reflect their deformities'.[1] Enid Welsford describes the trio as 'peculiarly odious grotesques whose only function in the play is to emphasize the luxury and selfishness of the Fox, and to perform an occasional jig, presumably to gratify the groundlings'.[2] In this chapter, I want to draw readers' attention to the signification of Nano the dwarf, suggesting how the study of his representation can enrich our reading of the play. I argue that the dwarf functions as a mirror to Volpone's own inner states. Using Lacan's theory, I suggest that he can be read as a figure of anamorphosis, signifying the presence of death and castration within Volpone/*Volpone*, challenging the audience to read the play in an anamorphic way. The dwarf is an important presence if we allow ourselves to think of the play from a different angle. Deciphering the signification of Nano, I will address how the representation of the dwarf contributes to the study of the comedy and its critique of the nascent early modern capitalism. Through the discussion of Velázquez and Holbein, and Shakespeare's portrayal of Richard III, with reference to the theoretical arguments of Michel Foucault and Jacques Lacan, I am going to discuss the representation of the dwarf as an anamorphic figure. I will then examine how, in Jonson, Volpone embodies the signification of the ape, arguing that the ultimate dwarfish character of the play is the gold in Volpone's shrine, which means that while the gold helps to create the feeling of possession in a capitalist subject, the power of death and impotence, or in other words, dispossession, is always present, challenging this illusion. Therefore, the dwarf should not just be seen as a character that provokes cheap laughter, but rather, in Lacanian terms, as one that works as an important 'stain' which serves as a *memento mori*. Finally, this chapter revisits some of the traditional arguments on *Volpone*, to see how the dwarf, as a comic figure, helps us to see Jonson and the early modern capitalist subject in a different way.

Velázquez and Holbein, Foucault and Lacan

In this section, I want to first discuss representations of dwarfs in two sixteenth- and seventeenth-century paintings, namely, Velázquez's *Las Meninas* (*The Maids of Honour*) (1656/7) and Holbein's *The Ambassadors* (1533), and show how they enable us to see the dwarf in Jonson's comedy as an anamorphic figure. From antiquity onwards, dwarfs seem to have been regarded as objects both of ridicule and of peculiar respect.[3] Presumably because they were regarded as non-threatening and quick-witted, they were close to power centres throughout history.[4] It was fashionable for Renaissance royal and noble families to keep dwarfs as intimates, and one such example can be seen from the paintings of Velázquez (1599–1660), Jonson's near contemporary, who seems to have had a fascination with dwarfs and jesters. From his paintings, we see the representation of dwarfs as repeatedly concerned with imitation and death. *Prince Baltasar Carlos with a Dwarf* (1631) shows a dwarf as the prince's playmate. While the two years and four months old prince dressed in ceremonial robes resembles a miniature adult, the dwarf raises similar associations, which connects his smallness with imitation and comedy. As the prince holds a baton and a dagger in his hands, the dwarf has a silver rattle and an apple as if he were imitating the prince. Such a gesture produces an ambiguity as the dwarf makes the symbols of power a toy and, potentially, undermines and ridicules their authority. While wearing dresses before breeching was conventional for boys of that age, the practice nonetheless introduces gender ambiguity into the painting. Their heights confuse their age difference, reflecting the dwarf's ability to confuse young and old; as Leslie Fiedler suggests, dwarfs 'have a disconcerting way of seeming both at once: old-young, young-old'.[5] The double relates to the feeling of the uncanny, which is the combination of both *heimlich* and *unheimlich*, something that is familiar yet foreign and strange, arousing alarm and fear. In his famous discussion of the uncanny, Freud uses the example of Olympia, the doll in E. T. A. Hoffmann's (1776–1822) 'The Sand-Man', to suggest how the effect is raised by an object which is ambiguously lifeless and animate. The fear in 'The Sand-Man' relates to the robbing of eyes, which, for Freud, signifies the fear of castration. Freud connects the uncanny with the double, suggesting that it functions both as 'an insurance against the destruction of the ego' and 'the uncanny harbinger of death'.[6] Thinking Velázquez's paintings with Freud's theory, perhaps the dwarf can be read as a figure of the uncanny. Standing next to the prince, he embodies both their similarities and differences simultaneously. He might look the same as the prince at first glance, but we realise there is nothing youthful in him once we read him more carefully. We might ignore his presence at first, but it also makes him more disturbing once we realise his existence. The dwarf creates an image of doubleness, and we cannot think of the prince without thinking of him. In other words, he becomes a haunting presence. The dwarf relates to the issue of death because he makes us wonder if the prince can be immune to his demise. He connects with comedy in an eerie way.

The dwarf questions our ordinary vision and challenges the notion of single subjectivity. Originally known as 'Portrait of the Empress with her Ladies and a Dwarf', Velázquez's *Las Meninas* (*The Maids of Honour*) shows the heiress to the throne, the Infanta Margarita, attended by two of the queen's maids of honour, Doña María Agustina Sarmiento and Doña Isabel de Velasco. Beside them are two dwarfs, the female Mari-Bárbola and the male Nicolasico Pertusato, with his foot resting on the mastiff. While the kneeling 'maid of honour' is about the same height as the princess, the female dwarf is slightly taller than both of them. Their seemingly equivalent size covers up their differences in age and social position. At the back of the room are different paintings and a mirror with King Philip IV and the queen's image, which may be what is being painted on the canvas to the left of the picture. Beside it is a doorway, in which stands José Nieto, the queen's palace marshal, leading to another space opposite to the direction that the painter is looking. In *The Order of Things*, Michel Foucault analysed in detail how the painting makes us question the classical concept of representation. The invisible side of the canvas in the painting and the gaze of the painter cause us to wonder if we, the spectators, are the subject of representation. Moreover, since anyone can be the spectator of the painting, everyone can be its subject:

> But, inversely, the painter's gaze, addressed to the void confronting him outside the picture, accepts as many models as there are spectators; in this precise but neutral space, the observer and the observed take part in a ceaseless exchange. No gaze is stable, or rather, in the neutral furrow of the gaze piercing at a right angle through the canvas, subject and object, the spectator and the model, reverse their roles to infinity.[7]

The gaze of the painter towards the outside of the painting opens up the space of representation. Focusing on the light coming from the window on the right, Foucault draws attention to the mirror at the back of the room, the one that reflects nothing in front of it, but something invisible, providing 'a metathesis of visibility that affects both the space represented in the picture and its nature as representation', allowing us to see 'what in the painting is of necessity doubly invisible'.[8] The gaze from the mirror shatters the differentiation between subject and object: while the figures in the painting are observing the people reflected in the mirror, they are objects of contemplation, which indicates that there is a centre and an origin outside the painting, making the concepts of centre and origin problematic. Commenting on Foucault's discussion, Gary Shapiro writes that 'Foucault's essay is a sustained meditation on the relationship between the visible and the invisible.'[9] Adding to this suggestion, perhaps we can say that the presence of the dwarfs contributes to this ambiguity. However, at the same time, we can also say that the disturbing factor of the dwarfs lies in their insistent visibility – in the sense of us 'not being able to take our eyes off them' – an effect that is accentuated by Velázquez's placing them front and centre.

With the display of the dwarf and the gaze of the painter, Velázquez's paintings challenge the concept of representation. The combination of the *memento mori* and the concept of gaze can be found in Lacan's discussion of the concept of anamorphosis in Hans Holbein's *The Ambassadors*. Holbein's painting shows Jean de Dinteville, Seigneur de Polisy (1504–55), the French Ambassador to the English court, on the left; and Georges de Selve (1508/9–41), the soon to be Bishop of Lavaur at that time, on the right. While the two men suggest their knowledge of the Trivium – the three topics at the heart of medieval education – the objects between them, such as the different astronomy and geometry instruments, a German book of arithmetic and a German hymn book, represent a mastery of the Quadrivium. Even though the painting exhibits the coexistence of different forms of knowledge and power (such as state and Church; Protestantism and Catholicism), it contains significantly an anamorphosis of a skull in the front. Lacan uses anamorphosis to illustrate the trap of the gaze:

> What, then, before this display of the domain of appearance in all its most fascinating forms, is this object, which from some angles appears to be flying through the air, at others to be tilted? You cannot know – for you turn away, thus escaping the fascination of the picture.
>
> Begin by walking out of the room in which no doubt it has long held your attention. It is then that, turning round as you leave – as the author of the *Anamorphoses* describes it – you apprehend in this form . . . What? A skull.[10]

For Lacan, identity comes from identification with what the subject feels is looking at him, and that which seems to hold the subject and give it a narcissistic completeness, he calls the gaze. The gaze confirms identity, yet it also disconfirms and annihilates the subject. The trap of the gaze means that the distorted skull, which is in the form of a stain, tempts the subject to wonder about it, until, just as he walks away from it, he realises that the power of death is looking at him, which unsettles and destroys subjectivity. Lacan argues that such an object signifies the phallus:

> All this shows that at the very heart of the period in which the subject emerged and geometral optics was an object of research, Holbein makes visible for us here something that is simply the subject as annihilated – annihilated in the form that is, strictly speaking, the imaged embodiment of the *minus-phi* [(-ϕ)] of castration, which for us, centres the whole organization of the desires through the framework of the fundamental drives.[11]

This quotation from Lacan indicates that while the sense of subjectivity comes from the vision of a world seen in perspective, there is a shadow within, which the subject identifies with the gaze, and which is here in the form of a death's head, acting as a force of castration, making the male subject a 'Sporus' (IV.ii.48), to use Jonson's term. Lacan reads the *memento mori* as a representation of the phallus, through its erection, and also as a symbol of castration, which means that the phallic and the castrative are identified with each other, ambivalent, disturbing any belief in single meaning or identity. We can say that the anamorphic skull in Holbein has a similar function to the dwarf in the paintings of Velázquez. Like the skull in Lacan's reading, the dwarf has been coded in European culture to mean both virile sexuality and death. In antiquity, Greek dwarfs were usually identified with the phallic, having an apotropaic power, meaning that they had the ability to avert ill power and ill luck.[12] Appearing to be a harmless playmate of the royal family, the dwarf's power of aping and imitation is a force of ridicule. In other words, the anamorphic body of the dwarf may escape our attention, yet it can be read as a stain with a gaze that challenges our subjectivity. Comparing the difference between the elongation of the skull (which is a linear anamorphosis) and the shortening of the dwarf, one can even treat the dwarf as the equivalent of the 'normal' skull, thereby making a so-called normally sized adult an anamorphically elongated stain.

Based on these theoretical arguments, I am going to argue that Nano, in *Volpone*, also embodies the signification of the anamorphic ape, and its representation is ultimately related to Volpone's gold, which means that while the gold gives a narcissistic completeness to a city subject, the force of death and castration, as embodied in the dwarf, is always present, challenging and making this illusion questionable. Understanding this, perhaps we can rewrite Volpone's first speech by having him say, 'Who can get thee, / He shall be noble, valiant, honest, wise, (and tall) –' (I.i.26–7); and, if we give a Jonsonian reading to Shakespeare, we can have Timon say, 'Thus much of this will make black white, four fair, wrong right, base noble, old young, coward valiant (and dwarfish tall)' (*Timon of Athens* IV.iii.28–30).[13]

The Dwarf and the Hunchback

> I would have saide, that the loose or disjoynted motion of a limping or crookebackt Woman, might adde some new kinde of pleasure unto that business or sweet sinne, and some un-assaid sensuall sweetnesse, to such as make triall of it: but I have lately learnt, that even ancient Philosophy hath decided the matter: Who saith, that the legs and thighs of the crooked-backt or halting-lame, by reason of their imperfection, not receiving the nourishment, due unto them, it followeth that the Genitall parts, that are above them, are more full, better nourished and more vigorous.[14]

Before returning to *Volpone*, I want to comment on one more important hunchback and ape figure, namely, Shakespeare's Richard III, who possibly existed in Jonson's mind as he may have once written a play called *Richard Crookback*. In *Oxford Dictionary of National Biography*, Ian Donaldson writes that Jonson received payment from Henslowe in 1602 for a play called 'Richard Crookback', but the play has vanished.[15] In Shakespeare's *King Richard III* (1592–3), the young Duke of York, when talking to the hunchback, says:

> Uncle, my brother mocks both you and me.
> Because that I am little like an ape,
> He thinks that you should bear me on your shoulders.

(III.i.129–31)

The suggestion of 'little like an ape' evokes the image of Nano, linking hunchbacks with dwarfs. A. P. Rossiter sees the hunchback as a middle term between Barabas in *The Jew of Malta* (1590) and Volpone because he

> inhabits a world where everyone deserves everything he can do to them; and in his murderous practical joking he is *inclusively* the comic exposer of the mental shortcomings (the intellectual and moral deformities) of this world of beings depraved and besotted.[16]

Laurence Olivier's *Richard III* (1955) makes a huge feature of the hunchback as Camp (a subject which I will return to in the final chapter).[17] Many times in the film the camera just focuses on the shadow on the ground instead of the characters' action, reminding us of how Richard has to 'spy my shadow in the sun / And descant on mine own deformity' (I.i.26–7). The focus on the shadow recalls the stain of the skull in *The Ambassadors*, highlighting Richard's relationship to death. Thriving on killing males and seducing females, the hunchback can be seen as another *memento mori*. Reading the figure in relationship to comedy, Marty Feldman's performance of Igor in Mel Brooks's *Young Frankenstein* (1974) parodies Olivier, exaggerating the comic potential of the hunchback.[18] The film connects to the grotesque body in several ways: not only does the law enforcer Inspector Kemp have a deformed hand, Dr Frankenstein, or 'Fronkensteen' (Gene Wilder), has a hunchbacked servant Igor, who can switch his hump from right to left. In response to the former's suggestion that 'Perhaps I could help you with that hump', the latter asks, 'What hump?' as if his deformed back, phallic in its protrusion, is invisible. Igor, like a Vice, sometimes talks straight to the camera as if he were talking to a live audience and commenting on the film. However, he also acts like a zany and a parasite. He signifies the crooked attempt of Frankenstein, who cannot escape from the name of the Father (with him crying, 'Destiny! Destiny! No escaping that for me!') that pushes him to produce a monster (Peter Boyle). The grotesque figure possesses different enlarged body parts, including an enormous 'schwanzstucker' that will make him very popular. He helps women to solve the mystery of their lives, recalling the hunchback saying to his master, 'It's gonna be a long night. If you need any help with the girls, I'll be . . .', indicating the ambiguity between phallic empowerment and impotence.

The hunchback is another anamorphic figure. As a comedian, he is not really 'deformed', because he has the power to undo inhibitions. Francis Bacon argues that the deformed person has 'a perpetual spur in himself to rescue and deliver himself from scorn', and hence, 'all deformed persons are extreme bold', which makes deformity 'an advantage to rising'.[19] Freud's discussion of people who are 'exceptions' is important to the understanding of Richard III as a comic figure. Using the hunchback as an example, he believes that the play's opening soliloquy means the following:

> Nature has done me a grievous wrong in denying me the beauty of form which wins human love. Life owes me reparation for this, and I will see that I get it. I have a right to be an exception, to disregard the scruples by which others let themselves be held back. I may do wrong myself, since wrong has been done to me.[20]

In psychoanalysis, Freud suggests that the patient, under the guidance of the doctor, is usually asked 'to make the advance from the pleasure principle to the reality principle by which the mature human being is distinguished from the child'. However, some may say that 'they have renounced enough and suffered enough, and have a claim to be spared any further demands'; and they will 'submit no longer to any disagreeable necessity, for they are *exceptions* and, moreover, intend to remain so'.[21] Refusing to submit himself to the reality principle, the hunchback becomes a figure who questions 'normal' behaviour and order.

Being a part of the tradition of folk play and popular theatre, the Vice inherits the speciality of manipulating language:[22]

> RICHARD GLOUCESTER [*aside*]   So wise so young, they say, do
> never live long.
> PRINCE EDWARD   What say you, uncle?
> RICHARD GLOUCESTER   I say, 'Without characters fame lives long'.
> [*Aside*] Thus like the formal Vice, Iniquity,
> I moralize two meanings in one word.
>
> (III.i.79–83)

In 'Structure, Sign and Play in the Discourse of the Human Sciences', Jacques Derrida argues that the language system cannot be regarded as fixed and unchangeable; it has to be understood on the level of *différance*.[23] Moralising two meanings into one word, Richard not only plays with double meanings, he blurs the differences between moral and immoral, just as he shatters the distinction between formal and informal with the suggestion that he is 'like' the formal Vice. Bernard Spivack argues that Richard

> is inviting the appreciation of the audience for his dexterity in deceit, for his skill in that kind of exhibition which evolved out of the moral metaphor of the Vice. He has become for the nonce the artist, his ornate duplicity an end in itself.[24]

Pretending to weep to beguile the fools, Richard clothes his naked villainy and acts like a saint when he plays the devil. Peter Happé argues that 'The Vice's weeping is an identifying feature. His grief is always insincere, since it was meant to be part of his showmanship', suggesting that the Vice 'derives from clowns, fools, and cheeky messengers, and inherits from the Devil a desire to humble all men'.[25] Discussing the Devil and the Vice, Spivack suggests that the Devil is the father of evil and the source of all vices.[26] However, the 'deformity' of Richard is disputable. On the alleged deformity of Richard III, Marjorie Garber argues that 'Richard is not only deformed, his deformity is itself a deformation. His twisted and misshapen body encodes the whole strategy of history as a necessary deforming and *un*forming – with the object of *re*forming – the past.'[27] Drawing attention to the difference between Charles Ross and Thomas More's descriptions of Richard III, Garber notes that while 'Ross describes Richard's right shoulder as being higher than his left', More 'asserts that "his left shoulder [was] much higher than his right"'.[28] Moreover, Garber writes that a portrait in the Royal Collection 'seems to emblematize the whole controversy', as 'X-ray examination reveals an original straight shoulder line, which was subsequently painted over to present the raised right shoulder silhouette so often copied by later portraitists.'[29] Therefore, one may argue that there is also an anamorphic nature in the alleged deformity of Richard III: similar to the skull in *The Ambassadors*, Richard's 'deformed' shoulder is also 'there' and 'not there' simultaneously. Recalling the relationship between the ape and the uncanny, the hunchback, as a Vice, de-forms with his ability of self-fashioning.

The Anamorphic Nano

With these figures from Velázquez, Holbein and Shakespeare in mind, I want to go back to discussing Jonson's dwarf. Can Nano be read as another anamorphic figure? Could he be seen as another de-formed Vice-like character? Many critics have discussed the importance of death in *Volpone*, but none of them has attempted to link it with the image of the dwarf. When Volpone asks his bastards to bring forth some sports (III.iii.1), Nano claims precedence over Androgyno and Castrone. Even though we cannot accept the dwarf's words at face value, he seems to be the most important character among Volpone's bastards:

> NANO   Dwarf, fool, and eunuch, well met here we be.
>   A question it were now, whether of us three,

> Being, all, the known delicates of a rich man,
>   In pleasing him claim the precedency can?
> CASTRONE   I claim for myself.
> ANDROGYNO   And so doth the fool.
> NANO   'Tis foolish indeed. Let me set you both to school.
>   First, for your dwarf, he's little and witty,
>   And everything, as it is little, is pretty;
>   Else why do men say to a creature (of my shape)
>   So soon as they see him, 'It's a pretty little ape'?
>   And why a pretty 'ape'? But for pleasing imitation
>   Of greater men's action, in a ridiculous fashion.
>   Beside, this feat body of mine doth not crave
>   Half the meat, drink, and cloth one of your bulks will have.
>   Admit your fool's face be the mother of laughter,
>   Yet, for his brain, it must always come after;
>   And though that do feed him, it's a pitiful case
>   His body is beholding to such a bad face.
>
> (III.iii.3–20)

Describing himself as 'little', 'witty' and 'pretty', Nano, saying he has the shape of an ape, suggests the power of imitation. Volpone says, 'Indeed, very many have assayed, like apes, in imitation of that which is really and essentially in me, to make of this oil' (II.ii.128–9). The relationship between apes and imitation reminds us that the dwarf acts as the zany Zan Fritada in the mountebank scene, which makes him an imitator, a counterfeiter and a swaggerer.[30]

Nano also performs a Vice-like part when Mosca is absent. When the parasite is still on the street (Act III scene iii), the dwarf twice speaks an aside and comments on the play. First, when Lady Would-be enters, he says, 'Now, St Mark / Deliver us! Anon, she'll beat her women / Because her nose is red' (III.iv.14–16): the woman's red nose makes her grotesque. When Lady Would-be says to other women, 'I, that have preached these things so oft unto you, / Read you the principles, argued all the grounds, / Disputed every fitness, every grace, / Called you to counsel of so frequent dressings' (III.iv.23–6), Nano interrupts again, like a Vice, 'More carefully than of your fame or honour' (III.iv.27).

The suggestion of 'little', 'witty' and 'pretty' has its sexual implications. Tricked by the parasite into believing that her husband is with a courtesan of Venice, Lady Would-be asks Mosca, 'I pray you, lend me your dwarf' (III.v.29). Whether she, or Jonson, thinks of a dwarf as a dildo must be left to the audience's imagination: perhaps the association may be no more than the audience's way of thinking. Borrowing the dwarf from Volpone questions the masculinity of Politic Would-be, foretelling how she mistakenly takes Peregrine as her husband's Sporus and a hermaphrodite (IV.ii.48). The relationship between Sporus and

Nero raises the issue of same-sex desire, recalling how Volpone wants to transform Mosca into a Venus (V.iii.104), making the supposed triumph of masculinity questionable.

At the end of the play, Volpone is punished in the hospital of the *Incurabili*, with his body 'cramped with irons' till he is really 'sick and lame':

FIRST AVOCATORE   Thou, Volpone,
    By blood and rank a gentleman, canst not fall
    Under like censure. But our judgement on thee
    Is that thy substance all be straight confiscate
    To the hospital of the *Incurabili*;
    And since the most was gotten by imposture,
    By feigning lame, gout, palsy, and such diseases,
    Thou art to lie in prison, cramped with irons,
    Till thou be'st sick and lame indeed.

(V.xii.116–24)

In contrast to the scene in which he stood on the platform in the open square outside Celia's window, Volpone has to be imprisoned and cramped in a confined space where he cannot stretch his body. He has to be compressed and bent over, like a hook, being turned into a dwarfish shape, and to become stiff and paralysed. He is to be tortured till he becomes a distortion, and his punishment, in other words, is to be anamorphic. Therefore, instead of keeping a dwarf in his house, he is, as it were, turned into one. The word 'hook', though it appears only once in the play, has a significant implication. Referring to Volpone's scheme, Mosca says: 'You know this hope is such a bait, it covers any hook' (I.iv.134–5). Within all the 'hopes' is a 'hook', which not only reminds us of Volpone's final punishment, but suggests that within the centre of the play is a hook, with its image of distortion and compression.

The hint that Volpone becomes an image of distortion and compression in the end tempts us to read the presence of the anamorphic shape in the earlier parts. Indeed, we can find Nano and his shadow in many places. Throughout *Volpone*, there is a constant image of bodies being hunched up, made to be distorted, stiffened by being unable to move: fusing oddly such images of the stiff (the dead body, the impotent phallic self), the dwarf, and the self as tortured. The Argument of the play suggests that Volpone is 'childless, rich, feigns sick, despairs, / Offers his state to hopes of several heirs, / Lies languishing' ('The Argument', lines 1–3). The 'lying' of Volpone relates to both his acting and his posture, linking to his shape of feigning sick, suggesting the ambivalent image of living and dying. Before his suitors come in, Volpone says:

Now, my feigned cough, my phthisic, and my gout,
My apoplexy, palsy, and catarrh,
Help, with your forcèd functions, this my posture,
Wherein this three year I have milked their hopes.

(I.ii.124–7)

Volpone's acting is inseparable from his 'dwarfish' posture – the idea of
his being a figure of death, that is, the *memento mori*. When we watch
his performance on his 'deathbed', we are seeing the shadow of Nano
on the stage. At the beginning of Act V, Volpone says:

'Fore God, my left leg 'gan to have the cramp,
And I appre'nded, straight, some power had struck me
With a dead palsy. Well, I must be merry
And shake it off. A many of these fears
Would put me into some villainous disease,
Should they come thick upon me;
...
I shall conquer.

(V.i.5–13)

The suggestion that Volpone is starting to feel the cramp demonstrates
that even he cannot avoid the power of the dwarf, and, therefore, he
is becoming another anamorphic figure. The suggestion of cramping
reminds us of Caliban, who is constantly threatened by similar punishment. For instance, Prospero says to him, 'For this be sure tonight thou
shalt have cramps' (*The Tempest* I.ii.328); and 'What I command, I'll
rack thee with old cramps, / Fill all thy bones with aches, make thee
roar, / That beasts shall tremble at thy din' (I.ii.372–4). At the end of
the play, Prospero says to Stefano (who is not Stefano, but a cramp
(V.i.289)), 'He is as disproportioned in his manners / As in his shape'
(V.i.294–5), and then he says to Caliban, 'Go, sirrah, to my cell. / Take
with you your companions' (V.i.295–6). The idea of cramping is linked
with being improper as the word 'disproportion' implies; and perhaps
the feeling of cramping is what 'prosperity' enforces on a capitalist
and a colonised subject. The scene in *Volpone* is in contrast with the
mountebank scene, in which he claims that he sells drugs which can
cure 'cramps, convulsions, paralyses, epilepsies . . .' (II.ii.90): symp-
toms that relate to losing control of the body. The suggestion of 'I shall
conquer' is contrasted with Mosca's earlier words 'age will conquer'
(I.iii.32), showing that Volpone thinks that he is an exception. What
he does not realise is that his parasite has already turned the joke
around and is setting the 'fox-trap' against him (V.v.18), which raises
the image of clasping and torturing. The image of distortion recalls
the words of Mosca that Volpone would not coffin people alive in a

'clasping prison' (I.i.46), which describes a prison as a confined space where people cannot stretch their bodies properly. The beginning of Act V suggests that the anamorphic shape of Volpone is no longer just a performance, echoing his words in front of Lady Would-be: 'Before, I feigned diseases; now I have one' (III.iv.62). Throughout this comedy, the anamorphic image of the dwarf is, like a shadow, a constant presence on the stage.

The idea that the dwarf signifies the *memento mori* that escapes our consciousness can be noticed in the scene in which Volpone dupes Corbaccio. When the raven sees the sickness of the fox, he says, 'Excellent, excellent, sure I shall outlast him! / This makes me young again, a score of years' (I.iv.55–6). Seeing the imminent death of the Venetian *Magnifico* makes Corbaccio jubilant, causing him to forget that he is facing his own. Volpone says:

> Nay, here was one
> Is now gone home, that wishes to live longer!
> Feels not his gout, nor palsy, feigns himself
> Younger by scores of years, flatters his age
> With confident belying it; hopes he may
> With charms, like Aeson, have his youth restored;
> And with these thoughts so battens, as if fate
> Would be as easily cheated on as he,
> And all turns air!
>
> (I.iv.151–9)

As a young man pretending to be old, Volpone laughs at old age, recalling how Mosca describes Corbaccio as an impotent who hopes to 'hop over his grave' (I.iv.4–5). The images of sickness and death remind us of the meaning of 'cramp', as both relate to the bending of the body and to the idea of becoming a hook. Commenting on old age, the fox and the fly link it with stiffened joints (I.iv.43) and fainting limbs (I.iv.147), connecting death with impotence, recalling how Politic Would-be laments the death of Stone the fool as 'Stone dead!': a double entendre 'opposing suggestions of death and generation'.[31] More importantly, Corbaccio is looking at himself – the image of a dying person – but fails to realise it, as if he sees only the gold but not Volpone, and the gold gives an excess to the fox, making him more than who he is.[32] The gold creates an illusion that 'blinds' Corbaccio, making him incapable of realising the power of death that is right in front of him.

Similar to the anamorphic image in *The Ambassadors*, Volpone reverses the gaze as he constantly blurs the difference between actor and spectator: while many critics assert the importance of Volpone's theatricality, we should be aware that in most parts of the play, he takes pleasure in watching his suitor while pretending to be watched. Therefore, we need to think twice if we just focus on Volpone being a 'consummate actor' and suggest that he is 'too inveterate an artist to be content with the role of the looker-on',[33] because it makes the relationship between subject and object one-dimensional:

> VOLPONE   I'll get up
> Behind the curtain, on a stool, and hearken;
> Sometime peep over, see how they do look,
> With what degrees their blood doth leave their faces!
> Oh, 'twill afford me a rare meal of laughter.
>
> (V.ii.83–7)

At the end, the fox becomes a voyeur openly. While we are mesmerised by his performance onstage, we should not forget that the fox's role allows him to watch back. This reminds us of how the fox repeatedly asks his parasite if he could see Celia when he first hears about her beauty (the same can be applied to the eagerness of Subtle and Face to see the face of Dame Pliant) – the suggestion is repeated three times at the end of Act I, which illustrates how Volpone has the constant urge to watch the other. The same happens when the fox is on his bed watching Mosca's performance, and in Act V scene iii when he speaks aside while enjoying his parasite's show. Therefore, while on the surface the audience enjoy watching Volpone playing dead, what really happens is that the shadow of the dwarf is watching us and laughing, recalling the quotation of Horace's *Epistles* which was printed on the title page of *Bartholomew Fair* in the 1640 folio:

> If he were still on earth, Democritus would laugh in scorn, for he would gaze at the audience more attentively than at the show itself, as offering him something more spectacular than the actor. As for the writers, however, he would reckon they were telling their tales to a deaf ass. (II.i.194–200)[34]

However, the representation of death in the play may be more than just the image of Volpone. If we go back to the beginning, we realise that right at the heart of the play is the gold. In other words, if we visualise a stage production of *Volpone* and compare it with paintings such as *Las Meninas* and *The Ambassadors*, we should notice that the key element, or the key object, that makes the play 'strange' is not the deathbed (with Volpone on it) at the centre of the stage. Instead, this curious object is the *gold* behind him that has the simultaneous effect of illuminating and alienating. Not only is gold an anamorphic object, it is the power to anamorphically transform other objects. To paraphrase Falstaff, gold is the object 'not only anamorphic in itself, but the cause that anamorphosis is in other men' (*2 Henry IV* I.ii.8–9). Therefore, the real dwarf, the real stain, or the real skull is not Volpone. Instead, it is the gold, the god that is dumb (I.i.22):

> VOLPONE   Good morning to the day; and next, my gold!
>   Open the shrine that I may see my saint.
>   *[Mosca reveals the treasure.]*
>   Hail the world's soul, and mine! More glad than is
>   The teeming earth to see the longed-for sun
>   Peep through the horns of the celestial Ram
>   Am I to view thy splendour, darkening his;
>   That lying here, amongst my other hoards,
>   Show'st like a flame by night, or like the day
>   Struck out of chaos, when all darkness fled
>   Unto the centre.
>
>   (I.i.1–10)

At the centre is the mute object, with its power of mutilation (a pun first suggested by Paul De Man),[35] and Volpone is metonymically linked to it. Therefore, while it is true that Nano represents the dwarfish quality of Volpone, its implication does not end here. Because at the heart of this quality is the concept that Volpone signifies the gold, which is the real 'dwarf' that haunts us while we are watching this comedy. When Corbaccio asks Mosca why Voltore is in Volpone's house, the parasite replies:

> He smelt a carcass, sir, when he but heard
> My master was about his testament;
> As I did urge him to it, for your good –
>
>   (I.iv.61–3)

Mosca strikes on the truth here. Volpone, as the signification of gold, is the carcass (I.ii.90), the thing 'from which the "life", "soul", or essence is gone' (*OED* 4). Another reference to the dead body is in Act V scene ii:

> MOSCA *[Dressing]*   But what, sir, if they ask
>   After the body?
> VOLPONE   Say it was corrupted.
> MOSCA   I'll say it stunk, sir; and was fain t' have it
>   Coffined up instantly and sent away.
>
>   (V.ii.76–9)

When Mosca says, 'I'll say it stunk', he is referring to Volpone and the gold as the dead object simultaneously. Gold is the foul and dead object that is at the heart of the play, and the comedy comes from there. In *The Odd One In: On Comedy*, Alenka Zupančič writes:

It is essential to tragedy that there is nothing behind, that the closet is empty; and it is precisely this nothing that becomes the space of the hero's infinite passion, which ultimately brings him down . . . On the other hand, what comedy puts in the place of this infinite passion is a finite, trivial object: instead of the abyssal negativity of the subject, it puts there its other, 'objective,' objectified side.[36]

If we 'shadow' the dwarf, we realise that *Volpone* originates from an object, and the centre is an abyss that lures us. In other words, at the centre of this comedy is a lack, or a dead object, which embodies this absence, making the concept of the 'fox hole' significant:

> MOSCA   My fox
>   Is out on his hole, and ere he shall re-enter,
>   I'll make him languish in his borrowed case,
>   Except he come to composition with me. (V.v.6–9)

Throughout the comedy, the dwarf and the cramping body of Volpone function as a reminder of this dead object. As such, it is extremely important when the parasite says:

>   True. They will not see't;
>   Too much light blinds 'em, I think
>
> (V.ii.22–3)

Mosca talks about the importance of the blinding light as if there is an absence illuminating from the fox hole and the gold is in the place of this emptiness. One can argue that the gold is not always present 'objectively' on the stage; however, it is important to see that the 'it' is hidden somewhere in the 'altar' of Volpone. The gold is the dead object that is hidden but always present. (An example from modern comedy can be seen in Joe Orton's *What the Butler Saw*: the 'object' – the missing part of Sir Winston Churchill – has always been kept in the box on the desk, but no one seems to pay attention to it throughout the play until the end.[37]) Commenting on Mosca's remark, 'You are not taken with it enough, methinks?' (V.ii.9) and Volpone's response, 'Oh, more than if I had enjoyed the wench. / The pleasure of all womankind's not like it' (V.ii.10–11), Ian Donaldson writes that the '"it" which lies at the very centre of the play – is the art of impersonation and deception: an art which for Volpone and Mosca is more thrilling than sex itself. This *it* is the ultimate end for which Volpone plays.'[38] If we consider the representation of the dwarf as an anamorphic ape, then this statement can perhaps be rewritten as the 'it' can be read as the gold, the object that drives the play forward.

The Dwarf as a Critique of Early Modern Capitalism

In the final part of this chapter, I will use the above discussion to rethink some of the traditional criticisms of *Volpone*, and, subsequently, its response to the nascent early modern capitalism, starting with Stephen Greenblatt's famous argument on the 'false ending', in which he suggests that the beginning of Act V shows how Volpone 'directs the audience, as it were, to reject the theatrical principles of displacement, mask, and metamorphosis'. Jonson's vision, he says, is even more radical: 'We reject not the abuse of playing but playing itself.'[39] This suggests the importance of a lack in the play:

> Indeed, with his ready disguises, he is liberated even from himself, uncommitted to a single, fixed role. He has the energy of Proteus. Yet in the lull following the false ending, we perceive the converse, as it were, of this splendid energy, a yawning emptiness which at once permits its flowering and swallows it up. 'We are all hollow and empty,' wrote Montaigne: 'It is not with wind and sound that we have to fill ourselves; we need more solid substance to repair us.'[40]

Considering the signification of the ape in the play, I would suggest that the sense of lack in *Volpone* is intricately linked with the city and the rise of early modern capitalism. It is such a society that produces an abyss that urges the suitors of the Venetian *Magnifico* to chase after property, in particular, the gold, as a fetish and a substitute. When Greenblatt writes that 'this play bitterly insists [that] you cannot stay in the theatre forever',[41] he seems to be suggesting that there should be a fixed subject and identity which is beyond theatre and role playing. However, to develop my argument, this 'solid substance' may not necessarily be related to the concept of a definite subject, it may just be the gold, the object that forever works as a substitute, which reminds us of how a capitalist subject is castrated and a fetishist.

Volpone critiques capitalism with the concept of possession. In the courtroom scene, after the three suitors realise that they have been fooled by Mosca, Voltore reverses what he had said earlier:

VOLTORE   Oh,
        I know not which to address myself to first,
        Whether Your Fatherhoods, or these innocents –
CORVINO   [*Aside*] Will he betray himself?
VOLTORE   Whom, equally,
        I have abused, out of most covetous ends –
CORVINO The man is mad!

| CORBACCIO | What's that? |
| CORVINO | He is possessed. |

(V.x.5–10)

Jonson puns on the word 'possession'. Voltore is mad because he is driven by the desire to possess. In other words, to be mad is related to ideas of property and inheritance. To be possessed means that a subject is haunted by the ideology of capitalism. Voltore alters his 'truth' based on his desire for possession and property.[42] To be a capitalist subject is to be mad, which reminds us of the ambiguity between folly and madness.

The play on possession continues. Corvino says, 'Grave fathers, he is possessed; again, I say, / Possessed; nay, if there be possession / And obsession, he has both' (V.xii.8–10). The twist in this scene comes when Volpone wants to get himself out of trouble by telling Voltore that he actually lives, that 'you [Voltore] are still the man; your hopes the same; / And this was only a jest' (V.xii.17–18). He tells Voltore:

> VOLPONE　　　Sir, you may redeem it.
> 　　　　They said, you were possessed; fall down and seem so:
> 　　　　I'll help to make it good.　　　　[*Voltore falls.*]
> 　[*Aloud to the court*]　　　　God bless the man!
> 　[*Aside to Voltore*] Stop your wind hard, and swell. [*Aloud*] See, see,
> 　　see, see!
> 　　　　He vomits crooked pins! His eyes are set
> 　　　　Like a dead hare's hung in a poulter's shop!
> 　　　　His mouth's running away! [*To Corvino*] Do you see, Signor?
> 　　　　Now 'tis in his belly!
>
> (V.xii.21–8)

Voltore 'dispossesses' himself because he thinks he has a chance to possess again. The scene shows the ambiguity between the two concepts: to 'possess' can at the same time mean to be 'dispossessed'. Voltore is 'possessed' and 'dispossessed' by the ideology of possession. By showing his 'possession' and 'dispossession', Voltore vomits a 'crooked pin', a reminder of the image of the dwarf, which suggests the crookedness within the ideology of capitalism. Finally, Volpone says, 'Take good heart; the worst is past, sir. / You are dispossessed' (V.xii.34–5). In reply, the avocatore says, 'If he were / Possessed, as it appears, all this is nothing' (V.xii.36–7). To possess, and therefore to be possessed, is to be nothing. Possession in capitalism makes a subject become no-thing, an image which links with the concept of castration.

Volpone plays with the concept of property with the theme of cuckoldry. In Act IV scene vi, Mosca asks Corvino to profess himself as a cuckold (IV.vi.70–1). Describing Celia to Volpone, Mosca says, 'As the true, fervent instance of his love / His own most fair and proper wife; the beauty / Only of price in Venice' (III.vii.77–9). He describes Celia as Corvino's 'proper' wife. The word 'proper' is linked with the concept of property, which relates to the functioning and mechanism of capitalism. His remark about Celia as a 'proper' wife means that to turn someone into a cuckold is to turn a wife from 'proper' into 'improper'. The cuckold is 'improper' because he hands over his own 'property'. Therefore, the act of cuckoldry turns both husband and wife into 'improper', or, to be more precise, into someone with the nature of bastardy.

In *Hamlet* (a play which I will discuss further in Chapter 5), the clown says that men in England are as mad as Hamlet (V.i.142–3). The clown's comment shows the ambiguity between folly and madness, since it is the clown who tells Hamlet that he is mad. There seems to be more sanity in the clown than in Hamlet; or, perhaps, there is only a thin line between folly and madness. From *Volpone*, we can deduce that the world of bastards, under Jonson's portrayal, is Britain. Even though he is writing about Venice, there is no bigger fool in the play than Politic Would-be, whose name implies a parrot, and, therefore, suggests the idea of imitation, and one who comes from England. Moreover, Jonson makes London the location of his next play, *Epicoene*. The fact that the Folio edition of *Every Man in His Humour* changes the play's location from Italy to London is another support. The importance of seeing the play as being related to London comes from its association with the establishment of the city and the rise of city power. A person who gains his status because of capitalism is a bastard of Volpone. The relation between London and the establishment of national identity should also be emphasised. The British East India Company was established in 1600, only six years before *Volpone* was written. The play was created during the rise of capitalism and imperialism. Venice was another trading nation, and thus, its relation to London was important.[43] Jonson's works seem to show his contempt towards capitalism and the China houses. For instance, in *Epicoene*, La Foole, who is 'a precious manikin',

> has a lodging in the Strand for the purpose, or to watch when the ladies are gone to the china-houses, or the Exchange, that he may meet 'em by chance and give 'em presents, some two or three hundred pounds' worth of toys, to be laughed at. (I.iii.26–9)

La Foole is closely associated with China houses and the Exchange. The China houses suggest Orientalism.[44] The Orient is a heterogeneous force that challenges the homogeneous imperial power. Jonson's attitude demonstrates his anxiety about heterogeneity; however, it also shows that it is impossible to sustain a homogenous identity. There is a tension between insistence and deferral within an individual and national identity. A country whose growing international status comes from coining is a world of bastards.

However, having said this, it is not certain whether Jonson is really only anti-theatrical and anti-capitalist, especially if we think of another of Mosca's famous speeches:

> Why, your gold
> Is such another med'cine; it dries up
> All those offensive savours! It transforms
> The most deformèd, and restores 'em lovely,
> As 'twere the strange poetical girdle.
>
> (V.ii.98–102)

This is a reference to Lucian's *The Dream* or *Dialogue of the Cobbler and the Cock* in which the cobbler says that gold 'transforms ugly people and renders them lovely'.[45] Recalling the image of the dwarf, perhaps Mosca's words mean that not only do we need to see how the gold, as the mute object, signifies the presence of death and castration within a capitalist subject, we also should realise how it works as the force that creates and empowers him. After all, the source of madness is also the origin of folly. Discussing the Lacanian concept of symbolic castration, Slavoj Žižek writes:

> This is what the infamous 'symbolic castration' means: the castration that occurs by the very fact of me being caught in the symbolic order, assuming a symbolic mask or title. Castration is the gap between what I immediately am and the symbolic title that confers on me a certain status and authority. In this precise sense, far from being the opposite of power, it is synonymous with power; it is what gives power to me. So one has to think of the phallus not as the organ that immediately expresses the vital force of my being, but as a kind of insignia, a mask that I put on in the same way that a king or judge puts on his insignia – phallus is a kind of organ without a body which I put on, which gets attached to my body, but never becomes an organic part, forever sticking out as its incoherent, excessive prosthesis.[46]

The phallus as an organ without a body reminds us of the skull in *The Ambassadors*, the image of Volpone/gold that lures Corbaccio, and the presence of gold, and its extension, the dwarf, on the stage when we are watching the play. Going back to the words of the parasite, we see that even though the gold represents the deformity within a capitalist subject, it creates him simultaneously.

Mosca's words on gold and deformity give us an insight into how we are 'deformed' as subjects: while the gold with its illumination gives us the illusion of a complete subjectivity, the dwarf, meanwhile, reminds us that it is merely a dead object, which 'de-forms' us from within. We are originally 'deformed', which means that the 'solid substance' cannot be a complete and unified centre. Instead, it is just a dead object, making us a fetishist. Not only can *Volpone* be read as a critique of the 'anti-acquisitive' attitude, as L. C. Knights famously argues, it thematises the 'dwarfishness' of a capitalist subject, and it is a text that talks to us: we are empowered by 'it', we are castrated by 'it'. Therefore, even though *Volpone* can be read as a text that criticises the nascent early modern capitalism, it recognises the power of transformation of a city subject simultaneously.

Notes

1. Herford and Simpson (eds), *Ben Jonson*, vol. 2, p. 58.
2. Welsford, *The Fool*, p. 246.
3. O'Connor, 'Physical Deformity and Chivalric Laughter', p. 60.
4. Garland, 'Disfigurement World', p. 43. There is also a dwarf in Spenser's *The Faerie Queene*: 'Behind her farre away a Dwarfe did lag, / That lasie seemd in being euer last, Or wearied with bearing of her bag / Or needments at his backe.' See Spenser, *Faerie Queene*, I.i.6.
5. Fiedler, *Freaks*, p. 43.
6. Freud, 'The Uncanny', p. 235.
7. Foucault, *Order of Things*, p. 5.
8. Foucault, *Order of Things*, p. 9.
9. Shapiro, *Archaeologies of Vision*, p. 260.
10. Lacan, *Four Fundamental Concepts*, p. 88.
11. Lacan, *Four Fundamental Concepts*, pp. 88–9.
12. Shapiro, 'Notes on Greek Dwarfs', p. 391. On the monstrous body, see also Fudge et al., *At the Borders of the Human*. Some dwarfs, however, are impotent, as they are the victims of Turner's Syndrome and so-called asexual ateliotics, and their deformities are induced by pituitary malfunction. See Fiedler, *Freaks*, p. 51. While discussing the representation of the dwarf, I am fully aware of the troubling nature of this subject. This chapter is merely an attempt to read how the dwarf as a representation exists as an ideology, and in art and literature, not in life.
13. In *Every Man Out of His Humour*, Shift says, 'Ay, as God shall have part of my soul, sir, I ne'er robbed any man, I; never stood by the highway side, sir, but only said so, because I would get myself a name and be counted a tall man' (V.ii.164–6).
14. Montaigne, 'Of the Lame or Crippel', p. 287.
15. For more details, see Jonson, *Cambridge Edition*, vol. 2, pp. 183–4.
16. Rossiter, 'Angel with Horns', p. 16.
17. *Richard III*, directed by Laurence Olivier.
18. *Young Frankenstein*, directed by Mel Brooks.
19. Bacon, 'Essay XLIV'.

20. Freud, 'Some Character-Types', pp. 314–15.

21. Freud, 'Some Character-Types', p. 312.

22. Peter Happé describes Richard III as one of the later developments of the figure of the Vice, and he argues for the relation between the popular theatre and the use of verbal words. See Happé, '"The Vice" and Popular Theatre', pp. 15–16. See also Happé, 'The Vice and the Folk-Drama'; Happé, 'The Vice: A Checklist'; Happé, 'Theatricality in Devils, Sinnekins, and the *Vice*'. See also Weimann, *Shakespeare and the Popular Tradition in the Theatre*. For a discussion of Richard III, see Burnett, *Constructing 'Monsters'*.

23. Derrida, 'Structure, Sign and Play', p. 352. On this point, we can also consider William Empson's suggestion: 'Thus a word may have several distinct meanings; several meanings connected with one another; several meanings which need one another to complete their meaning; or several meanings which unite together so that the word means one relation or one process ... "Ambiguity" itself can mean an indecision as to what you mean, an intention to mean several things, a probability that one or other or both of two things has been meant, and the fact that a statement has several meanings.' See Empson, *Seven Types of Ambiguity*, pp. 5–6.

24. Spivack, *Shakespeare and the Allegory of Evil*, pp. 394–5. Jeremy Tambling writes that the Vice 'interprets in dual senses' and with 'one moralization subverts the other moral'. See Tambling, '*Richard III*, Mourning and Memory', p. 194.

25. Happé, '"The Vice" and Popular Theatre', p. 21.

26. Spivack writes that 'Although the vices of the later moralities occasionally refer to the Devil as their father or godfather, their relationship to him is doctrinal and hierarchic rather than genetic.' See Spivack, *Shakespeare and the Allegory of Evil*, p. 132.

27. Garber, 'Descanting on Deformity', p. 36. The idea of reforming the past recalls the discussion of Walter Benjamin (1892–1940), who was fascinated by Richard III and the hunchback. Discussing the relation between the Vice and allegory, Benjamin writes that 'for *Richard III*, for *Hamlet*, as indeed for all Shakespearian "tragedies", the theory of the *Trauerspiel* is predestined to contain the prolegomena of interpretation'. See Benjamin, *Origin of German Tragic Drama*, p. 228. In 'Theses on the Philosophy of History' (his last work), he writes in Thesis I that there is a puppet who is controlled by a hunchback and wins every chess game, indicating the power of ideology. In Thesis IX, writing against the concept of progress, he describes that, for the angel of history, history is continuous trauma. While everyone sees history as a chain of events, the angel of history views it as 'one single catastrophe which keeps piling wreckage upon wreckage and hurls it in front of his feet'. There is a storm called progress that keeps pushing the angel of history forward, while the angel faces backward and continues to see piles of debris piling up. In every construction of homogeneous historical narrative, there must be some forgetting and exclusion of other heterogeneous elements. The piles of debris within progress recall the image of the hunchback. The crooked back signifies that which distorts history, makes it go astray, and brings about ruin. See Benjamin, 'Theses on the Philosophy of History'.

28. Garber, 'Descanting on Deformity', p. 31.
29. Garber, 'Descanting on Deformity', p. 35.
30. In *Every Man Out of His Humour*, Macilente describes Brisk as a 'poor fantastic' (IV.i.54), who 'apishly' imitates (IV.i.58) and counterfeits (IV.i.65), acting like a 'zany to a tumbler' (IV.i.69). In *Cynthia's Revels*, Mercury says, 'The other gallant [Cos] is his zany and doth most of these tricks after him, sweats to imitate him in everything to a hair, except a beard, which is not yet extant' (II.iii.78–80). In *Poetaster*, a play which is about poets as apes, Tucca says, 'Marry, you may bring Frisker, my zany; he's a good skipping swaggerer' (III.iv.243–4).
31. Donaldson, 'Volpone: Quick and Dead', p. 129.
32. An opposite comparison can be seen in *A Midsummer Night's Dream*: because of the juice of Oberon, the 'dwarfishness' of Hermia suddenly becomes a problem for Lysander. The latter says to her, 'Get you gone, you dwarf' (III.ii.329). While Corbaccio cannot see the 'dwarfishness' of Volpone (or himself) because of the illumination of gold, the juice of Oberon reveals it in Hermia.
33. Herford and Simpson (eds), *Ben Jonson*, vol. 2, pp. 58–9.
34. See Jonson, *Cambridge Edition*, vol. 4, pp. 269–70.
35. De Man, 'Autobiography as De-facement'.
36. Zupančič, *Odd One In*, p. 210.
37. Orton, *Complete Plays*.
38. Donaldson, 'Unknown Ends', p. 121.
39. Greenblatt, 'False Ending in *Volpone*', p. 103.
40. Greenblatt, 'False Ending in *Volpone*', pp. 95–6.
41. Greenblatt, 'False Ending in *Volpone*', p. 104.
42. In *Every Man in His Humour*, Kitely raises similar association when he talks about Wellbred: 'Methought he bare himself in such a fashion, / So full of man and sweetness in his carriage, / And – what was chief – it showed not borrowed in him, / But all he did became him as his own, / And seemed as perfect, proper, and possessed / As breath with life or colour with the blood' (II.i.43–8).
43. On Venice, see McPherson, *Shakespeare, Jonson, and the Myth of Venice*; Tanner, *Venice Desired*; Salingar, 'Idea of Venice in Shakespeare and Ben Jonson'.
44. See Said, *Orientalism*.
45. Lucian, *Lucian*, vol. 2, p. 201.
46. Žižek, *How to Read Lacan*, p. 34.

Chapter 3

'Think me cold, frozen, and impotent, and so report me?': Volpone and His 'Castrone' Complex

VOLPONE   No, no, worthy gentlemen: to tell you true, I cannot endure
to see the rabble of these ground *ciarlitani* that spread their
cloaks on the pavement as if they meant to do feats of activity, and then come in lamely with their mouldy tales out of
Boccaccio, like stale Tabarin, the fabulist – some of them
discoursing their travels and of their tedious captivity in the
Turks' galleys, when indeed, were the truth known, they were
the Christians' galleys, where very temperately they ate bread
and drunk water, as a wholesome penance, enjoined them by
their confessors, for base pilferies.

(II.ii.44–52)

What is the importance of castration in *Volpone*? Castrone, the eunuch,
is one of the Venetian *Magnifico*'s 'bastards'. In Renaissance theatre,
there are more castrated characters compared with the dwarf and
the androgyne: there are twelve plays which have a dwarf character;
Volpone is the only play that has a hermaphrodite character; and there
are at least twenty-five plays with a eunuch.[1] In *Volpone*, Castrone
appears in five scenes. The only lines that he speaks are 'here' with
Nano and Androgyno in Act V scene v and 'I claim for myself' in Act
III scene iii. He is probably the character who has the fewest lines in
Volpone, which makes him almost like a mute, a silent figure. Within
the play, there are two appearances of the word 'eunuch' which are particularly interesting. The first one is in Act I scene ii, where Nano says:

This learnèd opinion we celebrate will,
Fellow eunuch, as behoves us, with all our wit and art,
    To dignify that, whereof ourselves are so great and special a part.

(I.ii.60–2)

Apart from meaning the companionship between the three, 'fellow
eunuch' may mean that both the dwarf and the hermaphrodite are also
castrated. Is it possible that there is more than one castrated figure in

Volpone? If there is, how about Volpone? Another important reference to the word 'eunuch' appears in Act III scene vii when Volpone woos Celia:

> and my dwarf shall dance,
> My eunuch sing, my fool make up the antic,
> Whilst we, in changèd shapes, act Ovid's tales.

(III.vii.218–20)

The eunuch who sings points to the importance of castrati: the male singers who are castrated when they are in their boyhood to preserve their soprano or alto voice. The presence of Castrone in Volpone's house may signify that there is a certain 'lack' in Volpone's body. One of the most intriguing questions when reading *Volpone* appears in the 'rape' scene in Act III scene vii, in which Volpone successfully cuckolds Corvino. However, instead of immediately jumping into 'action' with Celia, he starts his song 'Come, my Celia, let us prove' (III.vii.165) and defers sex with his speech on transformation. The merchant's wife tries her best to resist him, and in the face of this rejection, the *Magnifico* asks angrily, 'Think me cold, / Frozen, and impotent, and so report me?' (III.vii.259–60). And just as it seems that Volpone is going to force himself on her, he is interrupted again by Bonario, which leaves him only with his words, 'I am unmasked, unspirited, undone, / Betrayed to beggary, to infamy –' (III.vii.277–8). What has happened? Can he really *do* it? After all, as the Argument of the play suggests, Volpone is 'childless, rich, feigns sick, despairs . . .'. The fact that he is childless may be a point that is worth noting. While the stopping of Volpone's potential rape of Celia can be attributed to the entrance of Bonario, this chapter argues that the presence of Castrone in the house of Volpone may equally be a significant factor. The question that Volpone asks Celia may reflect a certain kind of anxiety within him – a question that no man can hide away from. Though we generally perceive being castrated as a representation of the threat and the restriction of power, this chapter, through a psychoanalytic reading of Act III scene vii, argues that Volpone's joy in theatrical performance can be conceived in terms of his being 'castrated'. In other words, his transformation and castration perpetuate each other mutually. To discuss their relationships, this chapter will address Howard Bloch's argument in *The Scandal of the Fabliaux* as it argues that castration is the theme of fabliaux (thirteenth century). Afterwards, the image of two 'castrated' figures, namely, Cipolla in Boccaccio's *The Decameron* (1350–3) and the Pardoner in Chaucer's 'The Pardoner's Tale' (1380s–90s), will be examined.[2] The importance of castration in the comedy tradition can be seen from these examples. Finally, this chapter illustrates how the concept of castration in *Volpone* is related to Volpone's transformation, which means that his theatricality should be understood in terms of his being a 'castrated' man. Comparing the scene with another similar one in Philip Massinger's *The Renegado* (1624), this chapter will address why the subject of castration is important in early modern comedy; it will also compare the treatment of this theme in Jonson and in Massinger.

Reading the Fabliau Psychoanalytically

In *The Scandal of the Fabliaux*, Howard Bloch argues that there is a close relationship between fabliaux and castration. Through the tale of ill-fitting coat, he suggests that fabliaux are narratives of lack.[3] In 'L'estoire de Merlin', King Arthur 'will not sit down to dinner' until he hears 'a tale of adventure'.[4]

There is a connection between the fashioning of clothes and that of the story. Bloch suggests that, rather than covering as it should, 'the garment . . . work[s] instead to discover or expose' and 'constitutes an empty center of the story which it so strongly structures'.[5] The significance of the tale and the coat are linked 'in the assimilation of deceit – trickery, infidelity, lies, hiding – to poetic invention', and 'literary and sexual deception are equated'.[6] Within the *Roman de la Rose*, 'the robe of Nature is always in pieces'; thus the repeated use of the word 'deviser' means both 'to describe' and 'to divide'.[7] Narrative puts things in coherent order and separates things simultaneously. The disreputableness of the fabliaux comes from the insistent exposition of 'the scandal of their own production'.[8] In other words, the fashioning and writing relate to the concept of deception.

The mobility of poetic language is equated with that of sexual identity, as 'the loss of phonetic difference is a loss of sexual determinacy', which threatens 'the *straight*ness – *correct*ness, *regular*ity, *ortho*doxy – of grammar'.[9] Bloch links silence with transvestism, suggesting that 'Silence is the liar, the deceiver and trickster . . . who wears other clothes and takes other names in defiance of Nature's rule of difference . . . Silence embodies the pluralistic possibilities of fiction and assumes its multiple functions.'[10] The importance of silence could be linked with the word 'mute', which, as already noted, is a form of mutilation. Silence and castration are related to one another.

Bloch uses various examples to illustrate how the theme of mutilation is central to the understanding of fabliaux. He suggests that 'both actual castration and the motif of the detached member are limit cases of a more general fetishization of body parts within the fabliaux'.[11] The significance of mutilation does not only represent the detachability of body parts; it also points to the 'meditation upon the potential of language for detachment or deception'.[12] Based on the reading of *Recueil général et complet des fabliaux*, Bloch argues that 'the dismemberment of the body is in other words directly associated with the modes of linguistic disruption that are the essence of the fabliaux'.[13]

The erotic interest of the fabliaux consists 'neither of anything like a natural act (a naturalism of the body) nor of the use of direct speech to describe such an act (a naturalism of language)'; it derives from 'a deferral in speech, of speech, that substitutes for the object or act'.[14] Bloch emphasises that 'the narrative fixation upon the partial object is at the origin of sexual desire within the comic tale and not the reverse'.[15] He adds, 'This tale of dismemberment, desire, and the desire for dismemberment originates in a prior act of castration synonymous with narrative itself', and 'a narrative fixation upon the partial at once engenders desire and the desire for narrative'.[16]

Reading Cipolla: Narrative as the Mask of Same-Sex Desire

Bloch's analysis allows us to link the discussion with *The Decameron* and 'The Pardoner's Tale' (and, eventually, with *Volpone*) in which Cipolla's and the Pardoner's fashioning, in terms of both their clothes and narrative, can be associated with the concept of castration. Both stories focus on the significance of relics. The dismemberment of the body illustrates the Lacanian concept of the body in pieces, which relates to the fragmented body and the construction of subjectivity through the mirror image. Moreover, the relics can be seen as a supplement of the phallus. Both stories demonstrate the obsession with the objects which constitute a narrative full of sexual undertones.

To understand *The Decameron*, one must consider the importance of narrative in it. In *The Writer as Liar*, Guido Almansi suggests that

> the story of Madonna Oretta, in its strategic location at the very centre of the *Decameron*'s hundred stories, is a story about how to relate and how not to relate a story. It is therefore a *meta-novella*; in other words, a *novella* dealing with the art of telling a *novella*.[17]

The tenth story of the sixth day is about how Friar Cipolla turns around his narrative about the relic when he finds out some bits of coal have been substituted for the feather of Angel Gabriel. At the beginning, Cipolla asks the followers to kiss the cross after he gives his sermon. He tells them that he will show them a 'most sacred and beautiful relic', which he has brought back from 'the Holy Land across the sea'.[18] That relic is the feather of Angel Gabriel, which 'was left behind in the bedchamber of the Virgin Mary when he came to annunciate her in Nazareth' (p. 470). Aiming at having a good laugh at Friar Cipolla, his friends Giovanni del Bragoniera and Biagio Pizzini remove the feather and want to see how Cipolla can explain its disappearance (pp. 470–1). They substitute the feather, which comes from a parrot, with a few pieces of coal that they have found in a corner of the room (pp. 472–3). Completely unaware, Cipolla opens the caskets in front of his followers. After realising that the relic has been swapped, he does not change colour in the slightest. Instead, he 'raise[s] his eyes and hands to Heaven, and in a voice that could be heard by all the people present', he exclaims, 'Almighty God, may Thy power be forever praised!' (p. 474). Then he closes his casket and says:

> Ladies and gentlemen, I must explain to you that when I was still very young, I was sent by my superior into those parts where the sun appears, with express instructions to seek out the privileges of the Porcellana, which, though they cost nothing to seal and deliver, bring far more profit to others than to ourselves. (p. 474)

He begins to tell a story which is full of sexual implications. For instance, 'the privileges of the Porcellana' probably refers to the act of sodomy.[19] For Cipolla to 'seek out the privileges of the Porcellana' may mean that he is a sodomite. After Cipolla's trips to various countries, he came to the land of Abruzzi (p. 475). His claim that the inhabitants 'go climbing the hills in clogs' has a 'homosexual' undertone, and others such as 'clothe pigs in their own entrails', 'carrying bread on staves' and 'wine in pouches' all have obscene connotations (p. 844). Moreover, 'clogs (*zoccoli*) usually have sodomitic connotations in the literature of the period' (p. 837). Cipolla mentions his trip to the Holy Land, where he met 'the Reverend Father Besokindas Tocursemenot', who offers to show him his 'relics'. The sexual and blasphemous implications can be supported by the list of the relics: the finger of the Holy Ghost which is 'as straight and firm as it ever was', and 'one of the side-bits of the Word-made-flash-in-the-pan' (p. 844). These fragmented body parts are numerous and Cipolla is not able to give them a complete list. The relics represent the body but are not the body. They demonstrate the power of deferral and the supplement. While the authority of the 'holy' body is based on its being single, the scattered nature of the relics disperses the body and turns the single authority into plurality, which displaces the singleness of the body as the centre. The lack of authenticity of the relics further challenges the authority of the Church as the centre.

Cipolla says that he will mention some of the relics because he does not want to disappoint the ladies: the list, which is itself a narrative, is sexual, and it has a seductive power. Cipolla adds:

> And because I was able to place freely at his disposal certain portions of the *Rumpiad* in the vernacular, together with several extracts from Capretius, which he had long been anxious to acquire, he gave me a part-share in his holy relics, presenting me with one of the holes from the Holy Cross, and a small phial containing some of the sound from the bells of Solomon's temple, and the feather of the Angel Gabriel that I was telling you about, and one of Saint Gherardo da Villamagna's sandals, which not long ago in Florence I handed on to Gherardo di Bonsi, who holds him in the deepest veneration; and finally, he gave me some of the coals over which the blessed martyr Saint Lawrence was roasted. All these things I devoutly brought away with me, and I have them to this day. (pp. 475–6)

The suggestion that 'because I was able to place freely at his disposal certain portions of the *Rumpiad* in the vernacular, together with several extracts from Capretius' raises two names with the practice of sodomy in passive and active form, and by claiming that he has presented one of the saint's sandals to Gherardo di Bonsi, Cipolla implies that di Bonsi 'was given to homosexual practices' (pp. 844–5). The supplementary nature of the relics is exhibited because the caskets that kept the relics are so alike that even Cipolla has 'confused' one with the other.

In the end, the crowds are in awe in front of the coal, they beg to touch 'it'. According to Freud, 'the fetish is a substitute for the woman's (the mother's) penis that the little boy once believed in and – for reasons familiar to us – does not want to give up'.[20] Fetishism involves a process of disavowal. A fetishist admits and denies women's lack of phallus simultaneously. The fetishist creates a substitute. Fetishism comes from the fear of castration. It has a double function since it acts as 'a token of triumph over the threat of castration and a protection against it'.[21] It links with homosexuality because it 'saves the fetishist from becoming a homosexual, by endowing women with the characteristic which makes them tolerable as sexual objects'.[22]

OED traces the etymology of the word 'fetish' to mean something which is 'made by art, artificial, skillfully contrived', something which is factitious. This meaning helps us to link the word 'fetish' with the concept of fable/fabliaux and fiction. Bloch argues that the narrative of fabliaux comes from lack – from castration, which turns into an obsession with dead objects, which turns into a narrative, which is a deferral and a supplement of this lack. Fetishism and fabliaux derive from castration and the fear of it, and deriving from such lack is the fetish/fabliaux. Cipolla's narrative is full of undertones of same-sex desire. Reading Cipolla from a psychoanalytic perspective, the relics are his 'fetish', which prevents him from a 'homosexual' recognition. Of course, according to Foucault, to name Cipolla as a 'homosexual' is anachronistic.[23] However, such anachronism only marks the difference between folly (recalling Androgyno's song 'Fools, they are the only nation' (I.ii.66)) and the categorisation of madness as a disease. To suggest Cipolla as having same-sex desire exhibits his relation to folly and carnival, which is different from the category of homosexuality in the nineteenth century with its sense of marginalisation.

Reading the Pardoner: Mute and Mutilation in 'The Pardoner's Tale'

The importance of fashioning in 'The Pardoner's Tale' is suggested in the 'General Prologue' of *The Canterbury Tales*. There is also an undertone of same-sex desire in the 'General Prologue' between the Pardoner and the Summoner, as they are 'freend and compeer'.[24] *A Chaucer Glossary* suggests the 'stif burdoun' in 'this Somonour bar to hym a stif burdoun' (line 673) as an 'indecent pun'.[25] They sing together 'Com hider, love, to me!' (line 672) and it incites the suggestion of their mutual interest. The crucial line which implies the Pardoner's ambiguous sexuality is 'I trowe he were a geldyng or a mare' (line 691). The word 'gelding' shows someone who is castrated, which echoes with the description that the Pardoner has a voice as high as a goat, and he never has a beard, having a face as smooth as someone who has just had a shave (lines 688–90). According to *OED*, the word 'mare' means (1) a horse of either sex; (2) the female of the domestic horse; and (3) a woman, an effeminate man.[26] These three definitions explain the outlook of the Pardoner (which may be useful for us to think about Volpone's image):

> This Pardoner hadde heer as yelow as wex,
> But smothe it heeng as dooth a strike of flex;
> By ounces henge his lokkes that he hadde,
> And therwith he his shuldres overspradde;
> But thynne it lay, by colpons oon and oon.
> But hood, for jolitee, wered he noon,
> For it was trussed up in his walet.
> Hym thoughte he rood al of the newe jet;
> Dischevelee, save his cappe, he rood al bare.
> Swiche glarynge eyen hadde he as an hare.
> A vernycle hadde he sowed upon his cappe.
> His walet, biforn hym in his lappe,
> Bretful of pardoun comen from Rome al hoot.

(lines 675–87)

The Pardoner's hair is thin and smooth, and as yellow as wax. The line 'Hym thoughte he rood al of the newe jet' suggests that the Pardoner believes himself to be fashionable. His appearance is effeminate and his relationship to gender and sexuality is ambiguous.[27]

'The Pardoner's Tale' begins with the 'Pardoner's Prologue', which starts with the Pardoner confessing the lack of authenticity of his own status. Before he tells his moral tales, he stresses that he tells his story only to gain money. Starting his tale, he warns people against greed, gambling, swearing and perjury. The Pardoner tells the tale of three revellers, who decide to go out to hunt and kill Death. They meet an old man, who shows them the way in which they can locate Death. Instead of finding Death, they find some treasures under a tree. The tale continues with the three revellers tricking each other as each wants to possess the treasures alone. In the end, they all die through each other's tricks. After the Pardoner finishes his tale, he asks the pilgrims to come up and kiss the relics and offer their donation. Such a suggestion shows one of the similarities between the Pardoner and Cipolla. The invitation of the Pardoner to the Host makes him receive an angry insult from the latter. The fight between the two is particularly interesting:

> 'Com forth, sire Hoost, and offre first anon,
> And thou shalt kisse the relikes everychon,
> Ye, for a grote! Unbokele anon thy purs.'
>   'Nay, nay!' Quod he, 'thanne have I Cristes
>   curs!
> Lat be,' quod he, 'it shal nat be, so theech!
> Thou woldest make me kisse thyn olde breech,
> And swere it were a relyk of a seint,
> Though it were with thy fundement depeint!
> But, by the croys which that Seint Eleyne fond,
> I wolde I hadde thy coillons in myn hond
> In stide of relikes or of seintuarie.
> Lat kutte hem of, I wol thee helpe hem carie;
> They shul be shryned in an hogges toord!'

(lines 943–55)

The Pardoner asks the Host to kiss his 'relic' and unbuckle his purse, which suggests either he wants to practise sodomy with the Host or to castrate him (or both).[28] In return, the Host exposes the lack of authenticity of the Pardoner's relics, and, more importantly, he uncovers the 'lack' of the Pardoner.[29] He says that he will not kiss the breech – underpants – of the Pardoner as if it were the relic of a saint. The Host suggests that he wants to have the Pardoner's coillons – testicles – in his hands. He wishes to cut them off and enshrine them in a hog's turd. The conversation suggests the Pardoner and the Host's mutual desire to castrate each other. Moreover, what the Host says refers to the possibility that the Pardoner is a eunuch, as the latter has already been castrated.[30] Apart from this, the suggestion of the relics as an old breech implies the impotence of the Pardoner. When the Host uncovers the relics' lack of authenticity and when he suggests that the Pardoner is a castrated man, he immediately silences the latter: the uncovering of the lack stops his narrative. In other words, narrative and castration go together.

From the example of the Pardoner, we can see that the fashioning of clothes and that of narrative share the same function: they both aim at covering a gap, which signifies the lack of essence and meaning. However, the fact that the Pardoner can expose that there are no meanings beneath the letters does not mean that he can control his meaning, since his silence shows his inability to respond. The Pardoner exposes the nature of the floating signifier and he is part of it. By exposing the lack of authority and how the Church establishes authority through the power of narrative, the Pardoner turns the joke on himself. Comparing Cipolla with the Pardoner, even though both Boccaccio and Chaucer are concerned with relics and sexual narrative, Chaucer pushes his concern a little bit further as he focuses on the Pardoner's appearance, which helps to question the concept of gender in a more explicit way. While Boccaccio demonstrates the power of castration, Chaucer reduces the person who exhibits the power of mutilation to a mute. Chaucer uses the Host as a censoring force, which is a castrating force, to silence the gelded/mare Pardoner.[31] Even though the Pardoner, like Cipolla, is able to mutilate, the single authority has to be restored by the Host.

Reading *Volpone*: 'Think me cold, / Frozen, and impotent, and so report me?'

In this part, I will go back to the question raised at the beginning: why does Volpone not act immediately? Is there any possibility that he is really 'cold, frozen and impotent'? Moreover, adding Boccaccio and Chaucer to Jonson, does Volpone exhibit any sexual desire to his own sex? How about his image? Could he be a 'gelding or a mare'? In the following, I am going to reread Act III scene vii in detail, aiming to discuss Volpone as a 'castrated' man and how it can be seen, paradoxically, from this transformation.[32] The first point that allows us to link Volpone with Cipolla and the Pardoner is their shared obsession with relics:

> O thou son of Sol,
> – But brighter than thy father – let me kiss,
> With adoration, thee, and every relic
> Of sacred treasure in this blessèd room.
>
> (I.i.10–13)

Jonson opens the play with Volpone worshipping the gold in his shrine. If gold is the centre of the play, we can see that it is driven from the desire for relics.[33] The obsession with gold, as fragmented objects, demonstrates how Volpone can be seen as a fetishist. He and his suitors are obsessed with the pursuit of objects, which signifies the lack of the phallus.

The comic moment of Act III scene vii erupts when Volpone suddenly leaps from his sickbed, transforming himself from a dying old man into an energetic and lustful villain:

> Why art thou mazed to see me thus revived?
> Rather applaud thy beauty's miracle;
> 'Tis thy great work, that hath, not now alone
> But sundry times, raised me in several shapes,
> And but this morning like a mountebank,
> To see thee at thy window. Ay, before
> I would have left my practice for thy love,
> In varying figures I would have contended
> With the blue Proteus, or the hornèd flood.
> Now, art thou welcome.
>
> (III.vii.145–54)

He explains that he is 'revived' because of Celia's beauty, which reminds us of the cause of his attraction to her:

> VOLPONE   Has she so rare a face?
> MOSCA   Oh, sir, the wonder,
> The blazing star of Italy; a wench
> O'the first year, a beauty, ripe as harvest!
> Whose skin is whiter than a swan, all over!
> That silver, snow, or lilies! A soft lip,
> Would tempt you to eternity of kissing!
> And flesh that melteth in the touch to blood!
> Bright as your gold, and lovely as your gold!
>
> (I.v.107–14)

Volpone is attracted to her because the parasite describes her as gold, which makes it the object cause of desire that drives Volpone towards her. If the suitors of Volpone only see the presence of gold in his dying posture, the same can be said about Volpone's interest in Celia. Volpone never interests himself in Celia herself, for he wants to see her only because there is something 'extra' in her, something that makes her more than who she is – the gold.[34] In fact, we can see the same point in this scene, when in his pursuit of Celia, Volpone says:

> See, here, a rope of pearl, and each more orient
> Than that the brave Egyptian queen caroused:
> Dissolve and drink 'em. See, a carbuncle
> May put out both the eyes of our St Mark;
> A diamond would have bought Lollia Paulina
> When she came in like star-light, hid with jewels
> That were the spoils of provinces. Take these,
> And wear, and lose 'em. Yet remains an ear-ring
> To purchase them again, and this whole state.
>
> (III.vii.190–8)

He wants to 'add' something to Celia as if she has a lack.[35] However, in the language of Lacan, this 'lack' may belong to him because these requests suggest that he is a 'castrated' subject: there is no complete Other, and the subject needs the *objet a* in his Imaginary to fill the void.[36] This point is even more interesting if we continue to consider what Volpone says:

> A gem but worth a private patrimony
> Is nothing; we will eat such at a meal.
> The heads of parrots, tongues of nightingales,
> The brains of peacocks and of ostriches
> Shall be our food; and, could we get the phoenix,
> Though nature lost her kind, she were our dish.
>
> (III.vii.199–204)

The obsession with objects is followed by the eating of animal body parts. The words of Volpone illustrate how a capitalist subject is at the same time a 'castrated' one. The eating exhibits the repression of sexual desire, but it may also be his sole desire.

To transform is to live, and, to Volpone, it is the only way of living, and it originates from the gold, which is the dead object. The references to 'shapes', 'figures' and 'Proteus' point to the importance of changing shapes, and it is the only identit(ies) that one can have, which means that there is no original identity that a subject can return to. The fact that we are 'castrated' means that we are 'empowered' by it simultaneously in a paradoxical way. Let us reread Volpone's famous song to Celia:

> Come, my Celia, let us prove,
> While we can, the sports of love.
> Time will not be ours for ever;
> He, at length, our good will sever.
> Spend not then his gifts in vain.
> Suns that set may rise again,

But if once we lose this light,
'Tis with us perpetual night.
Why should we defer our joys?
Fame and rumour are but toys.
Cannot we delude the eyes
Of a few poor household spies?
Or his easier ears beguile,
Thus removèd by our wile?
'Tis no sin love's fruits to steal,
But the sweet thefts to reveal.
To be taken, to be seen,
These have crimes accounted been.

(III.vii.165–82)

The 'light' refers to the sun. However, we should remember that in *Volpone*, the light of the sun is related to gold. When Volpone talks about not losing the 'light' and not being in the perpetual 'night', he is referring to the power of gold and, its opposite, death. Moreover, we should take note of the question 'Why should we defer our joys?' For him, the transformation is not a deferral, it is an enjoyment in itself, which suggests that the postponement itself is an equivalent of the sexual act. Instead of saying, 'for in thy bed I purpose to destroy thee', as Tarquin does (*The Rape of Lucrece*, line 514), Volpone 'enjoys' himself by jumping into a speech about transformation as if it is a comedy segment. When Volpone says he would undergo different transformations with his 'hornèd flood', such a transformation is both theatrical and sexual, and the two cannot be isolated from one another. In fact, we should remember how, throughout the play, Volpone is acting on his bed, which means that his 'death' bed is his stage, fusing the concepts of sex, death and theatre together.

Interestingly, Volpone's sexual desire is very fluid during this trans-formation. The first transformation that Volpone undergoes is to be young Antinous:[37]

I acted young Antinous, and attracted
The eyes and ears of all the ladies present,
T' admire each graceful gesture, note, and footing.

(III.vii.162–4)

To act as young Antinous raises the confusion of Volpone's gender identity, as Antinous is the lover of the Roman Emperor Hadrian. To lure Celia, Volpone turns himself into a young 'homosexual' lover. According to Volpone, this figure is able to attract women, which means that he turns himself into a 'bisexual' figure. Therefore, we are watching the figure of a catamite, who possesses sexual appeal to both men and women.[38] There are many references which indicate an ambiguous relationship between the master and his servant.[39] For instance, Volpone calls the parasite 'Loving Mosca!' (I.ii.122). After the exit of Voltore, Volpone says, 'Excellent Mosca! / Come hither, let me kiss thee', to which the parasite replies, 'Keep you still, sir. / Here is Corbaccio' (I.iii.78–80). After Volpone sees Mosca dupe his suitors, he says, 'Let me embrace thee. Oh, that I could now / Transform thee to a Venus!' (V.iii.103–4). Perhaps Volpone is more 'excited' when he watches Mosca's act than when he faces Celia. Volpone continues to lure Celia by asking her to act with him in Ovid's tales:

> Thou like Europa now and I like Jove,
> Then I like Mars and thou like Erycine;
> So of the rest, till we have quite run through
> And wearied all the fables of the gods.

> (III.vii.221–4)

These transformations are theatrical and filled with sexual undertones. The first tale that they perform is the story of Jupiter and Europa. In *Metamorphoses*, under Saturn's order, Jupiter transforms himself into a bull to search for Europa. Attracted by the bull's beauty, even though Europa is fearful at first, she trusts him because of his gentleness and friendliness. She comes up to touch him and holds out flowers to his 'snow-white lips'. Then the two begin to join:

> Hardly any longer could he restrain his passion. And now he jumps spor-tively about on the grass, now lays his snowy body down on the yellow sands; and, when her fear has little by little been allayed, he yields his breast for her maiden hands to pat and his horns to entwine with garlands of fresh flowers. The princess even dares to sit upon his back, little knowing upon whom she rests ... She trembles with fear and looks back at the receding shore, holding fast a horn with one hand and resting the other on the crea-ture's back. And her fluttering garments stream behind her in the wind.[40]

To read these lines with sexual connotations, the horn of the bull can be read as Volpone's phallus, while for Europa to mount and ride on the bull's back implies sexual intercourse. Jonson is well aware of the sexual implication of this metamorphosis, as he writes the same joke in *Epicoene*:

> MRS OTTER   Well, I am contented for the horse. They love to be well horsed, I know. I love it myself.
> OTTER   And it is a delicate fine horse, this. *Poetarum Pegasus* [Pegasus of poets]. Under correction, princess, Jupiter did turn himself into a – *taurus* or bull, under correction, good princess.

> (III.i.16–20)

The sexual implication can be seen from the importance of 'horsed', with its meaning of riding and mounting. *Poetarum Pegasus* refers to

Jonson's poem on the Apollo room, lines 12–14, which says 'Wine it is the Milk of Venus, / And the Poets' Horse accounted. / Ply it, and you all are mounted.'[41] Again, we see the mutuality between theatre and sex, and Volpone thrives as a 'castrated' man. The speech is a supplement like the narrative of Cipolla and the Pardoner. The transformation covers up and exposes his lack simultaneously. The language constitutes the supplement of his lack, yet it is the language that seduces and rapes Celia. While Lavinia uses Titus's library to 'reveal the damned contriver of this deed' (*Titus Andronicus* IV.i.36), Volpone uses his to defer committing it.

Volpone does not just want to act as young Antinous, he wants to be Jupiter, and he asks Celia to be Europa, dame of France, Brave Tuscan lady, or proud Spanish beauty, and so forth. The role playing creates another deferral. The fashioning allows Volpone to go beyond the restriction of gender classification. He can be a young 'homosexual' lover at one point, and becomes a masculine bull at another. He can be feminine and masculine at different moments. In ancient Greece and Rome, the differentiation of masculinity and femininity was based on the activity and passivity of how a person behaved.[42] The speech turns this transformation into an androgynous moment. Not only is Volpone Castrone, he is Androgyno. If theatre is full of androgyny because of the existence of the boy actor representing both the male and female, sex is like theatre as it allows the androgynous moment to take place by the deferral within performance and the switching of roles between two lovers.

How can we imagine Volpone's body? The response of Celia to Volpone suggests him as an image of a dead object:

> If you have ears that will be pierced – or eyes,
> That can be opened – a heart, may be touched –
> Or any part that yet sounds man about you –
> If you have touch of holy saints – or heaven –
> Do me the grace to let me 'scape.

(III.vii.239–43)

Her words allow us to push the point further: Volpone is more than just a 'gelding or a mare', his body epitomises the gold as the fragmented and dead object, signifying the importance of 'castration' in the play. Of course, we cannot take Celia too seriously, as her words imply her fetishistic belief in moral values, for she says, 'but I, whose innocence / Is all I can think wealthy or worth th' enjoying, / And which, once lost, I have naught to lose beyond it, / Cannot be taken with these sensual baits' (III.vii.206–9). However, Volpone's response seems to imply a certain kind of paranoia within him:

Think me cold,
Frozen, and impotent, and so report me?
That I had Nestor's hernia thou wouldst think.
I do degenerate and abuse my nation
To play with opportunity thus long.
I should have done the act, and then have parleyed.
Yield, or I'll force thee.

(III.vii.259–65)

Harriet Hawkins suggests that 'Celia's refusal makes possible only the crudest of sexual experiences – a rape void of background music, audience, imaginative postures, mutual pleasure, or exotic context. And the entrance of Bonario at the crucial moment denies Volpone even the satisfaction of rape.'[43] This may be correct. However, Volpone's question 'Think me cold, / Frozen, and impotent, and so report me?' comes as if his 'impotence' has been exposed. It demonstrates the anxiety within him. Even though Celia may not be as eloquent as Marina, as the latter can 'freeze the god Priapus and undo the whole of generation' (*Pericles* xix.12–13), she is 'undoing' Volpone by revealing his 'deadness'. Moreover, just when the moment of rape is supposed to happen, the scene is interrupted again by the entrance of Bonario, much like the intrusion of Valentine on the potential rape by Proteus of Silvia in *The Two Gentlemen of Verona*. There is no suggestion in this scene that Volpone can really rape Celia. The interruption at such a moment makes the potency of Volpone remain in question. It is under such circumstance that he cries, 'I am unmasked, unspirited, undone, / Betrayed to beggary, to infamy –' (III.vii.277–8). To be unmasked is linked with the exposing of his lack, of Volpone's betraying to beggary, or buggery, and, once again, we see how transformation and castration are two interrelated concepts.

While Volpone in Act II scene ii says that he would not act like a *ciarlitani* and tell 'tales out of Boccaccio, like stale Tabarin, the fabulist', his disavowal may be more like a hint, allowing us to read the *Magnifico* in the tradition of the fabliau, Boccaccio and Chaucer. And if it is true that the theme of castration is important to the reading of *Volpone* (and maybe even to other Jonsonian comedies), we should rethink some of the usual criticisms against the dramatist. First, while some critics may disparage him for his portrayal of female characters (like the two extremes of Celia and Lady Would-be in *Volpone*), the almost 'character-less' Celia may not necessarily reflect his incapability to write about and understand women, since it signifies the importance of 'castration fear' in the play. The woman as a 'blank' represents a gap and an abyss that a man faces when he tries to impose his masculine authority. The silent woman is a mute, with her power of mutilation. The 'plain' woman says more about masculine fragility than feminine weakness. Second, while some critics, when comparing Jonson with Shakespeare, may criticise the former for the lack of reconciliation in his comedies, which reflects a certain kind of 'Moroseness' in him,[44] a Lacanian reading of his play suggests that we should see it as an exemplification of the psychoanalyst's dictum: 'There's no such thing as a sexual relationship.'[45] Volpone cannot have sex without using his imagination, without going back to the narrative of the theatre, without his transformation. He cannot do 'it' without his fixation on the dead object. Sex needs to be screened by the theatre, and it is the only way to achieve satisfaction for a 'castrated' subject.

'Castration' in Massinger's Tragicomedy

In the last part of this chapter, I want to discuss the importance of castration as a theme in early modern comedy by comparing the scene in *Volpone* with another similar one in Philip Massinger's *The Renegado*. Massinger's play has been discussed by critics for its relationship between the Turks, trading and castration. The play, called a tragicomedy, tells the story of the contact between Vitelli, a gentleman of Venice, and Donusa, the niece to Amurath, the Ottoman Sultan. The play starts with Vitelli, who is searching for his sister Paulina, who was abducted by Grimaldi, the double renegade. He goes to Tunis disguised as a merchant, because he believes she is there. He is attracted to Donusa, while she falls in love with him. Knowing the relationship between the two, Asambeg, Viceroy of Tunis, and Mustapha, Pasha of Aleppo, feel humiliated and sentence her to death.

As the play progresses, Donusa could free herself from death if she could convert Vitelli to Islam, only she is converted to Christianity in the end. Following the plot of Francisco, a Jesuit, Grimaldi helps the two to escape from the prison of the Turks, leaving Asambeg to 'hide [his] head among the deserts or some cave', 'filled with [his] shame', and to 'die without a partner in [his] moan' (V.viii.36–9).[46] The anxiety of 'turning Turk' is apparent in the text.[47] *OED* defines the word 'renegado' as referring to 'a person who has renounced his or her faith; an apostate; *esp.* a Christian who converts to Islam' (*OED* 2). Daniel Vitkus writes that:

> The term 'renegado,' used in early modern English, is derived from a Spanish form of 'renegade' and suggests a particularly Mediterranean phenomenon – the activities of European Christians who converted to Islam and lived

under Muslim authorities in the Ottoman empire or the Barbary ports of North Africa.[48]

Discussing Othello, Vitkus suggests that:

> Given the conventional association made by European Christians between Islam and promiscuity, it is not surprising that the English expression 'to turn Turk' carried a sexual connotation. Significantly, we find a series of contemporary uses of this phrase in the English drama of the early seventeenth century, where its meaning is 'to become a whore' or 'to commit adultery.' In Philip Massinger's *The Renegado, A Tragaecomedie*, for example, when the heroine Paulina threatens to convert, saying 'I will turne Turke,' Gazet's bawdy rejoinder makes the usual connection: 'Most of your tribe doe so / When they beginne in whore.'[49]

Referring to Othello's famous lines 'Are we turned Turks, and to ourselves do that / Which Heaven hath forbid the Ottomites?' (II.iii.161–2), Michael Neill annotates that:

> Strictly speaking to turn *Turk* meant to convert to Islam; but in common idiomatic usage it could mean simply 'betray', 'renege' or (as here) exhibit the barbarous behaviour attributed to Turks. In the mouth of a Moor-turned-Christian who will himself metaphorically 'turn Turk' at the end of the play the phrase is clearly ironic.[50]

Many critics have discussed the external political and economic circumstances surrounding the play, and the reason why the contact between the Europeans and the Moors would arouse the fear of castration within the former. However, while critics generally agree that castration is an important theme in the play, their understanding usually sees castration as a form of physical threat, a notion, in psychoanalytic analysis, relating more to a Freudian understanding. In the following, I will argue that while Freud's concept of castration is mainly related to the power of man, Massinger's play demonstrates a subtler form of castration, which is a power that comes from the Oriental woman.

Before I continue with the discussion, I want to underline again the importance of castration in the play. There is one scene in which the subject is addressed directly in a comical way. In Act III scene iv, when Gazet, the servant to Vitelli, meets Carazie, the eunuch of Donusa, we have the following conversation:

GAZET   What is your place I pray you?
CARAZIE   Sir, an eunuch.
GAZET   An eunuch! Very fine, i' faith, an eunuch!
          And what are your employments? Neat and easy?
CARAZIE   In the day I wait on my lady when she eats,
          Carry her pantofles, bear up her train;

```
                    Sing her asleep at night, and when she pleases
                    I am her bedfellow.
GAZET                                 How! Her bedfellow?
                    And lie with her?
CARAZIE                               Yes, and lie with her.
GAZET                                                Oh, rare!
                    I'll be eunuch, though I sell my shop for't
                    And all my wares.
CARAZIE                               It is but parting with
                    A precious stone or two. I know the price on't.
GAZET               I'll part with all my stones; and when I am
                    An eunuch, I'll so toss and touse the ladies!
                    Pray you, help me to a chapman.
CARAZIE                                       The court surgeon
                    Shall do you that favour.
GAZET                                 I am made! An eunuch!
```
                                                        (III.iv.42–56)

Many critics have discussed the thematic importance of castration in
The Renegado.[51] Adding to that, I want to suggest that there could be a
symbolic meaning in the presence of Carazie next to Donusa. Seemingly
unaware of the meaning of being a eunuch, Gazet says that he can 'toss
and touse the ladies' when he becomes one. The pun 'stone' joins the
concept of trading and castration together. Not only would the contact
between East and West lead to the exchange of money, it leads to the
concept of emasculation. Carazie's speech about lying with Donusa
implies that there is a force of castration within her: to be her bedfellow
one has to 'part with a precious stone or two'. His lack echoes with
hers, which is within the imagination of the Christians.

The encounter between Vitelli and Donusa in Act I scene iii is an
intriguing one. Different from Celia, one may argue that Donusa is
'moved' even before Vitelli commences his speech. She is enchanted by
Vitelli's words, as she says, 'He speaks well' (I.iii.109) and 'Poetical,
too!' (I.iii.115). In contrast with Celia, Donusa's response to Vitelli is
very positive. She says, 'How movingly could this fellow treat upon / A
worthy subject, that finds such discourse / To grace a trifle!' (I.iii.128–
30). Donusa seems to be mesmerised by Vitelli. The trifle can be interpreted with sexual meaning. In Act II scene iv, Donusa invites Vitelli to
visit her palace. Vitelli says:

Is not this Tempe or the blessed shades
Where innocent spirits reside? Or do I dream,
And this a heavenly vision? Howsoever,
It is a sight too glorious to behold
For such a wretch as I am. (*Stands amazed.*)

                                                        (II.iv.5–9)

The scene is like a sexual fantasy on the part of Vitelli, as indicated by words such as 'dream' and 'heavenly vision'. However, it seems that he also feels his impotence when he faces such a sight. He describes himself as a wretch, which suggests his feeling of inadequacy. A similar suggestion is raised again a few lines later:

> Can this be?
> May I believe my senses? Dare I think
> I have a memory, or that you are
> That excellent creature that of late disdained not
> To look on my poor trifles?

(II.iv.24–8)

Perhaps the poor 'trifles' suggests the sense of lack that Vitelli feels when he faces Donusa. This is part of the eroticised fantasy that the European has when he faces an exotic woman. Going back to the meeting between Donusa and Vitelli in Act I scene iii, she praises how the latter can 'find such discourse to grace a trifle'. She finds pleasure in Vitelli's speech and does not mind if there is only a 'trifle' behind. As Volpone does in Act III scene vii, Vitelli draws references ranging from Ganymede, Zeus and Hercules to Pygmalion (I.iii.118–36). The literary narrative constitutes a seduction. Different from Celia, Donusa is completely enamoured by it, as if she has a strong yearning for western customs.

Moreover, the scene highlights the contrast between the mirror and the veil:

> DONUSA   You are partial
>   In the cause of those you favour, I believe:
>   I instantly could show you one to theirs
>   Not much inferior.
> VITELLI   With your pardon, madam,
>   I am incredulous.
> DONUSA   Can you match me this?
>   (*Unveils herself.*)
>
> VITELLI
>   What wonder look I on! I'll search above
>   And suddenly attend you.   *Exit.*
> DONUSA   Are you amazed?
>   I'll bring you to yourself. (*Breaks the glasses.*)

(I.iii.138–44)

The veil is an important tool in the scene. In the contact between East and West, there is nothing more frightening to the West than the veiling of the face. Commenting on the French law which banned the full body veil of Muslim women on French streets in 2010, Žižek argues how the veil creates a castrating fear within Europeans:

From a Freudian perspective, the face is the ultimate mask that conceals the horror of the Neighbor-Thing: the face is what makes the Neighbor *le semblable*, a fellow-man with whom we can identify and empathize. (Not to mention the fact that, today, many faces are surgically modified and thus deprived of the last vestiges of natural authenticity.) This, then, is why the covered face causes such anxiety: because it confronts us directly with the abyss of the Other-Thing, with the Neighbor in its uncanny dimension. The very covering-up of the face obliterates a protective shield, so that the Other-Thing stares at us directly . . . 'Love thy neighbor!' means, at its most radical, precisely the impossible = real love for this de-subjectivized subject, for this monstrous dark blot cut with a slit/gaze . . . This is why, in psychoanalytic treatment, the patient does not sit face to face with the analyst: they both stare at a third point, since it is only this suspension of the face which opens up the space for the proper dimension of the Neighbor.[52]

In other words, the veil is a tool which allows the possibility of getting in touch with otherness. However, it is exactly the veil that people such as Francisco and Vitelli in *The Renegado* are afraid of. A 'real' contact with otherness should mean that there is a possibility for the questioning and even the breaking down of a person's subjectivity, which is the ultimate surrender of oneself. This is the reason why the contact with the Orient is so fearful for Europeans. Lacan describes the concept of the gaze in the following way:

In our relation to things, in so far as this relation is constituted by the way of vision, and ordered in the figures of representation, something slips, passes, is transmitted, from stage to stage, and is always to some degree eluded in it – that is what we call the gaze.[53]

For Lacan, a person's subjectivity is inseparable from the concept of seeing, the fact that a person feels that he or she is looked at. However, for him, there is a difference between the looking of an eye and that of the gaze. He says, 'What we have to circumscribe, by means of the path he indicates for us, is the pre-existence of a gaze – I see only from one point, but in my existence I am looked at from all sides.'[54] The difference between the seeing and the gaze is that while the former shows, the latter does not. Lacan says, 'The world is all-seeing, but it is not exhibitionistic – it does not provoke our gaze. When it begins to provoke it, the feeling of strangeness begins too.'[55] The gaze is a force that is not supposed to be realised, and the realisation of it makes a subject question his existence as a unique self. The strange feeling that Lacan refers to links with the concept of castration, as both the gaze and castration put the belief of subjectivity in doubt. Lacan says, 'The gaze is presented to us only in the form of a strange contingency, symbolic of what we find on the horizon, as the thrust of our experience, namely, the lack that constitutes castration anxiety.'[56] Following these suggestions, the fact that Donusa wants to visit the market, which is a metaphor of trading and castration, with a veil and be unseen makes her the embodiment of the gaze. In other words, the threat of castration in *The Renegado* is more than just the practice of circumcision and the association of it as a form of mutilation. The Turkish woman is a castrating power because she represents an unidentifiable and un-representable whole (hole) that threatens the existence and the safety of Christians.

There is an uncanny nature in this scene. It is a moment of enchantment as well as disenchantment. While the threat of Donusa comes from her veil, and from the fact that she is hiding her face and becomes a representation of the gaze, her mystic and seductive power also comes from it. Therefore, it is an extremely erotic moment when she takes off her veil and shows her face to Vitelli. She breaks the glasses after she unveils herself. The breaking of the glasses has a significant meaning as if she has broken down the subjectivity of the Europeans. However, it is a moment of arousal as much as a moment of challenge. Vitelli exits from the scene after the 'unveiling' of Donusa. His premature 'exit' may have a sexual implication as if it has an orgasmic effect on him. As Vitelli says to Donusa a few scenes later, 'You are too strong for flesh and blood to treat with' (III.v.9). However, when Donusa unveils herself, she also says, 'I'll bring you to yourself'. Perhaps what the glasses bring to people is just a fake identity, a stage role that is only suitable for the theatre. Donusa's words imply that if a person wants to know his 'true' self, he should get in touch with the 'other'.

Conclusion

Comparing *Volpone* with *The Renegado*, we can see that while Massinger's play illustrates the castrating threat of the Oriental woman to Europeans, Volpone shows his anxiety when he faces the 'plain' woman who does not give him any response. Moreover, we can use this subject to think more about the significance of trading and the city. At the beginning of the play, Volpone famously says, 'I use no trade, no venture . . . I turn no moneys in the public bank, / Nor usure private –' (I.i.33–40), showing his attempt to distance himself from Jews. In *The Renegado*, the threat of castration for the Europeans comes from their trading with the Turks and the Oriental woman. On the other hand, Volpone's words can be read as a denial, coinciding with his anxiety when he faces Celia. Discussing *The Merchant of Venice*, James Shapiro examines Shylock's desire to cut a pound of Antonio's flesh and its relationship to circumcision, and, therefore, to castration.[57] The act of circumcision becomes a mark that distinguishes the Jews from the Christians. However, it also becomes a recurring anxiety that threatens the distinction between them. Adding to this, Janet Adelman examines the role of the Jews as strangers among the Christians.[58] Again, we see how comedy is built upon the anxiety of castration. If circumcision is the little mark that separates the Jews from the Christians, then the idea that castration works as the little thing that signals the difference between the Christians and their 'strangers' could be interesting. Referring to the concept of *objet petit a*, Žižek explains:

> Are we not dealing with the same in our everyday racism? Although we are ready to accept the Jewish, Arab, Oriental other, there is some detail that bothers us in the West: the way they accentuate a certain word, the way they count money, the way they laugh. This tiny feature renders them aliens, no matter how they try to behave like us.[59]

The subject of castration is intricately linked with racial difference, and it continues to exist in modern-day society, especially in the form of jokes. Woody Allen once remarked that penis envy is not something that just applies to women ('I worked with Freud in Vienna. We broke over the concept of penis envy. Freud felt that it should be limited to women').[60] We should remember Allen's role as a Jewish comedian, which allows us to question if there is really such a 'tiny' difference between a Jew and a Christian. However, does Allen speak as a Jew or as a man? Can the joke be seen as a triumph over this racial stereotype because, after all, no man can exclude himself from it? More importantly, Allen's remark may indicate that there is a difference between a comedian and a psychoanalyst: the comedian thinks that comedy can go farther in revealing the fragility of masculinity.

Notes

1. For a detailed list of these plays, see Berger et al., *Index of Characters*.
2. There is a close relationship between Chaucer and fabliaux. Chaucer translated *Roman de la Rose* (begun c. 1225–40, completed c. 1270–8), and the *Roman* is studied by Bloch in his discussion of the fabliaux. Based on *The New Oxford Companion to Literature in French*, *Roman de la Rose* is a 'poem in octosyllabic couplets, cast as an allegorical dream-vision, that describes a young man's initiation into love and his efforts to possess the rosebud of which he is enamoured'. The question of genre should be noticed: while Bloch discusses fabliaux, *Roman de la Rose* is a romance. Fabliaux are 'short comic narratives, composed between the late 12th and the 14th c'. The characteristics of fabliaux are their explicitness about 'sexual behaviour' and 'sexual fantasy'. See France, *New Oxford Companion*, pp. 710, 295.

3. Bloch, *Scandal of the Fabliaux*, p. 22.
4. Bloch cites 'L'estoire de Merlin', in *The Vulgate Version of the Arthurian Romances*, ed. O. Sommer (Washington: Carnegie Institute, 1908), vol. 2, p. 320. See Bloch, *Scandal of the Fabliaux*, p. 22 and his notes on p. 134.
5. Bloch, *Scandal of the Fabliaux*, p. 23.
6. Bloch, *Scandal of the Fabliaux*, p. 26.
7. Bloch, *Scandal of the Fabliaux*, p. 33.
8. Bloch, *Scandal of the Fabliaux*, p. 35.
9. Bloch, *Scandal of the Fabliaux*, p. 43.
10. Bloch, *Scandal of the Fabliaux*, pp. 45–6. On transvestitism, see Garber, *Vested Interests*; see also Garber, *Vice Versa*.
11. Bloch, *Scandal of the Fabliaux*, p. 63.
12. Bloch, *Scandal of the Fabliaux*, p. 67.
13. Bloch, *Scandal of the Fabliaux*, pp. 69–70. Bloch quotes from A. de Courde de Montaiglon, *Recueil général et complet des fabliaux* (Paris: Librairie des Bibliophiles, 1872–90).
14. Bloch, *Scandal of the Fabliaux*, p. 90.
15. Bloch, *Scandal of the Fabliaux*, p. 90.
16. Bloch, *Scandal of the Fabliaux*, p. 91.
17. Almansi, *Writer as Liar*, p. 23.
18. Boccaccio, *Decameron*, p. 470. All the quotations from *The Decameron* are from this edition.
19. See G. H. McWilliam's notes in Boccaccio, *Decameron*, p. 844.
20. Freud, 'Fetishism', pp. 152–3.
21. Freud, 'Fetishism', p. 154.
22. Freud, 'Fetishism', p. 154.
23. Such a suggestion is anachronistic because the first record of the word 'homosexuality' in *OED* appears in 1892, thus the category does not exist in Boccaccio's time. Michel Foucault argues how the discourse of sex in the nineteenth century is different from previous centuries. See Foucault, *History of Sexuality: I*. On homoeroticism and sodomy, see Bray, *Homosexuality in Renaissance England*; Goldberg, *Sodometries*.
24. Chaucer, *Riverside Chaucer*, p. 34, line 670. All the quotations from *The Canterbury Tales* are from this edition.
25. See Davis, *Chaucer Glossary*, p. 19.
26. Monica McAlpine argues that mare 'must be a term commonly used in Chaucer's day to designate a male person who, though not necessarily sterile or impotent, exhibits physical traits suggestive of femaleness, visible characteristics that were also associated with eunuchry in medieval times and that were thought to have broad effects on the psyche and on character'. See McAlpine, 'Pardoner's Homosexuality', p. 11.
27. For more discussions, see Mann, *Chaucer and Medieval Estate Satire*; Cox, *Gender and Language in Chaucer*; Masi, *Chaucer and Gender*; Blamires, *Chaucer, Ethics, and Gender*.
28. For a gay affirmative reading, see Kruger, 'Claiming the Pardoner'.
29. Marshall Leicester, Jr. argues that the Pardoner 'continually makes himself a sign for privation or, as a Lacanian might say, for a lack. The indications are that he experiences this negation in himself as his own nothingness.' See Leicester, *Disenchanted Self*, p. 172.

30. Carolyn Dinshaw argues for the negation of identity of the Pardoner, calling it the eunuch hermeneutic, which 'proceeds by double affirmations, double truths, the incompatible positions of recognition and disavowal, knowledge and belief'. See Dinshaw, *Chaucer's Sexual Poetics*, p. 159.

31. Gary Taylor suggests that 'the English verb *castrate* derives from the Latin verb *castrare* (to castrate, prune, expurgate, deprive of vigour). It is used figuratively as early as 1627 to describe the mutilation of a text by censorship.' See Taylor, *Castration*, pp. 81–2.

32. For a historical discussion of this scene, see Peacock, 'Ben Jonson, Celia, and Ovid'.

33. On gold, see Levin, *Myth of the Golden Age*.

34. Ian Donaldson argues that Celia does not excite Volpone because of her 'physical desirability'; instead, what attracts Volpone is the thought that 'Celia is so difficult of access'. See Donaldson, 'Unknown Ends', p. 117.

35. Discussing this scene, Stephen Greenblatt links it with theatricality: 'The "changed shapes" Volpone lovingly describes are, in a sense, more important than sexual gratification itself, since that gratification is always succeeded by a pause. It is as if Volpone has displaced his sexual energy from its usual instinctual object onto masquerading.' See Greenblatt, 'False Ending in *Volpone*', p. 97.

36. Discussing *Hamlet*, Lacan writes: 'The object of the fantasy, image and pathos, is that other element that takes the place of what the subject is symbolically deprived of. Thus the imaginary object is in a position to condense in itself the virtues or the dimension of being and to become that veritable delusion of being that Simone Weil treats when she focuses on the very densest and most opaque relationship of a man to the object of his desire: the relationship of Molière's Miser to his strongbox. This is the culmination of the fetish character of the object of human desire. Indeed all objects of the human world have this character, from one angle at least.' See Lacan, 'Desire and the Interpretation of Desire in *Hamlet*', p. 15.

37. For more discussion on Antinous, see Fizdale, 'Jonson's Volpone and the "Real" Antinous'.

38. Richmond Barbour argues, 'If in men's eyes boys are women with agreeable pluck, then for women boys are a more companionable and pliable version of men.' See Barbour, '"When I acted young Antinous"', p. 1017.

39. Mario DiGangi argues that the homoeroticism can be seen from Volpone's reference to 'homoerotic role-playing', especially with his reference to young Antinous. See DiGangi, 'Asses and Wits', p. 189. For a discussion of homosexuality in Jonson's plays, see Hutson, 'Liking Men'.

40. Ovid, *Metamorphoses, Volume I*, trans. Miller, p. 121.

41. Holdsworth (ed.), *Epicoene, or, The Silent Woman*, p. 63. Holdsworth quotes here from Herford and Simpson (eds), *Ben Jonson*, vol. 8, p. 657.

42. Brisson, *Sexual Ambivalence*, p. 61.

43. Hawkins, 'Folly, Incurable Disease, and *Volpone*', p. 339.

44. Wilson, 'Morose Ben Jonson'.

45. Lacan, *On Feminine Sexuality*, p. 12.

46. Massinger, *Renegado*. All the quotations from *The Renegado* are from this edition.

47. In *Every Man Out of His Humour*, Puntarvolo says to a notary, 'Then, that

the intended point is the Turk's court in Constantinople; the time limited
for our return, a year; and that if either of us miscarry, the whole venture
is lost – these are general, conceiv'st thou? – or if either of us turn Turk'
(IV.iii.9–12).

48. See Daniel Vitkus's annotation in Vitkus, *Three Turk Plays from Early Modern England*, p. 234.
49. Vitkus, 'Turning Turk in *Othello*', p. 157.
50. Shakespeare, *Othello*, p. 268.
51. See Fuchs, 'Faithless Empires'; Burton, 'English Anxiety and the Muslim Power of Conversion'; Malieckal, '"Wanton irreligious madness"'; Bosman, '"Best play with Mardian"'.
52. Žižek, *Living in the End Times*, pp. 2–3.
53. Lacan, *Four Fundamental Concepts*, p. 73.
54. Lacan, *Four Fundamental Concepts*, p. 72.
55. Lacan, *Four Fundamental Concepts*, p. 75.
56. Lacan, *Four Fundamental Concepts*, pp. 72–3.
57. Shapiro, *Shakespeare and the Jews*.
58. Adelman, *Blood Relations*.
59. Žižek, *How to Read Lacan*, p. 67.
60. *Zelig*, directed by Woody Allen.

Chapter 4

'The case appears too liquid': The Two Sides of Androgyno

This chapter discusses Androgyno. Apart from Act I scene ii, the androgyne only briefly appears in Act III scene iii, Act V scene v and Act V scene xi. However, the lack of appearance does not mean that Androgyno carries no significance in *Volpone* or for other Jonsonian comedies. Two important points should be noted. First, Androgyno is a fool, and, second, the androgyne is characterised by Jonson as a hermaphrodite. These two points will be instrumental to my reading of the androgyne's significance as they suggest the ambiguous attitude of Jonson towards the figure: while the former suggests the importance of folly, the latter, if we follow the portrayal of Ovid, shows an anxiety about effeminacy and castration. To understand Jonson's androgyne, we should examine the figure of the epicene, which is the title of the play written three years after *Volpone*. Different from the dwarf and the eunuch, the androgyne, hermaphrodite and epicene were not popular characters in Renaissance drama. Jonson's *Volpone* and *Epicoene* were the only plays to have a hermaphrodite and an epicene character in them.[1]

OED suggests that androgynous means (1) someone who unites the (physical) characters of both male and female at once, a hermaphrodite; and (2) a womanish man, an effeminate. Hermaphrodite means (1) a person or animal (really or apparently) having both male and female sex organs; (2) an effeminate man or virile woman; (3) catamite; and (4) an animal in which the male and female sexual organs are (normally) present in the same individual, as in various molluscs and worms. Based on these definitions, it is difficult to draw a clear distinction between the androgyne and the hermaphrodite. They both refer to someone who has the physical characteristics of men and women, and relate to effeminate men. In Pushkin's 'A Journey to Arzrum at the Time of the 1829 Campaign', while among the Turks in the Caucasus region, he discovers a hermaphrodite among the prisoners. The hermaphrodite is described as follows:

I saw a tall, fairly stout man with the face of an old, snub-nosed Finnish woman. We examined him in the presence of a doctor. Erat vir, mammosus ut femina, habebat t. non evolutos, p. que parvum et puerilem. Quaerebamus, sit ne exsectus? – Deus, respondit, castravit me. [He was a man with the breasts of a woman, underdeveloped testicles, a small and boyish penis. We asked him if he had been castrated. 'God,' he replied, 'castrated me.']²

Pushkin's description demonstrates the ambiguity between hermaphrodite and eunuch: the Turk would rather be the latter. Moreover, the hermaphrodite is a foreigner, in other words, a heterogeneous creature, in front of the Russians.

In this chapter, I will illustrate how Jonson's representation of the androgyne combines the force of castration and folly. This chapter will first discuss Plato's *The Symposium* and Ovid's *Metamorphoses*, seeing how the androgyne and the hermaphrodite were portrayed in the Greek and Roman period. While Aristophanes's creature is more carnivalesque, Ovid's portrayal may not be too positive towards gender ambiguity. I will then examine Jonson's image of the androgyne in *Volpone*, followed by an analysis of *Epicoene*. In *Volpone*, with the presence of the dwarf, Lady Would-be seems to turn everyone she sees into a hermaphrodite and a eunuch, whereas in *Epicoene*, almost every character in the play is turned into an androgynous creature. Through a rereading of the play, I shall illustrate how Jonson's epicene more closely resembles Ovid's hermaphrodite, even though he also turns the potential anxiety into a force of folly and comedy. Moreover, this chapter will discuss the differences between Jonson's and Shakespeare's androgyny through a reading of *Twelfth Night*, a play which is full of many seemingly androgynous creatures. Compared with Jonson, Shakespeare's portrayal of androgyny resembles that of Aristophanes as his portrayal is carnivalesque and connects with the notion of doubleness. This chapter concludes with a distinction between the androgyne, the hermaphrodite and the epicene. Even though these three terms may suggest similar meanings, a reading of Aristophanes, Ovid and Jonson allows us to see their different implications. Finally, this chapter suggests the logic of comedy that can be seen in Jonson's androgyne, setting up the final reading of the bastards' interlude in the concluding chapter.

Androgyny in *The Symposium*

Julia Kristeva describes *The Symposium* as 'the first assertive apology for Western Eros under the guise of homosexual love'.[3] In Plato's eulogy to love, Aristophanes tells his understanding of Eros through the tale of the androgyne.[4] The beginning of his speech suggests that there were three kinds of human being: male–male, female–female and the combination of the two – the 'androgynous'. The three forms have 'surprising strength and vigour, and so lofty in their notions that they even conspired against gods', which makes Zeus cut each into two halves.[5] Zeus

> sliced each human being in two, just as they slice sorb-apples to make a dry preserve, or eggs with hairs; and at the cleaving of each he bade Apollo turn its face and half-neck to the section side, in order that every one might be made more orderly by the sight of the knife's work upon him.[6]

The wound of human beings represents the repression imposed by Zeus. After Zeus cuts the three genders, the two halves do not want to be separated from each other. Taking pity on such a sight, Zeus 'moved their privy parts to the front . . . so that if in their embracements a man should happen on a woman there might be conception and continuation of their kind'.[7] The cutting by Zeus creates desire. The two halves want to get back together and try to 'combine two in one and heal the human sore'.[8] Those cut from the androgynous are attracted to their opposite sex. Sexual activity is not limited to the love between male and female because the two halves can be male–male and female–female. This includes sodomy and lesbianism. Aristophanes says, 'if male met with male they might have some satiety of their union and a relief, and so might turn their hands to their labours and their interest to ordinary life'.[9] Similarly, those cut from the female gender are interested in women only.

To understand the figure of the androgyny described by Aristophanes, I will draw references to the discussion of Freud, Samuel Weber and Alenka Zupančič. In Freud's reading, he argues that it explains the origin of sexuality.[10] However, his interpretation assumes that the narrator behind the speech is Plato.[11] Samuel Weber challenges this point, arguing that Freud's interpretation attempts to 'authorize itself by appealing to the authority of the author, the "poet-philosopher." This gesture both repeats and initiates what it seeks to confirm: repetition as a movement of the same, originating and seeking to return to a founding identity.'[12] Such an appeal suggests that 'all repetition repeats an original identity, that it seeks to restore: the lovers, their original unity; life, its original death; the text, the original intention of its author'.[13] Weber argues that Freud sees the 'authorial consciousness and intention as the ground and guarantee of the meaning it attributes to the text'.[14] He says that it is difficult to trace the origin of the narrator of the tale.

The image of Aristophanes as a comedy writer allows us to put a touch of carnival on the interpretation. The androgyne is a creature of carnival before getting a 'human' shape. S/he represents the importance of doubleness and is the opposite of completeness. Weber suggests that the beginning of *The Symposium* demonstrates the impossibility of asserting an authority to the narrative. He sees that the recounting at the beginning of *The Symposium* represents 'a repetition of a repetition, Apollodorus recounting the words of Aristodemos. And what really was said may never be certain, for it all took place "long ago, when we were still children".'[15] This repetition signifies the desire to trace the origin, which is a 'disfigural representation' because each representation is a repetition of alteration.[16] What is derived from the desire of the origin are deformed representations.

Weber works from Wilamowitz's translation of *The Symposium*, which Freud cites in his argument and begins with 'our body, you see, was at first not formed as it is now; it was utterly different'. This text translates the Greek word 'physis' not as 'nature' but as 'body'.[17] He argues that 'Aristophanes' story concerns not abstract or incorporeal beings, a "self" or an "ego", but *bodies*.'[18] The androgyne does not refer only to a person's psychic state and is not just spiritual; s/he represents a body of doubleness. Weber suggests that the three genders are not that different from each other. The carnivalesque nature can be seen from 'the world of double-beings' or resemblances, and those beings are moved in circles, 'making cartwheels' like children.[19] The carnival world corresponds to the narrative of *The Symposium*, challenging the concept of singleness and completeness.

However, the androgyne remains a single-headed creature, which seems to represent the mastering of the carnival body by the use of reason. The carnivalesque nature of the androgyne seems to be repressed. Weber argues for the threat of doubleness through the splitting up of double bodies by Zeus. Zeus's action represents 'the economy of appropriation and assimilation that characterizes the organization of the ego; in short, the economy of narcissism'.[20] Such narcissism is an attempt to keep us in the proper place and 'to subordinate alterity to an economy of the same'.[21] The appropriation leaves a wound on the human body, which leads to the concept of castration. Castration comes from the fear of the double. The scar of this wound can be seen from the image of the navel. It serves as a trace of the splitting of the androgyne, signifying that the closure of the body can never be sealed.[22]

According to Weber, the interruption comes from Apollo,[23] who is the opposite of Dionysus. The scar recalls the wound of castration and shows that human bodies are cut, indicating the transition from Androgyno to Castrone. However, this castrated figure is not the opposite of the androgyne, since the wound reminds us that we were once a figure of the repressed carnival world. Weber draws attention to the silenced lovers who leave a wound of castration, a trace that is always there.[24] The muteness of the lovers is a form of mutilation; the mute and mutilation repress and draw out desire simultaneously.

Zupančič's interpretation of Aristophanes's tale allows us to see the difficulty of drawing a clear distinction between an androgynous body and a 'castrated' one. While Weber discusses how the second intervention of Zeus, namely, how Zeus moves the creatures' genitals to the front so that they can have sexual intercourse with each other, illustrates how displacement becomes the 'origin' of eros, Zupančič links it with the Lacanian concept of castration. For her, this latter intervention is important as it introduces the 'little surplus, unexpected, additional satisfaction'.[25] In other words, it is the notion of 'enjoyment as surplus enjoyment'.[26] It is only through this second split that sexual intercourse can take place. She writes:

> If we thus try to conceptually evaluate and grasp this aspect of Aristophanes' speech, we should say that it is only this second cut ('moving the genitals around') that brings us to the split in the strict sense of the term: that is to say, a split which is something other than simply halving or bisecting. It is a separation or a split that also adds or attaches to each 'half' something that (locally and indirectly) links them together, while at the same time making them (relatively) independent (so that they can go about their business and take care of themselves).[27]

Zupančič argues that Aristophanes's story allows us to understand the psychoanalytic notion of castration. Instead of simply seeing the notion of castration as bisection, it is 'a cut that comes in the form of an additional "appendix enjoyment"; it refers to the gap that separates the body; from within, from its enjoyment, and *at the same time* binds it to it'.[28] As we have seen in the previous chapter, Volpone's transformation is inseparable from the notion of reading him as a 'castrated' man. And, in a similar way, I shall discuss how the concepts of fashion and castration are inseparable in *Epicoene*.

Hermaphrodite in *Metamorphoses*

As a contrast to Aristophanes, Ovid's story about the hermaphrodite seems to be less positive towards the notion of gender ambiguity. In the latter's story about Hermaphroditus, there is a fountain called Salmacis that has the power to make men effeminate. The reason for the fountain's 'ill-repute' relates to Hermaphroditus, who is the infant son of Mercury and Venus.[29] Luc Brisson suggests that 'Ovid was the first to recount the myth of Hermaphroditus and the only writer to establish specific links between dual sexuality and masculine homosexuality of the passive kind.'[30] When Hermaphroditus reaches the age of fifteen, an age which suggests the blurring of gender distinction, he 'left his native mountains and abandoned his foster-mother, Ida, delighting to wander in unknown lands and to see strange rivers, his eagerness making light of toil' (p. 199). In the region of Lycia, Hermaphroditus finds 'a pool of water crystal clear to the very bottom' (p. 199), where he encounters a nymph. Representing a figure of excessive femininity, the nymph

> takes no hunting-spear, no painted quiver, nor does she vary her ease with the hardships of the hunt; but at times she bathes her shapely limbs in her own pool; often combs her hair with a boxwood comb, often looks in the mirror-like waters to see what best becomes her. (p. 201)

When she sees the boy, she 'longed to possess what she saw' (p. 201).[31] She takes the active role and seduces the boy with her words. When she asks him for 'a sister's kiss' and is 'in act to throw her arms round his snowy neck' (pp. 201–3), he refuses her request. Salmacis pretends to leave Hermaphroditus alone. Thinking he is unseen by anyone and charmed by the flowing coolness of the stream, the boy strips off his clothes. However, Salmacis has been watching him, making the boy the object of her gaze. Dazzled by what she sees, Salmacis leaps to follow him; she 'holds him fast though he strives against her, steals reluctant kisses, fondles him, touches his unwilling breast, clings to him on this side and on that' (p. 203). She cries, 'Grant me this, ye gods, and may no day ever come that shall separate him from me or me from him' (p. 205). Then their two bodies 'were merged in one, with one face and form for both ... they were no longer two, nor such as to be called, one, woman, and one, man. They seemed neither, and yet both' (p. 205). Brisson writes:

> By granting Salmacis's prayer, the gods thus allowed a reversion in the domain of anthropology, for the new being that emerged from the waters of the Salmacis spring was akin to the androgyne, one of the three

species of double beings from whom, according to Aristophanes in Plato's *Symposium*, the human beings of the present day were produced . . . The fusion of Salmacis with Hermaphroditus establishes a state of indifferentiation that blocks all activity, hence all generation, and arrests everything in a union that is permanent and so, perforce, sterile. The very notion of sex disappears, for to have both sexes is to have neither.[32]

When Hermaphroditus learns that 'the waters into which he had plunged had made him but half-man, and that his limbs had become enfeebled there', he cries, 'Oh, grant this boon, my father and my mother, to your son who bears the names of both: whoever comes into this pool as man may he go forth half-man, and may he weaken at touch of the water' (p. 205). His parents heard and 'charged the waters with that uncanny power' (p. 205).[33] This uncanny power of the water liquidates men and their masculinity. From Ovid's story, we see how the power of water makes men effeminate. Moreover, we should pay attention to the boy who functions as a figure of gender ambiguity. The threat of exaggerated femininity to men is also emphasised: it has power to make men impotent. Finally, the ambivalence between having both sexes and having neither is suggested: this image leads to the concept of epicene.

'The case appears too liquid': Androgyno in *Volpone*

After discussing the difference between Aristophanes's androgyny and Ovid's hermaphrodite, I will discuss how Jonson plays with these notions in *Volpone*. In Act I scene ii, Androgyno says that, after all the transmigration, he enjoys the state of being an androgyne most. When Nano asks, ''Cause here the delight of each sex thou canst vary?' (I.ii.54), Androgyno denies it and claims that being an androgyne is the same as being a fool, and being a fool is what he likes most. In the play, Androgyno is often accompanied by Castrone. In other words, being a fool and being a eunuch may be two notions that are inseparable from one another.

The important reference of *Volpone* relating to androgyny comes from its subplot. In order to get Lady Would-be away from Volpone, Mosca tells her that he sees Politic Would-be 'rowing upon the water in a gondole / With the most cunning courtesan of Venice' (III.v.19–20). Before leaving, she asks, 'I pray you, lend me your dwarf', to which Mosca replies, 'I pray you, take him' (III.v.29). With the dwarf beside her, Lady Would-be sees something different from what actually happens (a scene which recalls Chicolini's (Chico) famous line to Mrs. Teasdale (Margaret Dumont) in the Marx Brothers' *Duck Soup*: 'Who you gonna believe? Me or your own eyes?', even though in the case of Jonson, it makes no difference whether Lady Would-be is believing in Mosca or in her eyes[34]). Accusing Politic Would-be and Peregrine, she says, 'Since you provoke me with your impudence / And laughter of your light land-siren here, / Your Sporus, your hermaphrodite' (IV. ii.46–8). She suggests Peregrine as Sporus. Sporus is a favourite of Nero. Nero made Sporus a eunuch, dressed him as a woman, and publicly went through the form of marriage with him. Lady Would-be's words indicate that she sees Peregrine as a hermaphrodite and a eunuch. Moreover, by saying Peregrine is Sporus, she is categorising them as 'homosexuals'. Lady Would-be says that Peregrine comes from the 'Whitefriars nation' (IV.ii.51), which is a liberty outside law and order. The suggestion that the Whitefriars can be read as prostitutes means that Peregrine, who is 'a female devil in a male outside' (IV.ii.56), like Sporus to Nero, is a catamite of Politic Would-be. The meaning of prostitution is raised again through her use of words such as 'lewd harlot' and 'base fricatrice' (IV.ii.55). Lady Would-be continues her 'confusion' of gender, saying that, 'But for your carnival concupiscence, / Who here is fled for liberty of conscience / From furious persecution of the marshal, / Her will I disple' (IV.ii.60–3). There is a connection between androgyny and carnival, and the latter world is, possibly, what Jonson would call 'the world of bastards'. The carnivalesque nature of gender echoes the 'anarchic' condition of the Whitefriars Nation, recalling the 'baseness' of the fricatrice. The suggestion that Peregrine is 'fled for liberty of conscience' means that he has the freedom to practise bawdy trade. Lady Would-be suggests that she will 'disple': the need to 'discipline' is in opposition to the carnival of gender ambiguity. In the face of this gender confusion, Politic Would-be says, 'The case appears too liquid' (IV.ii.58). With the dwarf beside her, Lady Would-be seems to turn everyone she sees into a hermaphrodite or a eunuch.

'Your "*impotentes*", you whoreson lobster': The Comedy of Epicene

As mentioned earlier, *Epicoene* is the title of Jonson's play written three years after he wrote *Volpone*. The ambiguity between the androgyne and the eunuch was dealt with in a more explicit fashion in 1609. 'Epicene' was a comparatively new word at that time. The first record of the word in *OED* is 1450, about 150 years before Jonson's production. Jonson used the word 'epicene' in his poem 'An Epigram on the Court Pucell'. He describes Pucell as having a tribade lust and an epicene fury (7–8). The use of 'tribade' and 'epicene' both relate to concepts of gender ambiguity. According to *OED*, Epicene means 'people or animals having characteristics of both sexes, or of neither; indeterminate in respect of sex; androgynous; hermaphrodite; *spec.* (of a man) effeminate, effete'. The meaning of the word is similar to that of androgyny and hermaphrodite. However, as I shall describe, an epicene, for Jonson, represents a body that bridges the gap between the androgyne and the eunuch. It is different from Aristophanes's androgyny because, instead of signifying a body of doubleness, an epicene represents a body of nothingness. Epicene shows how Jonson understands the androgyne, which is a body that cannot be separated from the eunuch. If *Volpone* exhibits the nation of fools through the three bastards, Jonson is portraying the nation of epicenes in 1609.

There are at least six characters in *Epicoene* who have names and personalities related to gender and sexual ambiguity. Edward B. Partridge notes that 'nearly everyone in the play is epicene in some way'.[35] Not only does Epicene relate to gender ambiguity, the name Dauphine Eugenie conveys a similar implication. Roger Holdsworth suggests that the immediate meaning of the name is well-born heir, but it 'also associates him with the ideas of effeminate fashionableness and sexual ambivalence embodied in the more obviously satirized characters'.[36] The name

> connects him with things French (since Dauphin was the heir apparent to the King of France), and in the play France, fashion, and sexual unnaturalness are linked . . . also, it is given an 'incorrect', indeed impossible, feminine form by the addition of the *e* (cf. 'La Foole' and 'Centaure').[37]

The name Dauphine implies effeminacy, and by adding *e* to the name La Foole, the gender of the knight is confused. Moreover, there is a relation between inheritance and effeminacy. At the beginning of the play, Dauphine is in danger of being disinherited by Morose. The disinheritance means Dauphine 'has not a penny in his purse' (IV.iv.130). This suggestion has a sexual implication and relates to the epicene nature of Dauphine.

Apart from Epicene, Dauphine and La Foole, one of the collegiate ladies is called Madame Centaure. Centaure is the classical monster that is half human and half horse, and, characteristically, is savage and lustful.[38] The collegiate ladies are women with masculine features. Truewit describes the collegiate ladies as monsters. They have masculine brains and fashion, and create a hermaphroditical authority (I.i.63). Holdsworth adds that 'Centaurs mated with mares, or, usually by raping them, women.'[39] The mare recalls the image of Chaucer's

Pardoner (who was discussed in the previous chapter), who may be 'a geldyng or a mare' ('General Prologue', line 691).[40] This point echoes the fact that in the play, Madame Centaure is interested in Dauphine. Moreover, Morose's servant is called Mute, whose name relates to silence and castration. The sexual interest of Clerimont is also ambiguous. Truewit suggests that Clerimont keeps a mistress abroad and an ingle in his home (I.i.19). Discussing the ingles, Adam Zucker suggests:

> In the active life of this ingle, the transferable materials of gender inspire a number of homoerotic arrangements: in a woman's wig, the boy is kissed by women; in a boy's apparel, he lies 'above a man'. Clerimont seems nervous about his ability to compete with the academy of women and their dresses ('you shall go there no more, lest I be fain to seek your voice in my lady's rushes a fortnight hence'), and his lack of control over the costumes and visitations of the boy puts their master/servant relationship in danger of sliding into the disorderly realm of the sodomitical.[41]

With these names and characters in mind, I shall illustrate how the comedy of *Epicoene* is built upon the notion of castration.

Epicoene is strongly related to castration. The play makes fun of Morose's masculinity and, thus, his patriarchal power. The masculinity of Morose can be seen from his use of the long sword in Act IV scene ii, which scares away Mistress Otter, Daw and La Foole. Mistress Otter describes the long sword of Morose as a 'huge long naked weapon' (IV.iii.2), signifying Morose's phallus. Morose's fragile masculinity is shown from his fear of noise and his desire for silent women. His love of silence comes from his father's teaching (V.iii.36). The aim of such teaching is to collect and contain his mind, and not to make his mind suffer from flowing loosely (V.iii.37–8). The notion of preserving single identity can be seen here. Fear of noise equates to an anxiety of losing the position of a single subject. The need to avoid clamour and orators demonstrates his fear of narrative, that is, to apply what we have seen in the previous chapter, the fear of supplement. Morose particularly refers to his fear of woman's tongue (II.v.31–2). Such fear signifies the threat of castration. Morose's anxiety about being castrated can be seen in Act III scene vii where, referring to Epicene, he cries, 'Is that Gorgon, that Medusa, come? Hide me, hide me!' (III.vii.16). The Gorgons were three female monsters of classical legend; anyone who met their gaze was turned to stone, and Medusa was the most terrible of the three. The power of turning man into stone is the power of castration.[42] It is important to note that the supplement, tongue and speech that are associated with feminine power are also, deep down, the power of an epicene. In *Epicoene*, the agent of Epicene is a barber named Cutbeard: his profession and name are associated with castration.

Morose is extremely joyous when he meets Epicene: this raises questions about his sexuality. He is so thrilled to find Epicene that he kisses him (II.v.67). By claiming he wants a silent woman, he, in turn, wants and kisses an epicene. Steve Brown argues that

> when Morose scours the English countryside for a silent woman and finally marries what is seemingly a woman who is seemingly silent, he gets . . . what he actually wants, which is an ingle at home. In other words, if he is willing to accept a gender characterization of the female which renders all females repugnant and intolerable, then he never genuinely wants a female.[43]

When Morose first meets Epicene, he suggests that 'her temper of beauty has the true height of my blood' (II.v.14–15). Moreover, by suggesting that he wants to 'try her within' (II.v.16), Morose unconsciously turns the joke on himself, suggesting his same-sex desire and sodomitical tendency.

Along with the names and characters relating to epicene, the implication of castration surfaces in Act IV scene iv, in which Morose has married Epicene and wants to end the marriage:

MOROSE   Would I could redeem it with the loss of an eye, nephew, a
hand, or any other member!
DAUPHINE   Marry, God forbid, sir, that you should geld yourself to
anger your wife.

(IV.iv.6–9)

Morose tries to find a way to annul his marriage with Epicene. He says he is willing to suffer the loss of an eye, a hand or other member of his body. The 'other member' is his phallus, which is why Dauphine says, 'God forbid, sir, that you should geld yourself to anger your wife.' It suggests that Morose will need to 'geld' himself in order to get out of his marriage. The references to eye and hand in *Epicoene* are also supplements, indicating that the final resolution of the play (if there is one) comes with castration.

The theme of castration is related to the concept of fashion in *Epicoene*. At the beginning of the play, Clerimont and Truewit have a debate regarding women's beauty.[44] Clerimont suggests that the painted and perfumed faces of women are pieced beauty (I.i.67), and he shows his disgust when describing the women's oiled lips (I.i.69). 'Pieced beauty' demonstrates how seemingly attractive appearances are constituted of joints and gaps, exposing their fragmentary nature. Clerimont continues his condemnation with a song that shows his favour of simplicity. He describes their beauty as the adulteries of art (I.i.81). In contrast, Truewit seems to praise the importance of fashion in highlighting the beauty of women. However, we should not take

Truewit's comment without noticing its sarcastic tone; Truewit alludes to the ugliness underneath.

In *Epicoene*, fashion and sexual unnaturalness are linked to being French:

> TRUEWIT   [To Morose] If, after you are married, your wife do run away with a vaulter, or the Frenchman that walks upon ropes, or him that dances the jig, or a fencer for his skill at his weapon, why, it is not their fault; they have discharged their consciences when you know what may happen.
>
> (II.ii.44–7)

There are sexual implications within the dialogue. Vaulter, jig and weapon are all expressions with sexual innuendoes, and the fear of fashion is linked with the threat of being cuckolded.

Epicene fools Morose by his fashion, and even Morose is attracted to it. Morose's speech in Act II scene v shows his obsession, and he imposes his own fashion on Epicene. He suggests that he wants his heifer, that is, Epicene, to be the 'first and principal in all fashions, precede all the dames at court by a fortnight' (II.v.53–4). The reference to 'French intelligences' relates to 'news of the latest fashions' (II.v.55). This emphasis recalls the image of the Pardoner who thinks that he 'rood al of the newe jet' ('General Prologue', line 682). Morose's speech demonstrates how fashion, fetishism and the narrative are related. He says he wants to give an account of the details of his fashion through 'this frugality of speech' (II.v.58). He is obsessed with different items of clothing such as bodice, sleeves, skirts, cut, stitch, embroidery, lace, wire, knots, ruff, roses, girdle, fan, scarf and gloves (II.v.59–61). This detailed account of different parts of clothing shows Morose as a fetishist. His account becomes an endless list of supplements. Even though Morose is afraid of tongue, narrative and supplements, he is betrayed by his own speech.

The image of Dauphine and its relation to fashion and castration are suggested in Act IV scene vi. This scene shows how the collegiate ladies, including Madame Centaure, are attracted to Dauphine. The ladies see Dauphine as 'a very worthy gentleman in his exteriors' (IV.vi.20). They discuss his clothes, his face and his hair. Dauphine wears purer linen than the collegiate ladies (IV.vi.25) and is even more feminised than them. Dauphine is neater than the French hermaphrodite (IV.vi.25–6). Compared with the latter, Dauphine appears to be the most fashionable, the ultimate epicene. The conversations are sexual in nature. The collegiate ladies praise Dauphine for his nose, leg and eye (IV.vi.31–3). These different body parts can be seen as supplements to the phallus. The yearning for the supplement shows the desire of the collegiate ladies to have sex with Dauphine, as Centaure says, 'bring him to my chamber first' (IV.vi.35). The house and the chamber can be regarded as the sexual parts of women. Zucker makes the same point, but he also connects it to the relation between the economy and sexuality of women in that period. He argues:

> In case of the Collegiates, however, residential penetration is linked to sexual penetration, creating a forcefully eroticized urban identity. In Act V, Haughty, Centaure, and Mavis all attempt to seduce Dauphine, and all of them do so by offering him access to their 'chambers' (V.ii.15, 30, 34–6). The bawdy overtones are not coincidental. Private space, an expensive sign of wealth or economic status, becomes a figure for the Collegiates' private parts, linking this form of social power to fears of feminine sexual excess.[45]

The language of the collegiate ladies is another supplement and deferral, which demonstrates their desire to have sexual intercourse with Dauphine. However, the narrative questions the gender of Dauphine: the collegiate ladies only talk about the supplement, which perhaps implies the lack of Dauphine.

Many characters are turned into eunuchs in the end. The first example of this metaphorical castration appears in Act IV scene v. It demonstrates how Truewit, Dauphine and Clerimont trick Daw and La Foole by taking away their swords, symbolically castrating them. Truewit first plays his trick on Daw. Zucker suggests that 'Daw and La Foole undergo a symbolic castration when their swords are taken away from them, and Morose is made to proclaim his own impotence ("I am no man, ladies").'[46] Truewit says he will try to persuade La Foole to cut away Daw's leg or arm, also a castration metaphorically (IV.v.96). He continues by saying that perhaps Daw can substitute a thumb or a little finger for the leg or arm, which, again, is another metaphor for castration (IV.v.99–100). The 'conflict' between La Foole and Daw finally is 'settled' when they each allows the other (who in fact is Dauphine playing the part of the other) to take away his 'sword', demonstrating the power of the epicene. Later, Clerimont claims that 'They have forgot their rapiers!' (IV.vi.83), implying that they both are castrated, turning them into epicenes. In Act V scene i, Clerimont says to Daw that the latter carries the feminine gender afore him (V.i.25), to which Daw replies that the women [the collegiate ladies] carry us [masculine gender] afore them (V.i.26). The supposed gender relation is reversed: men are feminine while women are masculine. As well as both Dauphine and Epicene, La Foole, Daw and the collegiate ladies are epicenes within the play.

As the ultimate masculine figure, Morose is not immune to being 'transformed'. In order to end his marriage with Epicene, Morose is tricked by Truewit, Dauphine and Clerimont and trapped into castration. In the process of annulling the marriage, we have the following conversation:

> OTTER   That a boy or child under years is not fit for marriage because
> he cannot *reddere debitum*. So your *omnipotentes* –
> TRUEWIT   [*Aside to Otter*] Your '*impotentes*', you whoreson lobster.
> (V.iii.146–8)

To annul his marriage, Cutbeard and Truewit ask Morose to confess that he is a man unable, taking away his masculinity. Finally, Morose openly claims that he is no man (V.iv.35). Dauphine turns Morose into a 'castrated' man; he turns Morose into an epicene. By metaphorically castrating Morose, Truewit, Dauphine and Clerimont turn Morose's 'omnipotence' into impotence. The play on 'omnipotence' and 'impotence' captures the mechanism of Jonson's comedy nicely, resembling the joke on possession and dispossession in *Volpone*. While Jonson's comedies expose the impotence of the seemingly omnipotent figure through castration, the force of castration, of impotence, which is the power of epicene, is the source of folly and transformation. From the comedy of epicene, we can see why the androgyne, in Jonson, exemplifies the presence of both the hermaphrodite and the fool.

Epicoene has one more twist. Epicene is convinced that this is a device of Morose to claim that he is impotent, and she does not want to annul her marriage with him. Therefore, Dauphine asks La Foole and Daw to claim that they have committed adultery with Epicene to prove that she is not a chaste woman. This joke is twofold. First, since none of them can prove Epicene's lack of chastity, it seems likely that Morose has to 'Marry a whore! And so much noise!' (V.iv.122). Second, by discovering Epicene is a boy in the end, the joke is on Daw and La Foole because it means that they are sodomites and have slept with a catamite. By exposing Epicene as a boy, the sexuality of Morose, Daw and La Foole is questioned. *Epicoene* is similar to the fabliaux. It originates from the obsession with body parts. Its jokes are related to the dismemberment of the body. The play is centred on three characters whose sexualities cannot be clearly defined. Dauphine is an effeminate, Clerimont is interested in catamites, and even Truewit's sexuality is in question because of his companionship with Dauphine and Clerimont, as well as his hatred of women as noted in his narrative to Morose. Kate Levin argues that a love triangle exists among the three of them.[47] The centre of the play is a centre with gender ambiguity, that is, an epicene centre. Developing from this epicene centre is the plot that turns everyone in the play into an epicene. As Truewit says at the end, even the ladies are 'mute upon this new metamorphosis' (V.iv.197). The silence of Epicene turns everyone into a mute. If mute is a form of mutilation, then every character is castrated in *Epicoene*.

Shakespeare's Androgyny in *Twelfth Night*

In this part, I want to examine how the androgyne is represented in the works of Shakespeare through the example of *Twelfth Night* (a play that was written about eight years before *Epicoene*), showing the distinction between the two dramatists. A comparison of Jonson with Shakespeare allows us to see what is so special in Jonson's androgyne. More akin to the androgyny in *The Symposium*, *Twelfth Night* (as in *The Comedy of Errors*) is full of characters that are split in half, and tells of the characters' quest for their separated halves. For example, Orsino says, 'One face, one voice, one habit, and two persons, / A natural perspective, that is and is not' (V.i.208–9); and, with a similar image, Antonio asks, 'How have you made division of yourself?' (V.i.215). The search for the lost half reminds us of the search for the androgyne. Viola and her brother are split by the sea.[48] Later, we learn that Viola and Sebastian are the mirror image of each other. Their appearances are so alike that when Viola dresses as Cesario, she looks the same as Sebastian. The split of Viola and Sebastian is paralleled by the separation of Olivia and her brother because of her brother's death. The play poses two broken pairs. The incestuous undertone should be noted.[49] The search for the split half recalls the quest of the androgyne. Such a search, which is supposed to be a male–female love relationship, is substituted by the finding of siblings. Olivia rejects the pursuit of Orsino because she mourns her brother. The loss of her brother stops her from falling in love. The search for Sebastian leads Viola to Orsino. The difference between the quest for a brother and the need for a husband may be very small.

Twelfth Night is filled with separated halves, in terms of both their identity and their names. The names of the characters constitute another mirror image of the play. The names Viola, Olivia and Malvolio are virtual anagrams. They can be seen as the mirror image of each other. Joel Fineman writes:

> as the transposition of letters and sounds suggests, we are meant to understand them [Viola and Olivia] as a pair, each an incomplete rebus of the other, a system, as it were, of sisterly regret just the reverse of the organized fraternal rancor to be found in the two other plays [*As You Like It* and *Hamlet*].[50]

The mirror image of names between Viola and Olivia may suggest the combination of the female gender, and thus, the quest for a female–female relationship.

The names draw a connection between words and images and demonstrate the relation between language and identity. Greenblatt argues:

> For Shakespeare friction is specifically associated with verbal wit; indeed at moments the plays seem to imply that erotic friction originates in the wantonness of language and thus that the body itself is a tissue of metaphors or, conversely, that language is perfectly embodied.[51]

He suggests that sexual stimulation and the confrontation of verbal wit are similar and that repartee onstage becomes a visualisation of sexual intercourse. Moreover, the reversal of words causes the reconstruction of identity. Such reversibility in language demonstrates that identity is not inherent, but only a construction of language, as suggested by Feste, the clown who raises the concern of words as mirror images:

> FESTE   You have said, sir. To see this age! – A sentence is but a cheverel glove to a good wit, how quickly the wrong side may be turned outward.
>
> (III.i.10–12)

The clown suggests that words are like gloves; they can be turned inside out easily.[52] Since language and sexuality are interconnected, the fact that language can be inverted reflects the inversion of gender identity and sexual orientation.[53] This inversion recalls the image of the androgyne, which has 'the delight of each sex thou canst vary' (I.ii.54). However, the emphasis of Shakespeare's clown also marks the difference between Shakespeare's plays and Jonson's. While Shakespearean plays enact the visualisation of sexual intercourse through verbal wit, Jonson's main characters dislike talkative women and yearn for a silent woman, a characteristic shared by both Volpone and Morose. The refusal to have verbal communication with women and the desire for a silent woman suggest the possible impotence of Jonson's male characters. While these male figures establish themselves as strong masculine figures, they are threatened by talkative women, and their masculinity is fragile, a characteristic which is not unlike Ovid's representation of the hermaphrodite.

Viola is someone who can sympathise with the clown. She says:

> This fellow is wise enough to play the fool,
> And to do that well craves a kind of wit.
> He must observe their mood on whom he jests,
> The quality of persons, and the time,

And, like the haggard, check at every feather
That comes before his eye.

(III.i.53–8)

She knows what it takes to be a clown. The fool is wise and witty. Part of the reason why Viola is able to charm Olivia is because of her ability to master language. Viola shows her ability to play with language, and she demonstrates her capability to play with gender. The clown and Viola exhibit the androgynous nature of language and gender. While the clown upsets the hierarchy of identity, Viola upsets gender distinction. Coppélia Kahn draws attention to Viola/Cesario's ability to challenge gender norms. She suggests:

> At some level, Cesario is a homosexual object choice for each of them, and at another, a heterosexual one. Yet 'she' or 'he' is the same person, one person. Creatures whose sexual identity is not simply and clearly male or female – hermaphrodites or eunuchs – threaten the binary opposition on which sexual identity, and much else in culture, is based.[54]

Similarly, Robert Kimbrough writes that Shakespeare 'touches on homosexuality as well as heterosexuality in order to bring home to the audience that androgyny has no necessary connection with any particular kind of sexual orientation'.[55] The gender ambiguity of Viola can be seen from her own description:

> And I, poor monster, fond as much on him,
> And she, mistaken, seems to dote on me.
> What will become of this? As I am man,
> My state is desperate for my master's love.
> As I am woman, now, alas the day,
> What thriftless sighs shall poor Olivia breathe!
> O time, thou must untangle this, not I.
> It is too hard a knot for me t'untie.

(II.ii.32–9)

Viola is both a man and a woman. She describes herself as a monster.[56] Confusing gender and sexuality, she is able to attract both Orsino and Olivia, which questions whether we can define their sexuality. Speaking to Cesario, Orsino says, 'Diana's lip / Is not more smooth and rubious; thy small pipe / Is as the maiden's organ, shrill and sound, / And all is semblative a woman's part' (I.iv.30–3). His words expose his attraction to Viola. Viola/Cesario is also able to attract Olivia. Olivia says, 'Thy tongue, thy face, thy limbs, actions, and spirit / Do give thee five-fold blazon' (I.v.262–3). She is seduced by Cesario. Olivia's attraction to Viola can be read as her quest for a female–female relationship. She continues, 'Cesario, by the roses of the spring, / By maidhood, honour, truth, and everything, / I love thee so that, maugre all thy pride, / Nor wit nor reason can my passion hide' (III.i.140–3). She shows her love towards another woman unknowingly. The presence of Viola demonstrates that the boundary of 'heterosexuality' and 'homosexuality' is unsustainable.

Antonio's quest for Sebastian can be read as his love of the male. He calls attention to his love for Sebastian, and Sebastian replies, 'It were a bad recompense for your love to lay any of them on you' (II.i.6–7). Antonio says, 'if you will not murder me for my love, let me be your servant' (II.i.30–1). He adds, 'I do adore thee so' (II.i.41). Joseph Pequigney writes that the word 'servant' implies the meaning of 'lover'.[57] He argues that Antonio does not show any romantic or other interest in women, suggesting that the adoration that Antonio shows towards Sebastian 'must stem from passion'.[58] In Act III scene iii, Antonio indicates his love for Sebastian again. His suggestion that desire spurs him forth has sexual implications (III.iii.5). Pequigney argues that 'This impelling "desire" is sensual: the very word would connote libido even apart from the intensifying metaphor of the flesh-cutting metal spur.'[59] Valerie Traub writes that '*Twelfth Night* represents male homoerotic desire as phallic in the most active sense: erect, hard, penetrating.'[60] When Antonio loans his purse to Sebastian, the love is vivid in their relationship.

Associated with carnival because of the confrontation among several characters (Malvolio, Sir Toby Belch, Sir Andrew Aguecheek, Maria and Feste), *Twelfth Night* signifies the battle between Lent and carnival.[61] While Olivia is obsessed with the love triangle between Orsino and Viola/Cesario, Sir Toby and his companies become masterless subjects.[62] Interestingly, one of the company who represents carnival is Aguecheek, who, again, may recall the image of Chaucer's Pardoner:[63]

SIR TOBY   Then hadst thou had an excellent head of hair.
SIR ANDREW   Why, would that have mended my hair?
SIR TOBY   Past question, for thou seest it will not curl by nature.
SIR ANDREW   But it becomes me well enough, does't not?
SIR TOBY   Excellent, it hangs like flax on a distaff, and I hope to see a
   housewife take thee between her legs and spin it off.

(I.iii.81–6)

The suggestion that Aguecheek has hair that 'hangs like flax on a distaff' draws a comparison between him and the image of the Pardoner. The Pardoner has hair as yellow as wax; it is thin and smooth and hangs like 'a strike of flex' ('General Prologue', line 676). The importance of the Pardoner comes from the possibility of reading him as a gelding or a mare ('General Prologue', line 691). By comparing the images of the Pardoner and Aguecheek, it is possible that Aguecheek can be seen as 'castrated'. Indeed, we should pay attention to the importance of Aguecheek's sword. In Act I scene iii, Aguecheek, without realising the sexual implication, is tricked by Sir Toby into saying that he will 'never draw sword again' (I.iii.54–5). By saying this, Aguecheek symbolically castrates himself. The suggestion of Aguecheek being a 'castrated' figure can be seen from his failure to draw his sword in front of Viola/Cesario. Viola says:

> Pray God defend me. A little thing would make
> me tell them how much I lack of a man.

(III.iv.268–9)

The lack of the 'little thing' is the lack of the phallus and it can be read as Viola's suggesting that she is a woman in disguise. Traub argues for the relation between gender and theatricality: 'At this (phallic) point, Viola/Cesario's "lack" is upheld as the signifier of gender difference. And yet, to the extent that masculinity is embodied in the sword, it depends upon a particular kind of performance rather than any biological equipment.'[64] It is not difficult to understand why Viola fails to draw her sword since she indeed has no 'sword'. However, the failure to draw his sword shows that Aguecheek may be 'castrated'. As part of the carnival group, Aguecheek is the opposite of Malvolio, who is the embodiment of Lent and Puritanism and an anti-festive, anti-carnival figure. Even though Malvolio's name constitutes another anagram of Viola and Olivia, he is not a mirror image of other characters. Malvolio only possesses self-love. He is caught practising his behaviour with his shadow, thus forming his own mirror image and demonstrating his fear of doubleness or the fear of the androgyne.

Although the play is full of subversive qualities, it is interrupted violently. The relation between Olivia and Viola may demonstrate the tendency towards a female–female relationship, yet the play seems to reject this possibility. Viola hopes her appearance has not charmed Olivia. She says, 'Poor lady, she were better love a dream' (II.ii.24). Even though the play opens up various gender possibilities, they are closed out ultimately.[65] The end of the play seems to confirm patriarchal power. C. L. Barber suggests that the ending represents the moment 'when delusions and misapprehensions are resolved by the finding of objects appropriate to passions'.[66] He argues:

> The most fundamental distinction the play brings home to us is the difference between men and women . . . the disguising of a girl as a boy in *Twelfth Night* is exploited so as to renew in a special way our sense of the difference. Just as a saturnalian reversal of social roles need not threaten the social structure, but can serve instead to consolidate it, so a temporary, playful reversal of sexual roles can renew the meaning of the normal relation.[67]

Viola does not have to be punished because the name of her father, Sebastian, implies the quality of nobility in her blood. Through the name of the father, 'we learn that the threat to the social order and the threat to the sexual order were equally illusory'.[68] The Name-of-the-father 'sustains the structure of desire with the structure of the law'.[69] It signifies the upholding of the symbolic order. Lacan argues that 'There is no need of a signifier to be a father, any more than there is to be dead, but without a signifier, no one will ever know anything about either of these states of being.'[70] The upsetting of the symbolic order has to be repaired by another patriarchal figure, namely, Sebastian.

However, the violent interruption must leave a scar, a trace that draws out the desire for an androgyne. The ending of *Twelfth Night* is not without its ambiguity. For instance, it remains in question whether we can assign a definite sexuality to Orsino. The love of Orsino for Viola is not necessarily the one between male and female because it is not clear whether Orsino is in love with Viola or Cesario. As Orsino says:

> Cesario, come –
> For so you shall be while you are a man;
> But when in other habits you are seen,
> Orsino's mistress, and his fancy's queen.
>
> (V.i.372–5)

Orsino's words show the fluidity of gender. Viola can be a man, namely, Cesario, but, in other 'habits', she can be Orsino's mistress and his fancy's queen. 'Fancy' means something illusionary and imaginary. The gender of Viola is reversed. She is supposed to be a woman disguised as a man. However, the words of Orsino mean that he sees Cesario as the 'original' self and Viola as secondary (which reminds us of the presence of the boy actors). Orsino is in love with Cesario, but not Viola. His words raise the question of whether we can apply a definite sexual orientation to him, for he may be in love with both Cesario and Viola. The still-to-be-challenged sexuality of Orsino and Viola/Cesario and the affection that Sebastian seems to show towards Antonio demonstrate the impossibility of sustaining a 'heterosexual' patriarchy.

At the end, the play seems to divide the characters into two groups. Orsino, Olivia, Viola/Cesario, Sebastian, Fabian and Feste are on the stage, leaving Sir Toby and his company, Malvolio and Antonio off-stage. This separation suggests another scar (and trace). At the comedy's ending, the comic characters, such as Sir Toby, Aguecheek and Maria (who are the revellers), Malvolio (who is laughed at) and Antonio (who is the marginal, 'homosexual' figure), are absent. This absence demonstrates the failure of the resolution of comedy. Malvolio's famous last line 'I'll be revenged on the whole pack of you' (V.i.365) becomes a scar that haunts the violence of interruption. His line suggests that this battle goes on offstage, leaving the ending undecided and with the potential for tragedy.

Conclusion

This chapter discusses the representation of the androgyne, the hermaphrodite and the epicene in *The Symposium*, *Metamorphoses*, *Volpone*, *Epicoene* and *Twelfth Night*. From *The Symposium*, we see that the androgyne is a figure of doubleness before gender categorisations, relating to the importance of carnival. Ovid's hermaphrodite combines the characteristics of both sexes and represents the fear of exaggerated femininity. Shakespeare's use of androgyny is closer to that of Aristophanes since it is carnivalesque and relates to the importance of doubleness. Jonson's epicene is closer to Ovid's Hermaphroditus but he turns the power of castration into a force of folly. Indeed, we should notice the ambiguity in Jonson's portrayal of the subject. On one hand, the comedy of epicene is built upon the characteristics of being a hermaphrodite: the anxiety of becoming a sexless creature, of a man losing his masculinity due to castration. However, on the other hand, the joy of being a fool, namely, the importance of gender fluidity, of slipping from one identity to another, is apparent. Perhaps what is more important for Jonson, as said by Androgyno in the interlude, is the joy of being a fool instead of the pleasure of varying sexes. In the world of bastards, one slips from one identity into another. While such a state relates to the power of castration, one cannot ignore the comedy and transformation that come with it. The power cuts one down and makes one slip, yet it is the source of folly, one that relates to transformation, and, perhaps, to transmigration. Although it may mean madness for figures such as Lady Would-be and Morose, it is a praise of folly for the bastards and the epicenes (Truewit, Dauphine and Clerimont). The best way to deal with those who love to categorise others is to turn the joke on them, and to dissolve their madness into folly through the power of epicene, or the bastards. To use an analogy in modern films, Jonson's comedy is not unlike the scissors of Harpo Marx. It cuts everything, making one mad and laugh at the same time.

In sum, Jonson's comedies demonstrate the mechanism of madness and folly, and of insistence and deferral: the more one tries to insist on his/her own identity, the more he or she will be slipped by the power of the bastards. As suggested, Androgyno and Castrone are two creatures that seem to be inseparable. While in the previous chapter, we have seen how the notion of 'castration' in *Volpone* is paradoxically linked with Volpone's transformation, the discussion of the androgyne allows us to see that the logic of castration and folly are intertwined. The epicene is a creature that combines the characteristics of these two bastards. Portraying the androgyne, Jonson may have slipped into the figure of the epicene. The logic of epicene is the logic of Jonsonian comedies. More importantly, it is the logic that we shall see in the use of metempsychosis as a comedic metaphor in the interlude in Act I scene ii. Even though the transmigration seems to be about the debasement of souls, it exemplifies the slippage from one identity to another. This slippage is the mechanism of Jonson's city comedy, a notion that I shall return to in the discussion of the interlude in the final chapter.

Notes

1. Berger et al., *Index of Characters*.
2. Pushkin, 'Journey to Arzrum', p. 166. The translation of the Latin is from p. 194.
3. Kristeva, 'Manic Eros, Sublime Eros', p. 59.
4. On *The Symposium*, see Halperin, 'Why Is Diotima a Woman?'.
5. Plato, *Lysis; Symposium; Gorgias*, p. 137.
6. Plato, *Lysis; Symposium; Gorgias*, p. 139.
7. Plato, *Lysis; Symposium; Gorgias*, pp. 139–41.
8. Plato, *Lysis; Symposium; Gorgias*, p. 141.
9. Plato, *Lysis; Symposium; Gorgias*, p. 141.
10. Freud, 'Beyond the Pleasure Principle', p. 57.
11. Freud, 'Beyond the Pleasure Principle', p. 58.
12. Weber, *Legend of Freud*, p. 190.
13. Weber, *Legend of Freud*, p. 190.
14. Weber, *Legend of Freud*, p. 190.
15. Weber, *Legend of Freud*, p. 191.
16. Weber, *Legend of Freud*, p. 187.
17. Weber, *Legend of Freud*, p. 193.
18. Weber, *Legend of Freud*, p. 193.
19. Weber, *Legend of Freud*, p. 197.
20. Weber, *Legend of Freud*, p. 198.
21. Weber, *Legend of Freud*, p. 198.
22. Weber, *Legend of Freud*, p. 200.
23. Weber, *Legend of Freud*, p. 200.
24. Weber, *Legend of Freud*, p. 202.
25. Zupančič, *Odd One In*, p. 188.
26. Zupančič, *Odd One In*, p. 189.
27. Zupančič, *Odd One In*, p. 190.
28. Zupančič, *Odd One In*, pp. 191–2.

29. Frank Justus Miller's translation reads: 'How the fountain of Salmacis is of ill-repute, how it enervates with its enfeebling waters and renders soft and weak all men who bathe therein, you shall now hear.' See Ovid, *Metamorphoses, Volume I*, trans. Miller, p. 199. All the quotations from *Metamorphoses* are from this edition.

30. Brisson, *Sexual Ambivalence*, p. 42.

31. Arthur Golding translates this as 'when she first the yongman did espie, / And in beholding him desirde to have his companie.' See Ovid, *Ovid's Metamorphoses*, p. 96.

32. Brisson, *Sexual Ambivalence*, p. 58.

33. Arthur Golding's translation reads: 'Both Parentes moved with the chaunce did stablish this desire / The which their doubleshaped soone had made: and thereupon / Infected with an unknowne strength the sacred spring anon.' See Ovid, *Ovid's Metamorphoses*, p. 99.

34. *Duck Soup*, directed by Leo McCarey.

35. Partridge, 'Allusiveness of *Epicoene*', p. 94.

36. Holdsworth (ed.), *Epicoene, or, The Silent Woman*, p. 4.

37. Holdsworth (ed.), *Epicoene, or, The Silent Woman*, p. 4.

38. Holdsworth (ed.), *Epicoene, or, The Silent Woman*, p. 5.

39. Holdsworth (ed.), *Epicoene, or, The Silent Woman*, p. 5.

40. Chaucer, *Riverside Chaucer*, p. 34.

41. Zucker, 'Social Logic of Ben Jonson's *Epicoene*', p. 55.

42. See Freud, 'Medusa's Head'.

43. Brown, 'Boyhood of Shakespeare's Heroines', p. 258.

44. On the relation between fashion, aping and effeminacy, see Kay, '*Epicoene*'.

45. Zucker, 'Social Logic of Ben Jonson's *Epicoene*', p. 52.

46. Zucker, 'Social Logic of Ben Jonson's *Epicoene*', p. 51.

47. Levin, 'Unmasquing *Epicoene*'.

48. Coppélia Kahn argues that, 'As depicted in the plays, the tempest and shipwreck initiating the main action represent the violence, confusion, and even terror of passing from one stage of life to the next, the feeling of being estranged from a familiar world and sense of self without another to hang onto.' See Kahn, 'Providential Tempest', p. 218.

49. Joel Fineman argues that, 'being *specially* connected, as members of the same family, their coupling, the marriage of Shakespearean comic doubles – when it occurs or when it is deflected to a bifurcated mirror object – is incestuous in tone if not in fact, yet happily so, being the benign interpretation of a desire that links equals each to each'. See Fineman, 'Fratricide and Cuckoldry', p. 71.

50. Fineman, 'Fratricide and Cuckoldry', p. 74.

51. Greenblatt, 'Fiction and Friction', p. 49.

52. Of this Greenblatt says, 'The brief, almost schematic enactment of verbal friction leads to a perception of the suppleness of language, particularly its capacity to be inverted, a capacity imaged by the chev'ril glove.' See Greenblatt, 'Fiction and Friction', p. 49. On the language of Shakespeare, see Partridge, *Shakespeare's Bawdy*; Mahood, *Shakespeare's Wordplay*.

53. See Laqueur, *Making Sex*.

54. Kahn, 'Providential Tempest', p. 228.

55. Kimbrough, 'Androgyny Seen through Shakespeare's Disguise', p. 28.

56. Greenblatt suggests that 'prodigies paradoxically represent the disorder that their existence helps to negate. The monstrous is virtually defined by excess, by the improper, disordered fashioning of matter into misshapen lumps, uncanny conjunctions, gross and unnecessary excrescences. Hence in the moment that they celebrate nature's fecundity in producing prodigies, Renaissance scholars hasten to meditate upon the principle of order that may be discovered within the most uncanny oddity.' See Greenblatt, 'Fiction and Friction', p. 36.

57. Pequigney, 'Two Antonios and Same-Sex Love', p. 203.

58. Pequigney, 'Two Antonios and Same-Sex Love', pp. 201, 203.

59. Pequigney, 'Two Antonios and Same-Sex Love', p. 203.

60. Traub, 'Homoerotics of Shakespearean Comedy', p. 147.

61. Indira Ghose suggests that 'In the play *Twelfth Night* the structure of the sub-plot, the gulling of Malvolio, reflects exactly the motif of Carnival vs. Lent.' See Ghose, 'Licence to Laugh', p. 38.

62. Carol Thomas Neely argues that 'the master and the mistress are distracted by lovesickness'. See Neely, *Distracted Subjects*, p. 151.

63. See J. M Lothian and T. W. Craik's footnotes in the Arden Edition of Shakespeare, *Twelfth Night*.

64. Traub, 'Homoerotics of Shakespearean Comedy', p. 145.

65. Catherine Belsey suggests that 'Viola, addressing the audience, formulates both the enigma and the promise of closure.' See Belsey, 'Disrupting Sexual Difference', p. 185.

66. Barber, 'Testing Courtesy and Humanity', p. 244.

67. Barber, 'Testing Courtesy and Humanity', p. 245.

68. Greenblatt, *Shakespearean Negotiations*, p. 72.

69. Lacan, *Four Fundamental Concepts*, p. 34.

70. Lacan, *Écrits*, p. 464.

Chapter 5

'I fear I shall begin to grow in love with my dear self': The Parasite and His 'Mirror Stage'

I want to start my discussion of the parasite with an example from modern film comedy. In the Marx Brothers' *Duck Soup* (1933), there is a famous mirror scene in which the spies Pinky (Harpo) and Chicolini (Chico) try to steal the war plan from Rufus T. Firefly (Groucho).[1] When Pinky attempts to escape from Firefly, he accidently shatters the mirror. Without anywhere to go, Pinky pretends that he is Firefly's mirror image, imitating everything that the latter does. Not only can Pinky miraculously anticipate what Firefly does, the relationship between the subject and the mirror object becomes ambiguous as the scene goes on. When Firefly walks into the mirror, Pinky walks out from it. Intrigued by the image completely, Firefly acts as if he wants to sustain this illusion: when Pinky drops his straw hat on the floor, Firefly picks it up and hands it back to him. The scene ends when Chicolini barges in, creating the third image, breaking this illusion. Comparing this scene with another similar one in *Volpone*, this chapter attempts to explain the mechanism of comedy in these two scenes by proposing that their comedy can be explained through Lacan's concept of 'the mirror stage'. The psychoanalytic theory illustrates how human beings gain their identity through the recognition of the mirror image. The essence of it, in sum, is how we, as human beings, are constructed subjects, a point which this chapter will elaborate later. While we are seldom aware of the working of the 'mirror stage' in our daily existence, comedy highlights the functioning of it. The exposing of this concept explains why comedy is often built on the concept of narcissism: a comic character is often the subject who is driven by the logic of the mirror.

This chapter argues that the comedy of Mosca is related to his role as a parasite. While this role has its traditional and historical meaning, it can be understood through a breaking down of the word – 'para-site'. *OED* explains that 'para-', as a prefix, forms 'miscellaneous terms in the sense "analogous or parallel to, but separate from or going beyond, what is denoted by the root word"'. Therefore, the word 'para-site', as a theoretical concept, can, perhaps, mean the existence of a space which is parallel to or even beyond the original one. Moreover, the pun 'site' and 'sight' raises the question of whether this parallel space is related to a person's perception. In other words, because of his narcissism (the parasite acts as if he is looking at his mirror image in the scene), Mosca is a creature who thinks that he is living and existing in another zone. Although he is the servant, he thinks that he is the master. And, at the same time, he becomes who he claims he is not. To quote another famous line from the Marx Brothers: 'He may look like an idiot, and talk like an idiot, but don't let that fool you. He really is an idiot.' While the set-up of this joke makes us believe that there is a difference between 'he' and the 'idiot', the punchline says that there is none.

In order to justify this reading, I will examine Mosca's scene in great detail with the theory of Lacan. Throughout the discussion, I argue that the parasite's speech is full of internal inconsistencies and contradictions. Even though the parasite claims that he is different from the three 'bastards', his speech suggests that he is no different from the trio. He believes in his own words and their power because he is situated in his 'para-site'. In the final two parts of this chapter, the discussion will refer back to the mirror scene in *Duck Soup*, exemplifying the logic of comedy through the mechanism of the 'para-site'. Moreover, I will address the different functioning of the 'mirror stage' in comedy and tragedy through comparing *Duck Soup*, and more examples from modern film comedies, with, perhaps arguably, *the* representation of early modern tragedy, *Hamlet* (1600). While the gap and alienation that a subject feels may be essential to both genres, a comic subject would often end up following the logic of the mirror, while a tragic one might tend to resist and be traumatised by the difference between the belief in his 'self' and the mirror object.

The Traditional and Historical Meaning of Parasite

First, I want to give a brief note on the historical meaning of the role of parasite. In ancient Greek history, a parasite was 'permitted to eat at the table of a public official, or at the feast following a sacrifice'. He may have been 'a priest or priest's assistant who was permitted meals at the public expense' (*OED* 1b). In later periods, a parasite refers to a person who 'lives at the expense of another, or of society in general'; it especially relates to 'a person who obtains the hospitality or patronage of the wealthy or powerful by obsequiousness and flattery' (*OED*

1a). *OED* suggests that, in French, the parasite is a man who makes a profession of dining at another's table. Jonson inherits the role of the parasite from Greek culture. W. Geoffrey Arnott suggests that the word παράσιτος 'has a history going well back into the fifth century at least'.[2] It does not apply in the general sense of 'parasite', but 'in a technical sense belonging to the sphere of religious ritual'.[3] He writes:

> In this older, ritualistic use the παράσιτος was a temple acolyte who received free food and meals in return for services like that of the selection of the sacred grain for use in particular festivals. We hear of such παράσιτοι in the shrine of Heracles at Cynosarges in Attica and elsewhere in Greece. A suitable translation of παράσιτος in this application is 'companion of the holy feast', as Polemon suggests in the long fragment which is our main source of information about the subject, quoted by Athenaeus (6.234Dff).[4]

Enid Welsford suggests that, originally, the parasite 'was a dignified title applied to those associates of priests and magistrates who took part in official banquets not by right but by special invitation'.[5] However, the writers of the Middle and New Comedy 'used the word in a more degraded sense and applied it to those whose position at table was due neither to right nor to courtesy but to their own impudence', and, gradually, the more honourable meaning of parasite became something obsolete.[6] Parasites become those who have their own methods of gaining free meals; others are mere flatterers, while others gain favours from their master by 'a talent for mimicry, repartee, etc.', and they are especially associated with the type of buffoon that the Greeks call 'laughter-maker'.[7]

In *Volpone*, Mosca is a fly, a parasite and a Vice. The parasite is a classical figure, and the Vice is a Christian character. Robert Withington suggests that the parasite 'came from the classical drama to an English stage', while the Vice 'was originally the agent or servant of the Seven Deadly Sins, and sought to entrap "Mankind" – by whatever name he was known – into the power of evil'.[8] Bernard Spivack argues that the transformation of the Vice assimilates him with the parasite, making his performance opaque. He says that the Vice's performance

> loses its figurative and inward meaning and gets its explanation instead from what it appears to be – the cunning beguilements of a witty villain exerted upon everyone within reach. Furthermore it becomes flexible in respect to its objects, bending itself against a world of values and loyalties – social, political, sectarian, domestic, and romantic – that replace the original value of the Christian virtues and the original loyalty of the soul to God.[9]

Spivack adds that 'the world in which he [The Vice] now finds himself is to naturalize him to its human laws and conventions, to change him into a moral creature, in order to preserve his role on a stage very different from the one which brought it into being'.[10] There are many parasites or parasitical characters in Jonson's comedies. E. P. Vandiver, Jr. writes that there are three characters who are explicitly designated as parasites, namely, Mosca; Fly, in *The New Inn*; and Polish, in *The Magnetic Lady*. Other parasitical Jonsonian characters are Bobadill; Sejanus; Carlo Buffone and Shift, in *Every Man Out of His Humour*; and Tucca, in *Poetaster*.[11] On the creation of Mosca, Jonson may have been influenced by Lucian's *The Parasite*. In the story, Simon claims that he practises the art of the parasite, the 'art which is concerned with food and drink and what must be said and done to obtain them, and its end is pleasure'.[12] With the traditional and historical meaning of the parasite in mind, I will now re-examine the parasite's role in Jonson and his comedy from a psychoanalytic perspective. With a particular focus on the subject of narcissism, this chapter suggests how the parasite in Jonson can be read as a creature that lives in his 'para-site'.

Lacan and His Concept of the 'Mirror Stage'

Before I go into the discussion of *Volpone* and *Duck Soup*, I want to give a few words on Lacan and his theory of the 'mirror stage'. Freud defines narcissism as 'the libido that has been withdrawn from the external world' and which 'has been directed to the ego'.[13] As a concept related to narcissism, Jacques Lacan, in 'The Mirror Stage as Formative of the *I* Function', suggests the idea of the 'mirror stage':

> It suffices to understand the mirror stage in this context *as an identification*, in the full sense analysis gives to the term: namely, the transformation that takes place in the subject when he assumes [*assume*] an image – an image that is seemingly predestined to have an effect at this phase, as witnessed by the use in analytic theory of antiquity's term, 'imago'.[14]

The 'mirror stage' involves a subject's identification, which constructs his identity. For Lacan, an identity does not reflect or equal the subject. Instead, it transforms and constructs him. The word 'imago' links with the idea of imagination, meaning that a person's identity comes from his projection.[15] Moreover, the 'mirror stage' reveals the ambiguous relation between the subject and the object:

> For the total form of his body, by which the subject anticipates the maturation of his power in a mirage, is given to him only as a gestalt, that is, in an exteriority in which, to be sure, this form is more constitutive than constituted, but in which, above all, it appears to him as the contour of his stature that freezes it and in a symmetry that reverses it, in opposition to the turbulent movements with which the subject feels he animates it. Through

these two aspects of its appearance, this gestalt – whose power [*prégnance*] should be considered linked to the species, though its motor style is as yet unrecognizable – symbolizes the *I*'s mental permanence, at the same time as it prefigures its alienating destination.[16]

The mirror image creates an illusion of totality, giving the subject a gestalt, an exterior, a form that constitutes subjectivity. It 'freezes' the subject, making him believe in his having a fixed identity. Such an identity reverses the subject and object positions: while the subject feels that he is in an active position, the 'mirror image', as the subject's projection, is a controlling force. It 'symbolizes the *I*'s mental perma- nence', meaning that the construction of subjectivity is ideological and is an illusion. Moreover, it prefigures the subject's 'alienating destina- tion': identification is misrecognition, alienating the subject. The mirror image is a phantasm that dominates the subject, confusing the subject and object positions. Moreover, the image is a 'stage' since it is fictional:

the mirror stage is a drama whose internal pressure pushes precipitously from insufficiency to anticipation – and, for the subject caught up in the lure of spatial identification, turns out fantasies that proceed from a fragmented image of the body to what I will call an 'orthopedic' form of its totality – and to the finally donned armor of an alienating identity that will mark his entire mental development with its rigid structure.[17]

The 'insufficiency' points to the Lacanian idea of 'lack'. Turning empti- ness into a projection, it is a drama that turns the fragmented body into a totality. Putting the discussion of Lacan into the context of *Volpone*, the mirror would be the object that produces this 'para-site'. It repre- sents the existence of another space that gains control over the subject. Comedy, as it appears, often showcases the existence of these two spaces. The audience laugh when they are presented with this image of doubleness.

Volpone's Parasite and His 'Para-site'

In Act I scene v, when Corvino asks if Volpone has any children, Mosca says that the dwarf, the androgyne and the eunuch are Volpone's bas- tards, as if he is not one of them. Posing himself as someone outside, Mosca sounds as if he were another Vice figure, Richard III, who tells Buckingham to 'infer the bastardy of Edward's children' (*King Richard III* III.v.73). Richard bastardises Edward's children, proclaiming their illegitimacy. Even though Richard Dutton comments that 'Mosca dis- sociates himself from Volpone's paternity',[18] it remains unclear if the parasite's words are trustworthy.

Act III scene i marks the turning point of *Volpone*. The scene starts with Mosca's speech, contrasting with Volpone's soliloquy in Act I scene i that is interrupted by the parasite. Carol A. Carr argues:

> Mosca does not merely interrupt Volpone; he breaks a spell, and he does so sheerly through his tone of voice. He is not contradicting Volpone but merely summing up his speech into a concise maxim. Mosca's tone is dry, matter-of-fact, and detached; Volpone's is buoyant, imaginative, and impassioned.[19]

The audience witness that the parasite is waiting for his chance to subvert his master. However, the parasite's speech is full of contradictions. It illustrates the gap between what Mosca sees and what he is unable to see, suggesting that he, perhaps, is also just one of Volpone's bastards. The scene shows how Mosca is in the 'mirror stage', which is doomed to produce misrecognition of subjectivity:

> MOSCA   I fear I shall begin to grow in love
> With my dear self and my most prosp'rous parts,
> They do so spring and burgeon; I can feel
> A whimsy i' my blood. I know not how,
> Success hath made me wanton. I could skip
> Out of my skin, now, like a subtle snake,
> I am so limber.
>
> (III.i.1–7)

In this speech, Mosca shows his ambition for the first time, saying, 'I fear I shall begin to grow in love / With my dear self' (III.i.1–2), lines which suggest his narcissistic nature. His downfall might start from the moment when he begins to see the 'parasite' as an independent subject, misbelieving in the seeming omnipotence of his role. This scene shows Mosca as if he were looking at his mirror image. The words of the parasite represent his desire.

However, Mosca's narcissism is ironic and ambiguous. First of all, the parasite says he is in love with his 'prosperous parts'. Examining his speech with the Lacanian concept, these prosperous parts can be seen as the sum of the body as fragments. They are in contrast with his dear 'self', which implies a sense of completeness. Because of his narcissism, Mosca sees a double image. The complete, dear self of Mosca is contradicted by his fragmentary parts.[20] On the idea of a fragmented body, Lacan writes:

> This fragmented body . . . is regularly manifested in dreams when the movement of an analysis reaches a certain level of aggressive disintegration of the individual. It then appears in the form of disconnected limbs or of organs exoscopically represented, growing wings and taking up arms for internal persecutions that the visionary Hieronymus Bosch fixed for all time in painting, in their ascent in the fifteenth century to the imaginary zenith of modern man.[21]

The identification of subjectivity through the mirror image is simultaneously a construction and a repression. The fragmented body, which represents the disintegration of the individual, comes out in dreams and in art. Such a tendency of the disintegration of the body comes out from Mosca's language, which represents his unconscious. While celebrating his love for his 'complete' self, his language betrays him as it reveals a force of disintegration.

The prosperous parts of Mosca are sexual and phallic as they can 'spring' and 'burgeon'. Howard Marchitell links the theatrical with the sexual. He suggests that 'Mosca's celebration of his talent attest[s] to the phallic nature of the power to which he aspires, a power he understands as both protean and procreative, social and sexual.'[22] As Mosca 'grows' in love with himself, he 'erects' when he sees his own image, which corresponds with the suggestion of 'zany' in Jonson's *Poetaster* as the zany is 'a good skipping swaggerer' (III.iv.244). The word 'swag' means to 'move unsteadily or heavily from side to side or up and down' or 'to sway without control' with 'a pendulous part of the body' (*OED* 1). Although Mosca praises himself for being different from the zanies, he talks and acts like one.

Moreover, the prosperous parts can mean Mosca's theatrical parts: what Mosca sees in his mirror image is not necessarily Mosca per se, but Mosca as a Vice, a parasite and a servant. Jonas Barish links the soliloquy of Mosca with aping and counterfeiting. He argues:

> Mosca's opening soliloquy in Act III shows that this excellent counterfeiter is himself, like his master, obsessed by the notion of imitators. His contempt for ordinary parasites suggests that there is a hierarchy of counterfeits, ranging from those who are deeply and essentially false (like himself) to those who practice falsity out of mere affectation, who are, so to speak, falsely false and therefore, again, at two removes from nature.[23]

Norbert Greiner sees Mosca as 'the universal man of the theatre'.[24] He thinks that Mosca 'is one jump ahead of Volpone, because he is open for improvisation; he does not rely on literary tradition alone, but reacts *extempore* as required by the needs of the moment'.[25] Jonathan Dollimore suggests that Mosca is able to 'subvert social differentiation and identity'.[26] When Volpone asks Mosca to be 'a brave *clarissimo*', even though it is a pity that Mosca was 'not born one', Mosca replies, 'If I hold / My made one, 'twill be well' (V.v.3–5). Dollimore argues that Mosca's answer implies two meanings: on one level, ''Twill be well because he is not the real thing, never could be, and is not even now presuming to be'; but, on the other level, Mosca's answer implies that 'the imitation, the travesty, of the real thing can also usurp it and *to all intents and purposes* become it'. He sees that as a moment of 'ambiguity and irony' since it effortlessly abolishes the social differentiation. It is also a moment of appropriation since it incites knowledge and, at the same time, provokes the fear of the 'riot of the perverse, the antisocial and the anti-natural' within *Volpone*.[27] The word 'whimsy', in his speech, is linked with 'whim', which is 'a capricious notion or fancy; a fantastic or freakish idea; an odd fancy' (*OED* 3a). The 'whimsical blood' points to Mosca's capability to construct different plots and identities. However, the word 'whimsy' also means 'dizziness, giddiness, vertigo' (*OED* 1), which suggests an image of Mosca standing at the top and foreshadows his eventual downfall. The image of Mosca as a Vice standing at the top (and also of Volpone on his platform) recalls that of Lucifer, illustrating the danger of hubris. Isaiah 14 tells of the devil Lucifer's fall from heaven. Lucifer has to be cut down to the earth and brought down to the grave. Mosca's shape-changing ability indicates his power of de-forming. His 'self' is contradicted by his interchangeable roles. Even though he praises himself for his play-acting ability, the mirror image of what Mosca sees is and is not himself simultaneously.

The parasite suggests that 'success has made me wanton'. Being 'undisciplined' and 'ungoverned' (*OED* 1a), he thinks that he is no longer under anybody's control and cannot be managed. Having no regard for his master, his words correspond to the meaning of 'swaggerer' in *Poetaster*. The use of 'wanton' recalls the words between Feste and Viola in Shakespeare's *Twelfth Night*:

> FESTE   You have said, sir. To see this age! – A sentence is but a cheverel glove to a good wit, how quickly the wrong side may be turned outward.
> VIOLA   Nay, that's certain. They that dally nicely with words may quickly make them wanton.
> FESTE   I would therefore my sister had had no name, sir.
> VIOLA   Why, man?
> FESTE   Why, sir, her name's a word, and to dally with that word might make my sister wanton. But indeed, words are very rascals since bonds disgraced them.
>
> (III.i.10–19)

In addition to the sense of 'undisciplined' and 'unruly', 'wanton' can be used to refer to a person who is 'sexually promiscuous' (*OED* 3a). The linkage between 'wanton' and 'swaggerer' refers to Mosca's attitude towards sexuality.[28] The two words are contradictory since the use of 'wanton' puts him in a feminine position. This image contrasts with his phallic usage of words. Masculinity and femininity collide within the parasite's mind, which creates the image of the androgyne within him.

Mosca feels like a snake that can limberly skip out of his skin. The use of the word 'skip' instead of 'slough' raises the image of jumping, which echoes with Mosca's whimsy blood and his hubris. The power to skip out of skin represents an ability to separate the body from its surface. We are, therefore, reminded of the characters Subtle and Face in *The Alchemist*. If Subtle refers to the inner body, Face relates to the outer. Not only can Mosca skip out of his skin, he is a 'subtle' snake, making him both characters at once. The snake raises the importance of temptation and the image of the devil in Genesis 3: 1. Mosca makes others lose the meaning of words and identities: because of him, Lady Would-be confuses Peregrine with being Politic Would-be's catamite and calls him a hermaphrodite, and the avocatores have doubts over Bonario's and Celia's integrity. The parasite says he is so 'limber', meaning that he is easily bent, flexible, pliant and supple. However, the word also refers to things that are 'properly firm or crisp: limp, flaccid, flabby' (*OED* 1c). Commenting on Volpone, Stephen Greenblatt argues:

> The creature who can perform these feats has literally to be nothing, a bodiless fiction. Hence the terror lurking in a mere cramp: a sign that the body resists the will and thus that the fiction is collapsing. For Volpone, to sense the body's resistance is to sense death.[29]

He suggests that Volpone's fear is not an illusion but something physical, namely, 'the fear of real paralysis in place of feigned'.[30] His remark points out the bodilessness of Mosca and its relation to physical paralysis, which resonates with the two meanings of 'limber'. The parasite might think that he is capable of playing with words, but his hubris makes him blind to their opposite meanings:

> Oh! Your parasite
> Is a most precious thing, dropped from above,
> Not bred 'mongst clods and clodpolls here on earth.
> I muse the mystery was not made a science,
> It is so liberally professed! Almost
> All the wise world is little else in nature
> But parasites or sub-parasites.

(III.i.7–13)

The above suggestion shows the image of the parasite as an overreacher, a figure that breaks boundaries and reverses orders. Comparing this passage with the language of Richard III, Robert Jones suggests that Mosca does not engage the audience with the speaker as Richard does. Richard's speech holds up his behaviour for the audience's satirical inspection, and he consistently uses 'I'. This is in contrast with Mosca's distinction of himself from the other parasites and his objective tone of constantly referring to himself as 'parasite' or 'true parasite'.[31] While

Mosca puts himself in God's position, his words 'Oh! Your parasite' sound as if he were putting himself in a scientific demonstration, implying his own alienation. Mosca says that the parasite is the most precious thing that 'dropped from above'. Such an image has its religious meaning. The contrast between a figure dropping from above and clod or clodpolls demonstrates Mosca's superiority over others. He is different from others because of his wit, since 'clod' does not only mean soil or dust, it also means thickhead or clodhopper. However, to be dropped from above is the fate of Lucifer. Therefore, even though he thinks that he can pun, his words demonstrate that it is language that plays with him. Describing himself and his art as mystery, Mosca says, 'I muse the mystery was not made a science.' The word 'mystery', other than the meaning of 'craft' or 'trade', shows that there are certain 'mystic' qualities in his 'art'. The mystic quality puts him in God's position, which echoes with the suggestion of the parasite's religious function. Mosca's comment on making his art into science parallels his words 'Oh! Your parasite.' The final line pinpoints the parasite's spirit. He says, 'All the wise world is little else, in nature, / But parasites or sub-parasites.' This statement seems to suggest a breaking down of all categories, of all norms of hierarchy and all recognised positions of human society in a carnivalesque manner. Ian Donaldson argues:

> His [Mosca's] view of the 'wise world' as made up of an infinite regression of parasites is offered to us with an amused confidentiality. Mosca's delight at his recent success and at his present conception is a delight we feel tempted to share; and his view of the world is one which, in the light of the play's total action, is not entirely absurd.[32]

There is no distinction between master and servant. All dominations are trivialised because there is nothing but parasites or sub-parasites. Mosca unlocks the binary opposition between face and identity, signifier and signified, and the dominant and the dominated. If there is no other, there is no 'self'. Therefore, all 'selves' are heterogeneous in nature. Mosca's statement turns all people into parasites, which is the extinction of any form of independent identity. However, although he eliminates other people's belief in an independent subject, he embraces his identity as a parasite without recognising the illusion of this 'parasite'. Moreover, perhaps the very distinction between parasites and sub-parasites suggests that there is a hierarchical order in Mosca's mind after all.

The suggestion of 'wise world' raises another ambiguity. Although the word 'wise' relates to cleverness, the expression 'wise man' can be 'ironically applied to a fool or simpleton, as in *the wise men of Gotham*' (*OED* 1b). The use of 'wise' recalls Malvolio's words in *Twelfth Night*, who says, 'I protest I take these wise men that crow so at these set kind of fools no better than the fools' zanies' (I.v.75–6). While Malvolio, who is 'sick of self-love' (I.v.77), thinks that he is wise, he may just be a fool, or even a fool's zany. Mosca may turn himself into a fool without being aware of it. If all the wise world contains nothing but parasites and sub-parasites, he is no better than any of them:

> And yet
> I mean not those that have your bare town-art,
> To know who's fit to feed 'em; have no house,
> No family, no care, and therefore mould
> Tales for men's ears, to bait that sense, or get
> Kitchen-invention and some stale receipts
> To please the belly and the groin; nor those,
> With their court-dog-tricks, that can fawn and fleer,
> Make their revenue out of legs and faces,
> Echo my lord, and lick away a moth:
>
> (III.i.13–22)

Herford and Simpson suggest that 'If his [Mosca's] position and authority distinguish him from the vulgar parasite in the literal sense, his brilliant capacity equally distinguishes him from the professional jester.'[33] Even though Mosca may be neither a traditional parasite nor a traditional jester, there are ambiguities within his words. His claim is questionable because he moulds tales by describing Celia as gold to bait Volpone. Because of his tale, Volpone is 'lure[d] out of the safety of his own house and into the street', which leaves 'Mosca in possession of the keys, the house, and the goods of his master'.[34] Indeed, several times in the play we see Volpone giving Mosca money after the parasite flatters him. His suggestion of pleasing the groin raises another ambiguity. The groin can mean the one of the parasite or, perhaps, the master whom the parasite serves. The second interpretation suggests reading Mosca as Volpone's catamite, reminding readers of the similarity between the parasite and Castrone.

Mosca suggests that he differs from those 'With their court-dog-tricks, that can fawn and fleer, / Make their revenue out of legs and faces, / Echo my lord, and lick away a moth.' The 'court-dog-tricks' recalls Shakespeare's *Timon of Athens*, in which Timon suggests that his parasites are dogs. Although Mosca refuses to be a traditional parasite, these suggestions exhibit his awareness of his 'traditional' role:

> But your fine, elegant rascal, that can rise
> And stoop, almost together, like an arrow,
> Shoot through the air as nimbly as a star,
> Turn short as doth a swallow, and be here,
> And there, and here, and yonder, all at once;

Present to any humour, all occasion,
And change a visor swifter than a thought.
This is the creature had the art born with him;
Toils not to learn it, but doth practise it
Out of most excellent nature: and such sparks
Are the true parasites, others but their zanies.

(III.i.23–33)

The contradictory meanings between 'Fine and elegant' and 'rascal'
show Mosca's power to play with language. The use of 'rascal' recalls
Malvolio's description of zany, as he says, 'I marvel your ladyship
takes delight in such a barren rascal' (*Twelfth Night* I.v.71–2). The
fools' zanies are 'barren rascal[s]', contrasting with Feste's suggestion
that 'words are very rascals since bonds disgraced them' (III.i.18–19).
Mosca suggests that he can 'stoop' and 'rise' together, going in two
opposing directions. He says he can be an arrow and a swallow at the
same time. The importance of speed and swiftness recalls the use of
'limber' and 'spring'. He can be here and there, and present to 'any
humour and all occasion' at once.

The ability to be present to any humour and all occasion echoes with
the speech of Richard of Gloucester in *3 King Henry VI*:

Why, I can smile, and murder whiles I smile,
And cry 'Content!' to that which grieves my heart,
And wet my cheeks with artificial tears,
And frame my face to all occasions.

(III.ii.182–5)

His words point to the difference between heart and face. Buckingham,
in *King Richard III*, says:

We know each other's faces. For our hearts,
He knows no more of mine than I of yours,
Or I of his, my lord, than you of mine.

(III.iv.10–12)

Richard and Buckingham suggest a contradiction between face and
heart. The suggestion of crying with artificial tears is a reminder of
Bonario's reaction to Mosca:

What? Does he weep? The sign is soft and good;
I do repent me that I was so harsh.

(III.ii.18–19)

Richard says he will frame his face for all occasions, playing the orator
and deceiving others. The importance of Proteus and changing shapes
is raised, suggesting the concept of transformation. Richard's belief
that he can transcend Machiavelli parallels Mosca's projection of his

surpassing of Volpone. Interestingly, Richard's words come soon after he talks about deformity. His withered arm, his deformed back and his unequal legs are justifications for him to transform into a Vice. Richard's rhetoric on villainy can be compared with Mosca's words. After his soliloquy, in an attempt to convince Bonario, the parasite says:

> Sir, if I do it not, draw your just sword
> And score your vengeance on my front and face;
> Mark me your villain. You have too much wrong,
> And I do suffer for you, sir. My heart
> Weeps blood in anguish –
>
> (III.ii.66–70)

While Richard says that he is determined to prove a villain, Mosca asks Bonario to mark him a villain. Mosca asks Bonario to draw his sword, and 'score your vengeance on my front and face'. Richard says:

> Lo, here I lend thee this sharp-pointed sword,
> Which if thou please to hide in this true breast
> And let the soul forth that adoreth thee,
> I lay it naked to the deadly stroke
> And humbly beg the death upon my knee.
>
> (*King Richard III* I.ii.162–6)

Mosca says his heart 'weeps blood in anguish'. Richard says to Lady Anne:

> In that sad time
> My manly eyes did scorn an humble tear,
> And what these sorrows could not thence exhale
> Thy beauty hath, and made them blind with weeping.
>
> (*King Richard III* I.ii.154.9–12)

Not only does Mosca resemble the characteristics of the hermaphrodite and the eunuch, he is similar to the hunchback figure, recalling the image of the ape, or, to be more specific, Nano the dwarf in *Volpone*. Even though Mosca wants to separate himself from the dwarf, the androgyne and the eunuch, he shares some common qualities with the three bastards.

Finally, Mosca describes himself and his art as sparks. The word 'sparks' refers to men-about-town. The imagery is interesting because a spark is a glimpse of fire that no one can catch, implying the importance of fragments and something that exists for a second before being extinguished. The suggestion demonstrates the existence and the non-existence of the parasite's power, which shows itself only for a glimpse. Before any person can realise his power, it has already gone. Therefore, a true parasite plays with the art of presence and absence. Mosca claims to be a true parasite, saying that he is different from zanies. It means that those sub-parasites are nothing but fools, or some fools who act like or imitate others. If the true parasites are the imitators – as the proverb says, 'imitation is the sincerest form of flattery' – the zanies are imitators of imitators. The suggestion of being a true parasite shows his blindness once again because the idea is an oxymoron. It demonstrates his attempt to go beyond his role, suggesting that he takes being a parasite as a 'true' identity, an identity that, he thinks, does not need to depend on others. However, being a 'true' parasite, paradoxically, means that he needs to depend on others forever.

Duck Soup and *Volpone*: The Marx Brothers and Their 'Para-site'

The analysis of *Volpone* Act III scene i demonstrates that when the audience take pleasure in the parasite's seemingly magnificent speech, they should be conscious of the gap between what he sees and what he fails to see. The comedy of Mosca comes from three important factors. First, it derives from the 'mirror image', and the fact that this 'parasite' takes its own course and develops its own logic. When watching Mosca's performance in his 'mirror stage', the audience are indulging in his phantasmagorical creation. Therefore, applying the Lacanian concept, the scene is comical because the mirror object starts to gain control over the subject, which is essentially what the mirror image does in the construction of subjectivity. However, comedy highlights this fact, which leads to the second significant point: when letting the mirror object take control, comedy neither celebrates nor confirms any ideology. Instead, it brings the audience's attention to it by highlighting it. This is why it is important for the audience not only simply to follow Mosca's indulgence, but to see the gap within it and to witness Mosca's performance and his elimination simultaneously. This gap makes the audience aware of their subject position, allowing them to escape from their daily 'alienation', giving them superiority, albeit momentarily, which explains why the speech is comical. However, comedy is more than just the exposing of the mechanism of the 'mirror stage' and a subject's narcissism. There is one more issue at work, namely, a comic subject tends to be driven by the logic of the mirror, and he often ends up becoming someone who is beyond him.

Comparing Firefly's mirror scene with Mosca's, some similarities can be noticed between them. First of all, what is demonstrated in *Volpone* is the split between Mosca as a 'true parasite' and a zany. Moreover, Mosca and Volpone's three bastards are interchangeable, as he shares some common characteristics with them. This seeming oneness and the internal split of oneness create a comic effect. Zupančič writes:

> Comedy does not consist simply in the imaginary One falling apart, splitting into multiplicity or into two, but begins only at the moment when we see how these two can precisely not separate or part completely, and become simply 'two ones.' There is something like an invisible thread that keeps linking them, and it is this very thread that constitutes the true comic object.[35]

In a similar way, it is important for us to note that even though the Marx Brothers are different characters, they can also be seen as one. The mirror scene is the best illustration of this point. The scene draws our attention to the similarities between the three brothers, and, at the same time, their differences. The three bastards and the parasite, like the three Marx Brothers, can be seen as one and different.

Second, one of the reasons why the Marx Brothers' mirror scene is comical is because Firefly wants to sustain the illusion, but the audience know that it is only an illusion. Moreover, the reversal between subject and object in this scene highlights the relationship between comedy and the concept of the 'mirror stage'. Firefly is so intrigued by the image that he is fully taken control by it, which is interesting as the 'parasite' seems to have its own life and take its own flight. The audience can perhaps speculate about the motive behind Firefly's action. At the beginning of that scene, it would not be too hard for one to argue that Firefly wants to challenge this mirror object (Pinky) and tries to expose the latter as a fake. However, the situation gets more complicated as the scene goes on. Not only does Firefly walk into the mirror and Pinky walk out from it, the former even picks up the straw hat when the latter drops it on the floor. The audience could well suspect that Firefly in the latter part of the scene has started to believe in the 'real-ness' of this image. However, as the audience, we are made conscious of the internal inconsistencies within it. We are well aware that when Firefly pretends to sing and dance in front of the 'mirror', he twirls around while Pinky stands still. Moreover, we see that Pinky holds a black straw hat while Firefly holds a white one (the latter seems to be aware of it, but he again does not attempt to break the illusion and wants to continue to 'test' this image).[36] Chicolini is charged in the next scene with being a spy for Sylvania. In his essay on Lacan and the Marx Brothers, Paul Flaig argues that the mirror scene 'illustrates the limits of the mirror stage', writing:

> When the third term [Chicolini] erupts as identical to the first two [Firefly and Pinky], the abyss of all the terms is revealed so that the mask is nothing more than a contingent appearance, the very truth of their symbolic destitution.[37]

While this is true, I want to argue for the comic potential of this scene, as I believe that there is another reason why Chicolini is put on trial: he gets caught because his entrance breaks the illusion and, therefore, the comedy in the mirror scene. In other words, Chicolini creates a third space, breaking the functioning of the 'para-site'.

Another scene in the film which can be seen as a parallel comes from the dialogue before the Brothers sing 'This Country's Going to War'. In her attempt to prevent the war from happening between Freedonia and Sylvania, Mrs. Teasdale (Margaret Dumont) asks Ambassador Trentino to come and make peace with Firefly. Firefly agrees at first, but things start to change as he continues to consider the possible scenario:

> RUFUS T. FIREFLY   Mrs. Teasdale, you did a noble deed. I'd be unworthy of the high trust that's been placed in me if I didn't do everything in my power to keep our beloved Freedonia in peace with the world. I'd be only too happy to meet with Ambassador Trentino, and offer him on behalf of my country the right hand of good fellowship. And I feel sure he will accept this gesture in the spirit of which it is offered. But suppose he doesn't. A fine thing that'll be. I hold out my hand and he refuses to accept. That'll add a lot to my prestige, won't it? Me, the head of a country, snubbed by a foreign ambassador. Who does he think he is, that he can come here, and make a sap of me in front of all my people? Think of it – I hold out my hand and that hyena refuses to accept. Why, the cheap four-flushing swine, he'll never get away with it I tell you, he'll never get away with it.
> [*Trentino enters*]
> RUFUS T. FIREFLY   So, you refuse to shake hands with me, eh?
> [*Slaps Trentino with his glove*][38]

Firefly is led away by his imagination: another example of how a comic subject is the person who allows his or her projection to take its own flight. There is a sense of madness when a subject is obsessed with the lure of the mirror and words. Both *Volpone* and *Duck Soup* seem to suggest that there is an internal force within a subject's fantasy. While Mosca praises himself in his own 'mirror stage', he does not realise that this 'para-site' is driving him away from who he claims he is. Therefore, it is not enough to say that the mirror stage has the power to fix a subject, because Mosca's scene suggests that language and image are empowered by an internal force, causing a subject to drift away from any form of unchanged status. Even though Mosca considers himself as the 'true' parasite, he is also a parasite, a Vice, a zany, or even a dwarf, a hermaphrodite and a eunuch. While Firefly seems to be the head of Freedonia, he may be turned into Chicolini and Pinky easily. The more a person believes in his or her image and words, the more alienated and split he or she is. The Marx Brothers demonstrate the force of image and signifier in two scenes, and Jonson shows them in one.

Duck Soup vs Hamlet: The 'Para-site' in Comedy and Tragedy

The mechanism of the 'para-site' is not only applicable to the under-standing of comedy. However, it does function differently in comedy and its supposed opposite, namely, tragedy. In this last section, I want to draw in references to *Hamlet*, discussing how the 'para-site' often operates in a different way in the two genres. If one of the most crucial questions in tragedy is 'to be, or not to be', then the word 'or' may epito-mise the gap between the issue of 'being' and 'non-being'. Commenting on this line, Zupančič writes:

> As is otherwise blatantly clear from the play as a whole, its events stir up the question of Hamlet's being: *To be or not to be* is not simply a reflection on the possibility of suicide (as an action yet to be accomplished), it is also an articulation of another kind of vacillation between being and nonbeing: a vacillation in which the subject's nonbeing is already there, as part of his very existence. To be – no to be, here I am, and there I am not . . .[39]

To discuss this line in relation to comedy, the concept of the 'para-site' seems to imply that a person's identity, or his or her recognition of subjectivity (that comes from the mirror), is always a fake, and there is a 'true' sense of self who is in opposition to this mirror. However, Lacan's theory of the 'mirror stage' is telling us the opposite: we are constructed by this mirror image, so the fakeness of identity is always an inherent part of this so-called true self. Therefore, linking Lacan with *Hamlet*, it would be a mistake for someone to believe that he can separate his being (subject) from his non-being (mirror object), as if he could isolate his 'true' self from the mirror image. The 'not to be' is already a part of 'to be', and this might be what Hamlet is struggling with. In other words, this gap between what the subject sees and what he is not supposed to see is also relevant to the discussion of tragedy, only it works in a different way: in tragedy, the subject sees what he is not supposed to see, and not only does he see it, he keeps staring and is traumatised by it. Discussing the German tragic drama, Walter Benjamin writes: 'The Renaissance explores the universe; the baroque explores libraries.'[40] In a similar vein, perhaps we can say that while comedy explores the universe, tragedy explores libraries. Comedy tries to find its answer through searching the outside world, while tragedy tries to find it from within.

The interesting point about Hamlet is that throughout the whole play he keeps looking at this gap (the Queen says, 'Alas, how is't with you, / That you do bend your eye on vacancy, / And with th'incorporal air do hold discourse?' (III.iv.107–9)). This split is essential for us to understand Hamlet, and it can be interpreted on many levels. Hamlet is supposed to be the Prince of Denmark, and the son of King Hamlet. However, since the death of his father, while he is still the prince, he cannot feel that he is the son of Claudius, even though Claudius implies that he is. He feels a sense of alienation when he is in front of his uncle. As he says, 'The time is out of joint' (I.v.189). For him, the whole of existence has broken down. On the other hand, while a tragic figure keeps staring at the gap between himself and the para-site, a comic figure is driven by the force of the 'para-site'. Going back to *Duck Soup*, Groucho does not think too much before he follows the movement of Harpo in the mirror. He might, for a second, wonder, 'Who is this guy? Why does he look like me? But he is not me . . .'. However, the reaction that he has is to test this image, challenge it. Of course, it does not take long for him to fall for the lure of this image, and he even starts having fun with it. Žižek once compared Groucho, Chico and Harpo to superego, ego and id. Adding to his comment, perhaps we can say that Groucho, as a comic figure, cannot help himself but start having fun with *id*; and comedy showcases the power of *id* within the mirror.

To give another example, there is nothing funny when Hamlet asks the question 'To be, or not to be'; however, it is funny when Joseph Tura asks it in *To Be or Not To Be* (1942).[41] Mladen Dolar uses this scene to illustrate comedy's answer to the question, writing, 'What does comedy do with the question? *To Be or Not to Be* provides the brilliant answer: walk out on it.'[42] He argues:

> It (comedy) stands up, like the spectator in the second row, or rather springs up, and then persists, keeps springing up with clockwork regularity at precisely the same spot. Comedy hinges on this curtailed part which on either side of the choice was doomed to fall out – something that neither is nor is not, a partial object.[43]

An interesting comparison can be seen in Woody Allen's *Bullets Over Broadway* (1994), in which Eden (Tracey Ullman) says to Olive (Jennifer Tilly), 'Darling, could you give me that cue a little quicker in Act II? You know the one where your character is quoting Hamlet . . . It's "or not to be". Okay?' To which Olive replies, 'Oh, well, you know, it's hard, 'cause I always forget the second part.'[44] While it is a joke on Olive, there may be a point on comedy in her response. Although we, obviously, can point out the difference between Jacky Benny and Laurence Olivier as an easy explanation of why one is comedy and another one is tragedy, there might be something more sophisticated relating to the difference between the two genres. In Benny's version, an audience member (who was called 'the little thing in the second row' in the film) would leave his seat whenever Tura performed his soliloquy.

In Mel Brooks's remake of the film, not only does this 'little thing' upset Frederick Bronski (Brooks) whenever he performs his 'Highlights from *Hamlet*', 'it' actually makes him a better actor, as the film brings out by having another actor say, 'What happened? He's good tonight.'[45] In other words, instead of focusing on the important question, Bronski, because of his narcissism, is driven away by this little thing, which, ironically, makes him even more Hamlet than Hamlet. This 'little thing' can be perceived as both onstage and offstage at the same time. While 'it' is sitting literally offstage, the audience feed the narcissistic imagination of the actor. In other words, it is the 'offstage', the blind spot, on the 'stage'. Comedy is often about this heterogeneous driving force, and a comic subject will often follow it.

While Hamlet says he only sees words, words, words (II.ii.192), as if he is troubled by the gap between the signifier and the signified, the Marx Brothers tell you that in the world of comedy, there are only words, words, words. The punning of the Marx Brothers is important because it shows us how comedy allows the meaning of a sentence to flow with the movement of the signifiers. In the courtroom scene, after a series of puns such as 'secret war code and plans' and 'a pair of pants', 'irrelevant' and 'elephant', 'eliminate' and 'lemonade', and so on, Chicolini says to Firefly, 'Hey boss, I'm goin' good!' There is no sense in Chicolini whatsoever that he is going to be charged with treason and sentenced to death. Death (and war) is supposed to be the subject underlying this scene, only Chicolini, and even the audience, is/are completely oblivious to it. It is at this point that Firefly says, 'Gentlemen . . . Chicolini here may talk like an idiot, and look like an idiot, but don't let that fool you . . . He really is an idiot.' Firefly's words do not refuse the possibility that there are two layers of existence: one on the surface, and one that is deep inside. However, the tricky point that comedy tells us is that we should not expect that there is anything essential within, and what you get is what you see on the surface. Perhaps, if we can express it in another way, it means that the essence is already there on the surface. Or, to put it in the language of linguistic theory, comedy does not tell us that there is no signified, it simply suggests that the signified is there in the signifier. Therefore, one of the most astonishing scenes in *Duck Soup* is the one when the Brothers sing 'This Country's Going to War'. It is funny and challenging to watch because it does not moan and lament the suffering and the tragic nature of war. Instead, it forces the audience to react by making them laugh (a point to which I shall return in the final chapter). Comedy is not interested in 'telling' the truth. If the truth is really too much for anyone to handle, it may be due to the reason that it is already here, naked. Perhaps the act of 'telling' makes the truth become too distant. Comedy 'presents' the truth to its audience, it makes the truth present, and more imminent; and the 'truth', perhaps, is that in this world there is only acting and role-playing (remember how Groucho appears in different costumes in the subsequent war scenes). The 'para-site' is the only reality. If a tragic character is the person who refuses to accept the unbearable lightness of being, a comic character would be the one who thrives on it.

A tragedy, then, would be characterised by its inaction; and comedy is characterised by its action and movement. The discussion of movement and comedy brings us to the realm of Henri Bergson, who argues for the relationship between the comic and the machine. He writes that 'The attitudes, gestures and movements of the human body are laughable in exact proportion as that body reminds us of a mere machine.'[46] From the perspective of Bergson, the Marx Brothers' mirror scene can perhaps be explained by the following passage:

> But the suggestion must also be a subtle one, for the general appearance of the person, whose every limb has been made rigid as a machine, must continue to give us the impression of a living being. The more exactly these two images, that of a person and that of a machine, fit into each other, the more striking is the comic effect, and the more consummate the art of the draughtsman. The originality of a comic artist is thus expressed in the special kind of life he imparts to a mere puppet.[47]

Bergson draws a clear distinction between human and machine/puppet. In his words, something is comic when there is no longer life, but an 'automatism established in life and imitating it'.[48] He argues that 'To imitate any one is to bring out the element of automatism he has allowed to creep into his person. And as this is the very essence of the ludicrous, it is no wonder that imitation gives rise to laughter.'[49] In the example of the mirror scene, perhaps Firefly can be seen as the human and Pinky as the puppet who imitates the former's actions. Therefore, Firefly is ludicrous because he allows the mechanical side (Pinky as a puppet) to 'creep into his person'. However, Lacan's theory may teach us something more in regard to comedy. Perhaps the existence of the 'para-site' implies that imitation is already a part of life, and there is no easy distinction between life and puppet/machine. In the mirror scene, the idea of imitation should not be seen as a simple active and passive relationship. As the scene goes on, there are certain occasions when it is simply impossible for Pinky to imitate Firefly (and yet he is still able to do so). For instance, Pinky can still anticipate Firefly's action even when the latter is outside the mirror frame. Moreover, the fact that Firefly walks into the mirror and Pinky walks out from it also makes their relationship ambiguous. Finally, as the scene goes on, there is a certain moment when Pinky actually acts before Firefly (when the former puts on his straw hat, for example). Therefore, it is not easy to argue that Firefly is the human and Pinky is the automaton that imitates the human. There is no identity without imitation, and the two brothers perhaps are intertwined, leaving the audience to wonder who is human and who is puppet. Instead of rejecting this fact, comedy seems to imply that the only way to deal with it is to embrace this mechanism of the 'para-site' as part of life. Linking this discussion back to Jonson, the ambiguity between life and puppet recalls the role of Dionysus in *Bartholomew Fair*. Indeed, we can see Dionysus as the embodiment of the three bastards, a notion which I shall explore in the next chapter.

In the gravedigger scene, Hamlet says to Horatio, 'To what base uses we may return, Horatio!' (V.i.187). The word 'base' reminds us of Edmund in *King Lear*. Referring to his status as a bastard, Edmund says, 'Why brand they us / with base? With baseness? Bastardy? Base, base?' (I.ii.9–10). Thinking Shakespeare with Jonson, Hamlet's predicament can perhaps be defined as a refusal to be a bastard. Things might be different if Hamlet were happily to accept his uncle as his father, and to have no problem seeing his mother sleeping with his uncle. In other words, he might simply accept his new status as being a 'bastard'. Having said that, I am not suggesting that if Hamlet were to become a bit more 'immoral', he could live happily ever after and we could have a comedy about him. What the logic of the 'para-site' tells us is that any possibility of going beyond is to be driven by its flight. Mosca becomes the three bastards by believing himself to be a 'true' parasite; Firefly turns himself into Pinky as he tries to hold his ground; and Bronski, by seeing himself as a bad actor (as implied by seeing an audience member leaving), actually becomes a good actor.[50] Discussing Brecht's *The Resistible Rise of Arturo Ui* and Chaplin's *The Great Dictator*, Theodor Adorno famously questions the power of comedy, writing that 'For the sake of political commitment, political reality is trivialized: which then reduces the political effect.'[51] If morality is related to the discussion of comedy, I would say that perhaps there is a stronger moral courage in following the logic of the para-site than not following it. After all, are we not living in the space of 'para-site' one way or another? Lacan tells us that the construction of identity all depends on others. When the tragic figure resists the temptation of the para-site, perhaps he believes in his own identity too much as if his existence is not a construction. When Hamlet refuses to accept Claudius, does he realise that he is under the power of his father? He may question whether the image of his father is only an illusion and a figment of his imagination, but he never challenges the

Ghost of the father. 'There is nothing either good or bad but thinking makes it so' (II.ii.244–5) – despite his own avowal of this statement, Hamlet cannot accept this, he sees this as the breaking down of the world, leaving no hope left; comedy embraces this logic, but it is also characterised by movement, by twists and turns, driven by the silent, little thing from within. At the end of *Duck Soup*, when Mrs. Teasdale starts singing after she claims 'victory is ours', the brothers start throwing things at her. Comedy does not assert or confirm any single subject position. As soon as it looks like it is going to stop and end, it starts again. The key words for understanding comedy are 'drive' and 'movement'. Drawing references to the muteness of Harpo, Simon Critchley discusses comedy and tragedy with the notion of finitude. He writes: 'Tragedy is insufficiently tragic because it is too heroic. Only comedy is truly tragic. Comedy is tragic by not being a tragedy.'[52] Adding to this, I would suggest that tragedy seems to be related to the subject of death, but, in many cases, it is related to the resistance to death. On the other hand, comedy can be seen as closer to death, because it is defined by movement, and, therefore, it runs the risk of exhaustion.

Conclusion

Through comparing *Duck Soup*'s mirror scene with *Volpone*'s Act III scene i, this chapter demonstrates how both scenes are built on the mechanism of the 'para-site', meaning how their comedy is strongly related to Jacques Lacan's theory of the 'mirror stage'. Not only is their comedy based upon the exposing of a subject's narcissism, it tells us how a comic character is often the person who drifts along the logic of the mirror (and even the symbolic, with punning as an example). Comparing *Duck Soup* with *Hamlet*, we see that while a comic character would embrace this logic, a tragic one may be the person who tries to resist it, as, perhaps, he refuses to accept that the mirror object (non-being) is already part of the construction of the subject (being). However, having said this, I must emphasise that I am not trying to claim an all-inclusive theory of comedy, as, obviously, Jonson's and the Marx Brothers' comedies are unique in their own ways. Moreover, if comedy is developed from its drive and movement, from its twists and turns, then any attempt to pin it down to a single definition would be doomed to failure, and is, in itself, counter comedy.

Notes

1. *Duck Soup*, directed by Leo McCarey.
2. Arnott, 'Studies in Comedy, I', p. 162.
3. Arnott, 'Studies in Comedy, I', p. 162.
4. Arnott, 'Studies in Comedy, I', pp. 162–3.
5. Welsford, *The Fool*, p. 4.
6. Welsford, *The Fool*, p. 4.
7. Welsford, *The Fool*, p. 4.
8. Withington, '"Vice" and "Parasite"', p. 743.
9. Spivack, *Shakespeare and the Allegory of Evil*, pp. 311–12.
10. Spivack, *Shakespeare and the Allegory of Evil*, pp. 311–12.
11. Vandiver, 'Elizabethan Dramatic Parasite', p. 424.
12. Lucian, *Lucian*, vol. 3, p. 255.
13. Freud, 'On Narcissism', p. 75.
14. Lacan, 'Mirror Stage', p. 76.
15. Using Woody Allen's *Play It Again, Sam* as an example, Žižek explains the transition from imaginary to symbolic. He suggests that the withdrawal of the Bogart figure in the end means that Allen's character 'becomes an "autonomous personality" *through* his identification with Bogart'. He writes: 'The only difference is that now identification is no longer imaginary (Bogart as a model to imitate) but, at least in its fundamental dimension, symbolic – that is, structural: the hero realizes this identification by enacting in reality Bogart's role from *Casablanca* – by assuming a certain "mandate", by occupying a certain place in the intersubjective symbolic network (sacrificing a woman for friendship . . .). It is this symbolic identification that dissolves the imaginary identification (makes the Bogart figure disappear) – more precisely: that radically changes its contents.' See Žižek, *Sublime Object of Ideology*, pp. 121–2.
16. Lacan, 'Mirror Stage', p. 76.
17. Lacan, 'Mirror Stage', p. 78.
18. See the footnote in *Volpone* I.v.49 in Jonson, *Cambridge Edition*, vol. 3, p. 69.
19. Carr, 'Volpone and Mosca', p. 146.
20. Otter makes a similar remark on Mistress Otter's assembly and disassembly of her fragmentary body parts in *Epicoene* Act IV scene ii.
21. Lacan, 'Mirror Stage', p. 78.
22. Marchitell, 'Desire and Domination in *Volpone*', p. 293.
23. Barish, 'Double Plot in *Volpone*', p. 105.
24. Greiner, 'Scenic Laughter', p. 168.
25. Greiner, 'Scenic Laughter', p. 168.
26. Dollimore, *Sexual Dissidence*, pp. 291–2.
27. Dollimore, *Sexual Dissidence*, pp. 291–2.
28. Hostess Quickly says in *2 Henry IV*: 'I cannot abide swaggerers' (II.iv.93).
29. Greenblatt, 'False Ending in *Volpone*', p. 101.
30. Greenblatt, 'False Ending in *Volpone*', p. 101.
31. Jones, 'Volpone', p. 114.
32. Donaldson, 'Volpone: Quick and Dead', p. 125.

33. Herford and Simpson (eds), *Ben Jonson*, vol. 2, p. 61.

34. Donaldson, 'Unknown Ends', pp. 115–16.

35. Zupančič, *Odd One In*, p. 78.

36. Perhaps part of the joke here is that just as mirrors reverse left and right, so they can reverse black and white.

37. Flaig, 'Lacan's Harpo', p. 106.

38. *Duck Soup*, directed by Leo McCarey.

39. Zupančič, *Odd One In*, p. 170.

40. Benjamin, *Origin of German Tragic Drama*, p. 140.

41. *To Be or Not to Be*, directed by Ernst Lubitsch.

42. Dolar, 'To Be or Not to Be?', p. 123.

43. Dolar, 'To Be or Not to Be?', p. 125.

44. *Bullets Over Broadway*, directed by Woody Allen.

45. *To Be or Not to Be*, directed by Alan Johnson.

46. Bergson, *Laughter*, p. 32.

47. Bergson, *Laughter*, pp. 32–3.

48. Bergson, *Laughter*, p. 34.

49. Bergson, *Laughter*, pp. 34–5.

50. The treatment of Falstaff in *The Merry Wives of Windsor* may be a bit different. Quickly says to him, 'Corrupt, corrupt, and tainted in desire.' (V.v.88) and the fairies sing, 'Lust is but a bloody fire, / Kindled with unchaste desire' (V.v.92–3). Finally, Evans says to Falstaff, 'Sir John Falstaff, serve Got and leave your desires, and fairies will not pinse you' (V.v.124–5).

51. Adorno, 'Commitment', pp. 184–5.

52. Critchley, 'Comedy and Finitude', p. 235.

Chapter 6

Jonson's Comedy of Bastardy

In previous chapters, I have examined how the dwarf as a representation embodies the notion of phallic empowerment on one hand, and death and castration on the other. The androgyne and the eunuch are two figures that are interconnected: both signify the importance of folly and castration in their ways. Moreover, while the parasite may think that he is thriving on his stage, he may slip into being one of Volpone's bastards. Therefore, we should understand Jonson's comedies from two perspectives simultaneously: while it is true that the bastards represent a critical attitude of Jonson towards the city, the dramatist recognises their comic power. Moreover, if we see these figures together, we notice how they can be easily slipped into one another, meaning that a person's subjectivity in the city is built upon a series of misrecognitions, which is what the comedy is based upon. Even though there is 'nothing' beneath a person's identity, the creation and the transformation on the surface is 'everything' that he or she can have. As a continuation of the discussion, this chapter examines how the comedy of bastardy can be seen in *The Alchemist* and *Bartholomew Fair*. While Jonson makes fun of the city subjects, and suggests that to be possessed is to be melancholic, to be a fool, for him, is a liberation. The city helps to create and construct different identities.

This chapter is divided into two parts. The first part focuses on *The Alchemist*, arguing that while the critique of the city is still present, there seems to be a stronger indulgence in its logic. I am going to suggest that the representations and implications of Volpone's bastards can be found in *The Alchemist*, showing how alchemy becomes the metaphor of their comic logic: while on the one hand it is just a stone and a dead object, on the other hand, it is the gold with its magnificence. I shall argue for the importance of Lovewit's absence in most parts of the play, and his indulgence when he eventually comes back. Compared with Volpone, Lovewit seems to be more than willing to follow the plots of his servant, which may be the will of the audience members, a hetero-geneous crowd that cannot be clearly defined.

The second part of this chapter develops from Harry Levin's sug-gestion in 'Jonson's Metempsychosis', which proposes that 'Possibly Mosca's interlude was written before the rest of the play, like the puppet-show in *Bartholomew Fair*.'[1] It argues that the puppet embod-ies the characteristics of Volpone's bastards; and that its representation is instrumental for us to read the aforementioned doubleness within the 1614 comedy. While the puppet unveils its garment and reveals the nothingness beneath, its representation simultaneously relates to the importance of folly and transformation. Indeed, perhaps Jonson may have found the puppet to be the embodiment of the bastards. As my discussion is going to show, *Bartholomew Fair* is a play that highlights the fun that builds upon the notion of emptiness and nothingness. If the phallus is still present at the end of *Epicoene* (though I believe it is more an epicene centre than a male centre), then the *it* is absolutely gone in *Bartholomew Fair*. A rereading of these two plays shows how the significations of the dwarf, the androgyne and the eunuch remain important in this period of Jonson's comedy, and how he evolves as a comedy writer.

'Come near, my *terrae fili*': The Three Bastards in *The Alchemist*

First of all, I will focus my discussion on *The Alchemist*. Similar to *Volpone*, *The Alchemist* is a play that is filled with the encounters between the tricksters (Face, Subtle and Doll Common) and the gulls (such as Dapper, Abel Drugger, Epicure Mammon, Kastril and numer-ous others). While intending to lure Dame Pliant (Kastril's sister, who is a widow), Face (along with Subtle) makes Kastril believe that Subtle can 'make matches for rich widows' (III.iv.101). In Act IV scene ii, when Kastril brings his sister to Face and Subtle, we have the following dialogue:

> SUBTLE   Come near, my worshipful boy, my *terrae fili*,
> That is, my boy of land. Make thy approaches.
> Welcome. I know thy lusts and thy desires,
> And I will serve and satisfy 'em.
>
> (IV.ii.13–16)

On *terrae fili*, Peter Holland and William Sherman, in *The Cambridge Edition of the Works of Ben Jonson*, annotate:

The Lat. Phrase ('son of earth') meant someone without family property rights (e.g. a bastard). Subtle ought to call him [Kastril] *'terrae filius'*. Subtle, making a joke that Kastril will not understand, uses it, as if it were a term of praise, to mean the reverse: a son with lands.[2]

This wordplay is a trick that Jonson often uses in his comedies. It reminds us of how he plays with the tension between 'possession' and 'dispossession' in *Volpone*, a notion that cannot be separated from the play as a city comedy. Similarly, as discussed in Chapter 4, Jonson plays with the concepts of 'omnipotence' and 'impotence' in *Epicoene*. This confusion exemplifies the logic of the bastards: even though the notion of 'impotence' seems to represent a critique of nascent early modern capitalism, Jonson's tone towards the city may not be completely negative because the transformation also makes a subject 'omnipotent'. Among these examples, Subtle's words point directly to the subject of bastardy. His words suggest that Jonson's comedy plays on the thin line between being a 'son with lands' and being a 'son of earth'. In other words, 'dispossession', 'impotence' and 'bastardy' are three concepts that are interrelated, and Jonson exhibits them in these three plays through different means.

If we try to understand how Jonson treats the subject of alchemy through his poems and masques, we may come to the conclusion that he does not have a positive view towards it. For instance, Jonson touches on this subject in his poem 'To Alchemists':

If all you boast of your great art be true,
Sure, willing poverty lives most in you.

(*Epigrams* 6)

Similarly, when introducing the masque *Mercury Vindicated from the Alchemists at Court*, Martin Butler writes that it

tracks back to territory that Jonson had already explored in detail in *The Alchemist*. Its central conceit is a contrast between the King – here identified with Nature herself, the parent of all things and the 'spring whence order flows' (line 187) – and the alchemists, impoverished devotees of a false science, who have set up their Art in competition with Nature.[3]

However, while Jonson criticises the alchemist in his poems and masques, his attitude in his play seems to be more ambivalent. Anne Barton writes that

Like most of Jonson's masques, *Mercury Vindicated From the Alchemists at Court* deals in absolute values, sharply dividing a world of beauty, order and goodness from one of ugliness, chaos and vice. In the comedy he called *The Alchemist*, written five years earlier, the situation is nothing like so clear-cut.[4]

Indeed, if we consider the importance of bastardy in Jonson's comedy, we may say that although *The Alchemist* addresses the 'poverty' within the alchemist (as represented by the stone as an image of nothingness), his 'boasting' may be too appealing for the audience to ignore. In this part, I am going to compare *The Alchemist* with *Volpone*, suggesting that while the two plays share similar themes, the 'bastards' have a more significant role in the 1610 play. I am going to draw attention to the fact that Lovewit, as a master figure in this comedy, is absent most of the time, leaving Face, Subtle and Doll to be in charge of the house. In other words, if we compare this with *Volpone*, it would mean that Mosca, or even Nano, Androgyno and Castrone, are the central figures of this comedy. Moreover, I am going to address how the representations and implications of Volpone's bastards are present in *The Alchemist*. I will also compare Face with Mosca, and Lovewit with Volpone, arguing that while themes such as nothingness and castration are still important, the play demonstrates an indulgence in the logic of transformation and folly.[5]

First, if the centre of *Volpone* is the gold in the shrine, the one in *The Alchemist*, by contrast, would be the philosopher's stone, a barren object. Subtle says:

> Oh, I did look for him
> With the sun's rising. 'Marvel he could sleep!
> This is the day I am to perfect for him
> The *magisterium*, our great work, the stone,
> And yield it, made, into his hands, of which
> He has this month talked as he were possessed.
> And now he's dealing pieces on't away.
> Methinks I see him entering ordinaries
> Dispensing for the pox, and plaguy-houses,
> Reaching his dose, walking Moorfields for lepers,
> And offering citizens' wives pomander bracelets
> As his preservative made of the elixir,
> Searching the spital to make old bawds young
> And the highways for beggars to make rich.
> I see no end of his labours. He will make
> Nature ashamed of her long sleep, when art,
> Who's but a stepdame, shall do more than she,
> In her best love to mankind, ever could.
> If his dream last, he'll turn the age to gold.

(I.iv.11–29)

In the play, the speech of Epicure Mammon evokes the image of Volpone, reminding the audience, 'Good morning to the day; and next, my gold! Open the shrine that I may see my saint' (*Volpone* I.i.1–2). The suggestions of possession, of making old bawds young, of making nature ashamed of her long sleep, and of the 'golden' age can all be read as references to the 1606 play. However, the difference between the two is the more apparent 'presence' of the philosopher's stone in *The Alchemist*. Comparing *Volpone* with *The Alchemist*, Jonathan Haynes writes:

> Alchemy makes a neat metaphor for nascent capitalism, and *The Alchemist* fits neatly in the development of Jonson's economic thought between *Volpone*, in which a real pile of gold draws 'interest' in the old centre of mercantilism, and the direct satiric exploration of capitalist 'projection' in *The Devil is an Ass*.[6]

If the images of death and castration are epitomised by the three bastards in *Volpone*, which is subtler, the dead object is presented directly to the audience in the 1610 play. In other words, as if the glorification of gold and the performance of Volpone are too dazzling to the audience, the subject (and object) of nothingness is 'highlighted' in *The Alchemist*:

ANANIAS   He bears
The visible mark of the beast in his forehead.
And for his stone it is a work of darkness,
And with philosophy blinds the eyes of man.

                                                    (III.i.7–10)

The stone is described as an image of darkness, recalling similar representations in *Volpone*. Moreover, the suggestion that the philosopher's stone can blind the eyes of man is a reminder of Mosca's words: 'True. They will not see't; Too much light blinds 'em, I think' (V.ii.22–3). More importantly, the 'stone' cannot merely be read as the philosopher's stone, as there is a sexual implication in it. Therefore, similar to *Volpone*, the power of the stone in *The Alchemist* refers to money as much as to sex, meaning that its barrenness is both economic and sexual. However, the attitude of the play is more ambiguous, as one cannot argue for any moral authority in Ananias or Tribulation, and they are simply objects of laughter in it.

Even though Jonson seems to demonstrate a concern for the city and its trades in *The Alchemist*, its treatment is not exactly the same as that in *Volpone*. The play is situated in London, and it makes direct references to the social context of the time, pointing to the plague during 1609 and in the summer of 1610. More importantly, its Argument suggests that the master has quit the house to escape from the sickness:

> The sickness hot, a master quit, for fear,
> His house in town, and left one servant there.
> Ease him corrupted, and gave means to know
> A cheater and his punk, who, now brought low,

Leaving their narrow practice, were become
Cozeners at large; and, only wanting some
House to set up, with him they here contract,
Each for a share, and all begin to act.
Much company they draw and much abuse
In casting figures, telling fortunes, news,
Selling of flies, flat bawdry, with the stone,
Till it and they and all in fume are gone.

('The Argument', lines 1–12)

In other words, the figure of the master is not present in *The Alchemist* (though Lovewit does come back in the end, a point to which I shall return later). Therefore, if we compare it with *Volpone*, it would mean that the 1606 play would not have Volpone as its protagonist. *Volpone* would become a play that is led by Mosca, or even Nano, Androgyno and Castrone. Indeed, perhaps the title of the play should be *The Bastards*: Androgyno, being a fool, can be linked with Face; whereas Castrone, as the cutting force from within, is more like Subtle; and Nano could be both Face and Subtle at once. Being a masterless comedy, *The Alchemist* suggests a different attitude of Jonson towards theatre and the city. If Jonson is struggling with the tension between the critique of the city and the acknowledgement of it as a site of enjoyment in *Volpone*, he seems to be more relaxed towards this subject by 1610.

The beginning of the play shows the fight between Face, Subtle and Doll, and a certain parallel can be noticed between this scene and *Volpone*:

DOLL   [*To Subtle*] And you too
         Will give the cause, forsooth? You will insult
         And claim a primacy in the divisions?
         You must be chief? And if you only had
         The powder to project with? And the work
         Were not begun out of equality?
         The venture tripartite? All things in common?
         Without priority?

(I.i.129–36)

The scene reminds us of another similar one in *Volpone*, in which Nano says:

         Dwarf, fool, and eunuch, well met here we be.
             A question it were now, whether of us three,
         Being, all, the known delicates of a rich man,
             In pleasing him claim the precedency can?

(III.iii.3–6)

Nano goes on to say that it would be foolish for the androgyne and the eunuch to claim the precedency as, by being a dwarf, he is 'little and witty' (III.iii.9). Different from this scene, Doll tries to convince Face and Subtle that neither of them can claim any precedency. She says that no one is the chief and they are all equal.[7] Interestingly, these words are said by Doll, the woman among these 1610 bastards. Julie Sanders writes that 'In this very practical version of theatre, the ensemble rather than individual characters proves to be the driving force and a woman, an articulate and active woman, is very much a part of that ensemble.'[8] While this scene suggests how Volpone's bastards have taken centre stage in 1610, it demonstrates the differences between the two plays. If it is true that in *Volpone* Jonson establishes a hierarchal order between Volpone and Mosca, and between Nano and Androgyno and Castrone, *The Alchemist* suggests a more egalitarian attitude. The play addresses the subject of division in a more direct way:

> DOLL   Oh, me!
> We are ruined! Lost! Ha' you no more regard
> To your reputations? Where's your judgements? 'Slight,
> Have yet some care of me, o' your republic –
>
> (I.i.107–10)

This 'republic' that Doll refers to may equate to the nation of fools in *Volpone*. While the shattering force of the bastards is embedded within and subtler in *Volpone*, the opening of *The Alchemist* addresses this subject openly. For example, Subtle says to Face, 'I'll thunder you in pieces' (I.i.60); and Doll, while trying to stop the fight between them, keeps saying, 'Will you mar all?' (I.i.81), 'will you undo yourselves with civil war?' (I.i.82), 'Oh, this'll o'erthrow all' (I.i.92) and 'Will you be your own destructions, gentlemen?' (I.i.104–5). The 'civil war' represents an internal force within this 'republic' that goes against itself. It can be compared with the power of death, castration and nothingness within *Volpone*, resembling the alienating drive that is imbued within Mosca's speech.

We can also compare Face with Mosca. Reading them together, Face is different from the parasite because of his attitude towards his role and character. As argued in the previous chapter, Mosca mistakenly believes in his power as a parasite. However, the same cannot be said about Face. When the trio realises that Lovewit is coming back, Face says:

> I'll into mine old shape again, and meet him,
> Of Jeremy the butler.
>
> (IV.vii.120–1)

To him, Jeremy the butler is just another shape, a role that is borrowed. He says later:

> But, Doll,
> Pray thee, go heat a little water quickly.
> Subtle must shave me. All my Captain's beard
> Must off to make me appear smooth Jeremy.
>
> (IV.vii.128–31)

While Face talks about his beard when he says that he needs to 'appear' as 'smooth Jeremy', the word 'smooth' can be interpreted as a reference to his skill and dexterity, as if he is the one who can truly 'change a visor swifter than a thought' (*Volpone* III.i.29). In other words, by turning himself into Jeremy, he is and literally has a smooth Face.[9] When Face is accused in front of Lovewit by Mammon, Surly and Kastril, he says:

> If I can hear of him, sir, I'll bring you word
> Unto your lodging; for in truth, they were strangers
> To me. I thought 'em honest as myself, sir.
>
> (V.v.87–9)

Perhaps Face is telling the truth here: not only are Subtle and Doll 'strangers' to him in some sense (as represented by their fight at the beginning and the fact that they are preparing to gull him in the end), Face is a stranger to Jeremy the butler, and vice versa. In fact, if we follow Lacan's concept of the 'mirror stage', the subject and the mirror object are never a coherent one (as a subject tends to believe), and they are doomed to be strangers. The belief in the mirror object causes alienation within a subject, and it would cause the feeling of estrangement within him. There is nothing 'honest' within 'myself', for being a 'self', as in the case of the parasite, would lead to deviation and alienation. Face clearly has a better sense of self-awareness than Mosca, and that is why he is able to gain the trust of Lovewit in the end: instead of attempting to take over the keys and gain the possessions of his master, he offers Dame Pliant to him.

Even though Lovewit does come back in the end and order seems to be restored, he may have shown that he is different from Volpone. From the moment when he comes back to his house, Lovewit has already shown a different attitude:

> Come, sir,
> You know that I am an indulgent master,
> And therefore conceal nothing.
>
> (V.iii.76–8)

On the return of Lovewit, Cheryl Lynn Ross writes that 'Lovewit does not return London to its original, pre-plague state; he does not restore Subtle's booty to its rightful owners. Instead, he appropriates it himself, turning Subtle's productive efforts to his own advantage: he colonizes the colonist.'[10] Mathew Martin suggests that 'Lovewit's return seems to set a period to the time of play, illusion, and transformative possibilities and to re-establish everyday society and everyday, public organs of knowledge', though he immediately adds 'Yet illusion is not so easily contained.'[11] James Mardock argues:

> we can look beyond the specific character of Face to a more general assertion of theatrical power ... Face, after all, has submitted as much as Lovewit has; the impromptu arrangement he strikes with Lovewit constitutes another theatrical 'venture,' with Lovewit this time controlling the place of the house and Face/Jeremy in charge of the theatrical spatial practices therein.[12]

While the above dialogue suggests Lovewit's demand to Face to conceal nothing, it may also mean that as an 'indulgent' master, he will conceal 'nothing'. As I argued earlier, Jonson's comedies rely on the tension between 'nothing' and 'everything'. Therefore, not only does the phrase 'conceal nothing' mean 'not hiding anything', it might mean the opposite, as it suggests that he is willing to help Face to conceal his act/art of 'nothingness'. In other words, the master intends to accept theatricality as part of life and as a state of existence. In fact, he uses the word 'indulgent' again in the final part:

LOVEWIT   That master
That had received such happiness by a servant,
In such a widow and with so much wealth,
Were very ungrateful if he would not be
A little indulgent to that servant's wit,
And help his fortune, though with some small strain
Of his own candour.

(V.v.146–52)

Even though we can see how Mosca thrives in his para-site, he is still 'disrobed' in the end (V.xii.103). And although the parasite, as the servant, attempts to reverse the master–servant relationship, the order is nonetheless restored. Different from Volpone, Lovewit, as his name implies, is willing to follow the servant, as it would be ungrateful for the master not to do so since the servant has given him joy, woman and wealth. Referring his words to my reading of *Volpone*, it would mean that while it is true to say that the 'para-site' is just an illusion and reverses the subject–object relationship, it is still a site/sight of joy, happiness and, in Jonson's term, an indulgence. It would be too puritanical to condemn this 'para-site', as, perhaps, Jonson has recognised that it is all a city subject could have.

Indeed, Jonson seems to be more playful on the concept of nothingness in *The Alchemist*:

TRIBULATION   Ay, but stay,
    This act of coining, is it lawful?
ANANIAS   Lawful?
    We know no magistrate. Or, if we did,
    This's foreign coin.
SUBTLE   It's no coining, sir.
    It's but casting.

                                          (III.ii.148–52)

The word 'casting' can be read as a theatrical term, as the play's Argument
suggests 'Each for a share, and all begin to act' ('The Argument', line 8).
Therefore, upon this nothingness is a stage which allows the actors to
perform, or, in Volpone's word, to transform. Subtle's language shows
a comic attitude to his business. Indeed, Jonson plays with the tension
between 'nothing' and 'everything' in a more relaxed style in the scene
between Subtle, Face and Dapper:

FACE   She need not doubt him, sir. Alas, he has nothing
       But what he will part withal as willingly
       Upon her Grace's word – [*To Dapper*] Throw away your purse –
       As she would ask it – [*To Dapper*] Handkerchiefs and all –
       She cannot bid that thing but he'll obey.

                                          (III.v.19–23)

The word 'nothing' is constantly used in the scene. The meaning of the
above lines is ambiguous. When Face says, 'he [Dapper] has nothing
/ but what he will part withal as willingly', he may not simply mean
that Dapper has nothing except the possessions that the latter is going
to surrender. He may also be implying that Dapper never has anything, since the possessions (including the reference to his purse and
its sexual implication) are something that he can part with, which
means that he has never really owned them. In other words, Dapper is
already 'castrated' since his existence is defined by his possessions and
he literally has no-thing. Face continues the joke as he says to Dapper,
'Keep nothing that is transitory about you' (III.v.30), which, apart from
its surface meaning, could suggest that Dapper should keep being a
'eunuch'. In the end, there is the following conversation between them:

DAPPER   By this good light, I ha' nothing.
SUBTLE   *Ti ti, ti ti to ta*! He does equivocate, she says –
       Ti, to do ti, ti ti do, ti da! – and swears by the light when he is
       blinded.
DAPPER   By this good dark, I ha' nothing but a half crown
       Of gold about my wrist that my love gave me,
       And a leaden heart I wore sin' she forsook me.
FACE   I thought 'twas something.

                                          (III.v.40–6)

The reference to light reminds us of the image of gold, which is why Dapper is blinded by *its* light. The gold is in contrast to the notion of nothingness, darkness and a leaden heart. To possess gold is the same as owning nothing. However, the suggestion of equivocation shows how Jonson is aware of the doubleness within: a capitalist subject sees darkness as light and is literally a no-thing. At the same time, Face turns the supposedly moral attitude upside down. When Dapper says that he finds a half crown of gold, Face says it is indeed something. After all, in a capitalist city, the gold represents all the possessions that a person can have. These words, suitably, are spoken by Face, as if a person's sense of self and identity can only be found through his mask.

Moreover, this thinking may not simply be read as a compromise to ideology and illusion on the dramatist's part because it can be interpreted as surrender to the public and the people. Face says:

> My part a little fell in this last scene,
> Yet 'twas decorum. And though I am clean
> Got off from Subtle, Surly, Mammon, Doll,
> Hot Ananias, Dapper, Drugger, all
> With whom I traded, yet I put myself
> On you, that are my country, and this pelf,
> Which I have got, if you do quit me, rests
> To feast you often, and invite new guests.
>
> (V.v.158–65)

The final words are spoken by Face, whose name signifies an equivalent of mirror. It is a confirmation of the significance of the theatre, of illusion and, even, of fakeness. Face says that the audience members are his country, which means that while the master is following the will of the servant, he is following those of the audience. Therefore, *The Alchemist*, as a comedy, allows itself to drift along the logic of the text, of the theatre and, ultimately, of the audience. It would be as if, in *Duck Soup*, Chicolini has never come in, the mirror interaction continues within the scene, and somehow Pinky has taken over the role of Firefly and finished the film. In 1610, Jonson had 'surrendered' himself to the public and liberated the carnivalesque side within him. Face uses his loot to feast the audience, making them accomplices. However, the origin of the 'crime', if there is one, is not clear anyway, as, according to Face, he is just following the desire of the audience, a heterogeneous crowd that can never be clearly defined and identified.

The last lines of *The Alchemist* invoke another Jonson poem, 'Inviting a Friend to Supper':

> Tonight, grave sir, both my poor house and I
>   Do equally desire your company;

Not that we think us worthy such a guest,
  But that your worth will dignify our feast

                                      (*Epigrams* 101, lines 1–4)

From this example, we see how the poetic language of Jonson is used in his drama, as if Face, representing Jonson the dramatist, has taken over the role of Jonson the poet, and the public has become his patron.[13] In *The Alchemist*, there are times when the characters invoke certain phrases and imageries which reminds us of Jonson's poems as if it can be seen as a comment on, or even a parody of, the seriousness and the dignity of the latter. For instance, when Kastril and Dame Pliant see Subtle as Master Doctor and Face as the Captain, they say:

PLIANT   Brother,
     He's a rare man, believe me!
KASTRIL   Hold your peace.
     [Enter FACE as *Captain*.]
     Here comes the t'other rare man. – Save you, Captain.

                                          (IV.ii.49–51)

The word 'rare' is important to Jonson (a point that, perhaps, can be summed up by his epitaph 'O Rare Ben Jonson'). Its usage reminds us of one of Jonson's most famous poems, 'To Lucy, Countess of Bedford, with Master Donne's Satires':

Lucy, you brightness of our sphere, who are
  Life of the muses' day, their morning-star!
If works (not th'authors) their own grace should look,
  Whose poems would not wish to be your book?
But these, desired by you, the maker's ends
  Crown with their own. Rare poems ask rare friends.

                                  (*Epigrams* 94, lines 1–6)

Jonson uses this famous line to praise Donne and his patron Lucy, Countess of Bedford. However, when the word is uttered by Dame Pliant and Kastril about Face and Subtle, it becomes a joke, allowing us to see the differences between Jonson's poems and plays, and to appreciate the twists and turns between them. This example shows how the seemingly similar language develops its own life and logic onstage. When the word 'rare' is used of Face and Subtle, it can be read as a joke on both of them, and on Pliant and Kastril. However, it can also be read as a reference to the dramatist himself, as a parody of his own work and a mocking of its usage. Its usage puts the meaning of the signifier into question, detaching the signifier from the signified. Going back to the last words of Face, when Face says to the audience that he would 'feast you often, and invite new guests', the tone is egalitarian as if he is humbling himself in front of the public. The 'country' of the audience is the one that acknowledges no boundary.

'For we have neither male nor female amongst us': The Puppet Dionysus in *Bartholomew Fair*

After discussing *The Alchemist*, I shall move on to *Bartholomew Fair*. Having more than thirty speaking parts with several plots between them, *Bartholomew Fair* is a play that is famous for its carnivalesque quality. As Anne Barton writes:

> Structurally, *Bartholomew Fair* sustains the most delicate balance between order and chaos, between form and a seemingly undisciplined flow which sets out to imitate the random, haphazard nature of life itself, while maintaining an artistic control so tight that no episode, no character, however minor, can be removed without causing irreparable damage to the whole.[14]

The play was only performed twice in Jonson's lifetime (the first time at Hope Theatre in Southwark on 31 October 1614; the second one at Whitehall on the very next day before King James), for which reason Ian Donaldson describes it as an occasional play. Donaldson writes: 'In several senses of the term, *Bartholomew Fair* is an occasional play: it is designed for performance upon two particular holiday occasions, and it takes for its theme the events of another particular holiday occasion, St. Bartholomew's Day.'[15]

However, Jonson's critics have different opinions about the subject of carnival. For example, Michael McCanles argues for the difference between Jonson and Bakhtin, saying that in Jonson there is a distinction between a true festivity and a false one. He writes: 'Unlike the description of Renaissance festive given by Mikhail Bakhtin, for Jonson, to equate festival with the reduction of all human motivations to bodily appetite is to pervert it.'[16] Discussing city comedy, Susan Wells argues:

> while Bakhtin's Rabelais can present the marketplace as the place where the rights of the 'lower bodily stratum' are legitimated, and where the popular subversive tradition of laughter, parody, skepticism, and utopian hope could be preserved, so straightforward a relationship to the marketplace was impossible for Marston, Middleton, and Jonson. Their marketplace, their city, and their space of celebration, were different.[17]

Similarly, Mathew Martin suggests:

> the play is ultimately not a festive comedy ending with the renewal and reassertion of community. Rather, *Bartholomew Fair*, like the fairs of Jonson's

day, is a space in which boundaries of community are asserted only to be distorted, reversed, and disintegrated in a process of exchange that creates the laughter not of the pedagogue but of the con artist. The play is a fooling, both for people's laughter and their fooling.[18]

As I argue in this book, Jonson's bastards propel us to read the seemingly conflicting forces in the city; and in *Bartholomew Fair*, we have another figure which embodies the representations of Volpone's bastards, namely, the puppet Dionysus. In other words, the representation of the puppet embodies the presence of the dwarf, the androgyne and the eunuch in *Bartholomew Fair* because it highlights the interrelation between castration and carnival. In the following, I shall draw readers' attention to the puppet scene in Act V and argue for the importance of castration and carnival within the play. After the encounters between the characters in previous acts, they gather in the final act for the purpose of watching Littlewit's puppet show. To Leo Salingar, this puppet play is no more than a sideshow in *Bartholomew Fair*.[19] However, referring to the interlude in *Volpone* Act I Scene ii, Harry Levin, in his article 'Jonson's Metempsychosis', writes that 'Possibly Mosca's interlude was written before the rest of the play, like the puppet-show in *Bartholomew Fair*.'[20] Therefore, I want to follow Levin's suggestion and to see how this small scene is instrumental for us to understand the play.[21]

Indeed, the image of the puppet reminds us of the figure of the androgyne in *Volpone*. When Nano asks if the hermaphrodite enjoys 'the delight of each sex thou canst vary' (I.ii.54), the latter answers that the pleasure is 'stale and forsaken', and what s/he enjoys most is being the Fool. As I will demonstrate, similar to the Fool in *Volpone*, the notion of gender ambiguity in the puppet Dionysus in *Bartholomew Fair* is also being deflected, and what takes place instead is perhaps something more radical, namely, it exhibits the power of nothingness and castration that lies within performance. With a close rereading of the text, I am going to demonstrate how the puppet suggests the theme of castration, and how, with such an emphasis, the puppet scene can ironically be interpreted as the climax of *Bartholomew Fair*. In other words, the puppet Dionysus exposes the impotence of the seemingly omnipotent, dispossessing the possessed, and the play turns madness into folly by asking Overdo to invite everybody to supper. Moreover, by doing so, it suggests that the seemingly impotent are indeed the real omnipotent, much like the power of epicene that was discussed in Chapter 4. All these points demonstrate that we need to treat the importance of castration, with its implications of nothingness, as the 'centre' of the play and the driving force of the comedy of *Bartholomew Fair*, and other Jonsonian comedies.

Before I continue with my discussion, I want to highlight, perhaps once again, the relationship between the puppet show and *Bartholomew Fair* as a city comedy. This scene is a theatre within theatre. While it is a performance about Hero and Leander, Littlewit, who helps Leatherhead in the scene, says clearly that it has more to do with the city than with any type of romance:

> JOHN   I have only made it a little easy and modern for the times, sir,
> that's all: as, for the Hellespont I imagine our Thames here; and then
> Leander, I make a dyer's son about Puddle Wharf and Hero a wench
> o' the Bankside, who, going over one morning to Old Fish Street,
> Leander spies her land at Trig Stairs, and falls in love with her. Now do
> I introduce Cupid, having metamorphosed himself into a drawer, and
> he strikes Hero in love, with a pint of sherry – and other pretty passages
> there are o' the friendship that will delight you, sir, and please you of
> judgment.
>
> (V.iii.92–9)

The puppet show is intricately linked with theatre and city comedy, meaning that the characters in *Bartholomew Fair*, which is a city comedy about London, gather in Act V to watch a performance about themselves.

With this in mind, we can start to examine the 'body' of the puppet. As the characters are watching the puppet show, Zeal-of-the-land Busy suddenly barges in, claiming that the show itself is a profanation:

> BUSY   Yes, and my main argument against you is that you are an
> abomination: for the male among you putteth on the apparel of the
> female, and the female of the male.
> PUPPET DIONYSIUS   *You lie, you lie, you lie abominably.*
> COKES   Good, by my troth, he has given him the lie thrice.
> PUPPET DIONYSIUS   *It is your old stale argument against the players,*
> *but it will not hold against the puppets; for we have neither male*
> *nor female amongst us. And that thou mayst see if thou wilt, like a*
> *malicious purblind zeal as thou art!*
> *The puppet takes up his garment.*
> EDGWORTH   By the faith, there he has answered you, friend – by plain
> demonstration.
>
> (V.v.77–86)

The fact that Jonson uses Edgworth to utter the above lines should not be seen as only a coincidence, for the character is a cutpurse.[22] The suggestion of a 'plain' demonstration is a pun, because in face of the challenge posed by Busy, the puppet Dionysius shows that it has neither male nor female within, representing a thing that has no gender categorisation. Compared with *Epicoene*, which ends with Dauphine showing that Epicene is actually a male within a female body (and which, for this reason, was questioned by some critics), Jonson takes another approach five years later in *Bartholomew Fair*.[23] The plain demonstration can be interpreted from a Freudian perspective: Freud argues that a boy's fear is raised when he realises that the woman does not have a penis:

> The observation which finally breaks down his unbelief is the sight of the female genitals. Sooner or later the child, who is so proud of his possession of a penis, has a view of the genital region of a little girl, and cannot help being convinced of the absence of a penis in a creature who is so like himself. With this, the loss of his own penis becomes imaginable, and the threat of castration takes its deferred effect.[24]

While the puppet Dionysius has no gender underneath its garment, *it* reminds us of what Freud would think of the genital region of a little girl. In other words, they are both a site of nothingness, a sight that alarms the male with the thought that the penis, and, therefore, the supposed power that comes with it, does not necessarily exist. Freud argues that the boy is still 'castrated' even though he can preserve his penis, as he has paralysed it by removing its function because of his castration fear.[25] However, the threat works in another way for Jonson, as the puritan Busy is converted after he sees this 'plain demonstration'. Therefore, the conversion of Busy might not be so difficult to believe, because by demonstrating its 'plainness', what the puppet does is to make Busy 'tongue-tied'. If the gold is the centre of *Volpone*, the philosopher's stone is in *The Alchemist*, and the troupe of epicenes is in *Epicoene*, then in *Bartholomew Fair*, what we have is the puppet Dionysus, another figure that combines the presence of hermaphrodite and fool.

Using the puppet to rethink the play, we can perhaps highlight the idea of emptiness and nothingness in *Bartholomew Fair*. From the previous acts, we can see different examples demonstrating the idea of a lack. As established earlier, we need to understand *Bartholomew Fair* and its genre as a city comedy. The fair relates to the idea of buying and selling, and Jonson seems to connect buying with a lack, time and again:

> LEATHERHEAD What do you lack, gentlemen, what is't you lack? A fine horse? A lion? A bull? A bear? A dog, or a cat? An excellent fine Barthol'mew-bird? Or an instrument? What is't you lack? (II.v.3–5)
> ...
> What do you lack? What do you buy, pretty mistress? A fine hobby-horse, to make your son a tilter? A drum, to make him a soldier? A fiddle, to make him a reveller? What is't you lack? Little dogs for your daughters? Or babies, male or female? (III.ii.28–31)
> ...
> What do you lack, gentlemen? Fine purses, pouches, pin-cases, pipes?

What is't you lack? A pair o' smiths to wake you i' the morning? Or a
fine whistling bird? (III.iv.14–16)

From Leatherhead's words, one might think that there is always a sense
of lack within a buyer. A man does not become a gentleman 'naturally',
he needs a horse, a lion, a bull, or a bear. These little objects, which
extend to dogs, cats, birds, hobby-horses, drums, and so on, become a
list of supplements, questioning the belief in any original and complete
subjectivity.

This sense of lack does not only relate to the act of buying and
selling, it has to do with the power that comes with it. More than
once, the play exhibits and yet questions the nature of language and
its power. For example, there is a suggestion that Bartholomew Cokes
thinks that the fair belongs to him because they share the same name.
When we see Littlewit in the First Act, he is already amusing himself
with the pun of Bartholomew:

Here's Master Barthol'mew Cokes, of Harrow o' th' Hill, i' th' County
of Middlesex, Esquire, takes forth his licence to marry Mistress Grace
Wellborn of the said place and county. And when does he take it forth?
Today! The four and twentieth of August! Barthol'mew Day! Barthol'mew
upon Barthol'mew! That's the device! (I.i.2–6)

When we see Cokes later in the same act, he claims that the fair belongs
to him because of his name:

Nay, never fidge up and down, Numps, and vex itself. I am resolute
Barthol'mew in this; I'll make no suit on't to you. 'Twas all the end of my
journey, indeed, to show Mistress Grace my fair: I call't my fair, because of
Barthol'mew: you know my name is Barthol'mew, and Barthol'mew Fair.
(I.v.50–3)

Cokes is a fool because he enjoys such a bad pun. And as if he is afraid
that the point is not obvious enough, he repeats it four times in the
whole dialogue. The dialogue itself shows an obsession with the word
and its meaning. The fact that Cokes thinks that the fair belongs to
him suggests his blind belief in the symbolic, and he thinks that he can
fit right in, or even claim possession of the fair because they share the
same signifier. However, at the same time, the dialogue shows that
the signifier has its power of deferral: as the word 'Bartholomew' is
uttered four times, its meaning keeps changing with each utterance,
making the meaning of the word slip farther and farther away from
Cokes's intended meaning. The word 'resolute' gives us a clue here,
as it suggests Cokes's belief that the name Bartholomew gives him
certain power. However, as he keeps insisting and repeating his name,
we start to see him as a fool instead. In fact, if we link the two scenes

in Act I and Act IV together, we may have an interesting reading of *Bartholomew Fair* and its comedy: the signifier and signified are never a perfect match, they rob you blind instead of giving you any concrete significant meaning. While Cokes at first thinks that he and the fair are a perfect match, he says in Act IV that there is nothing but thieving and cozening in it:

> Would I might lose my doublet and hose, too, as I am an honest man, and never stir, if I think there be anything but thieving and cozening i' this whole Fair. Barthol'mew Fair, quoth he: an ever any Barthol'mew had that luck in't that I have had, I'll be martyred for him, and in Smithfield, too. I ha' paid for my pears, a rot on 'em, I'll keep 'em no longer.
> ...
> Friend, do you know who I am? Or where I lie? I do not myself, I'll be sworn. Do but carry me home, and I'll please thee: I ha' money enough there. I ha' lost myself, and my cloak and my hat; and my fine sword, and my sister, and Numps, and Mistress Grace (a gentlewoman that I should ha' married) and a cut-work handkerchief she ga' me, and two purses today. And my bargain o' hobby-horses and gingerbread, which grieves me worst of all. (IV.ii.55–69)

We can further interpret Cokes's predicament if we think of Lacan and his idea of symbolic castration. Explaining the concept, Slavoj Žižek writes:

> This gap between my direct psychological identity and my symbolic identity (the symbolic mask or title I wear, defining what I am for and in the big Other) is what Lacan (for complex reasons that we can here ignore) calls 'symbolic castration', with the phallus as its signifier.[26]

He adds that the Lacanian concept means:

> the castration that occurs by the very fact of me being caught in the symbolic order, assuming a symbolic mask or title. Castration is the gap between what I immediately am and the symbolic title that confers on me a certain status and authority.[27]

Instead of feeling at home in the fair, Cokes is completely lost in Act IV. The feeling of not knowing yourself is what happens to a person when he blindly believes in the symbolic and its power. Deceiving by the name and the appearance of power makes a person lose something bit by bit, and it is seen in Jonson with the image of cloak and hat, his fine sword (with its signification as phallic power), his relations, his servants, and even Mistress Grace (with the implication of turning himself into a cuckold). Through the example of Bartholomew Cokes, Jonson seems to tell us that a comic figure is a castrated figure who blindly believes in the connection between the signifier and the signified, not knowing that there is always a gap between them. More importantly, it also seems that the more someone insists on the importance of words and their powers, the more he is losing ground, because the signifier has its own logic, causing people to drift away from any kind of fixed subject position.

However, just as the puppet Dionysus is not only about nothingness and castration, this recognition of 'nothingness' does not only entail a negative meaning. Similar to the representations of Volpone's bastards, the puppet highlights the importance of folly and transformation. In *Bartholomew Fair*, another example which suggests the relationship between the word and its emptiness can be seen in the game of vapour.[28] According to the play, the game is 'nonsense', as it requires 'every man to oppose the last man that spoke, whether it concerned him or no' (IV. iv.24–8). Seeing this ludicrous situation, Quarlous says to Edgworth, 'Call you this vapours? This is such belching of quarrel as I never heard' (IV.iv.62–3). Indeed, what we see is a series of seemingly nonsensical conversations, as each character just keeps contradicting the previous speaker. However, given the previous discussion of language and the gap within it, perhaps we can reconsider its significance:

> KNOCKEM   Fight for him, Whit? A gross vapour, he can fight for himself.
> WASP   It may be I can, but it may be I wu' not. How then?
> CUTTING   Why, then you may choose.
> WASP   Why, and I'll choose whether I'll choose or no.
> KNOCKEM   I think you may, and 'tis true; and I allow it for a resolute vapour.
> WASP   Nay, then, I do think you do not think, and it is no resolute vapour.
> CUTTING   Yes, in some sort he may allow you.
> KNOCKEM   In no sort, sir, pardon me, I can allow him nothing. You mistake the vapour.
> WASP   He mistakes nothing, sir, in no sort.
> WHIT   Yes, I pre dee now, let him mistake.
> WASP   A turd i' your teeth, never 'pre dee' me, for I will have nothing mistaken.
> KNOCKEM   Turd, ha, turd? a noisome vapour – strike, Whit.
>
> (IV.iv.76–88)

The game of vapour highlights the importance of nothingness in *Bartholomew Fair*. It addresses the presence of 'no', 'nothing', with its gaps and contradictions within our daily use of language. The 'no' can be seen as referring to the Name-of-the-Father, as a fact that we are already under the patriarchal order when we use language, and, therefore, barred by it as we are within it. Lacan writes: 'It is in the *name of the father* that we must recognize the basis of the symbolic function which, since the dawn of historical time, has identified his person with the figure of the law.'[29] However, the comic use of 'no' in the game of vapour can also be read as a rejection of it, and comedy challenges it by highlighting it, drawing the readers' attention to it. The game addresses and acknowledges the gap within our existence. When Knockem says, 'I can allow him nothing', it does not necessarily only mean 'I cannot allow him anything'. Instead, it means that 'nothing' is the only thing he (or any patriarchal subject) could be allowed to get in life, and it is this game of vapour that one 'mis-takes', or 'must take'. Not only is a subject taking 'nothing', this 'nothing' is something that one 'must take' by 'mistake'. The 'mis-take' highlights the sense of missing, and slippage, in our use of language; just as the more Bartholomew Cokes says his name, the more he is farther from his intended meaning, but the closer he is to its hidden 'truth'. Discussing *Bartholomew Fair*, Heather C. Easterling suggests that 'language is a game people play with themselves and each other, and nothing more'.[30] She argues that the game of vapour shows that 'language's object here is that it has no object beyond the game; exigencies of productive communication or significance are beside the point'.[31] While I agree with the importance of playing and gaming, I believe that they, at the same time, are productive and significant. In other words, they are productive, and even constructive and constitutive, exactly because they are a game. When Wasp says that 'he mistakes nothing, sir, in no sort', he has hit on the 'truth' by accident, because he has confirmed the previous statement unknowingly. Therefore, what follows is the fight for nothingness, as Whit says, 'let him mis-take', to which Wasp responds, 'for I will have nothing mis-taken'. The comic truth, in sum, is the truth of mis-take, which is why, as the famous line goes, 'no-body is perfect'.[32]

With these reflections in mind, I will now go back to the last act of the play. The attention to language and its gap goes deeper than these examples. From the first speech of Littlewit, we learn that Cokes wants to take the licence in order to marry Grace Wellborn. Therefore, we see from the play the obsession of the licence and the box that carries it. Referring to the licence, Wasp says that 'there's nothing in't but hard words' (I.v.29), which combines the images of the phallic and the impotent. As a typical comic device (and even as a MacGuffin of sorts), the box is used to produce the effect of hiding and concealing. When Quarlous asks Edgworth to steal the box from Wasp, the cutpurse responds:

> Would you ha' the box and all, sir? Or only that, that is in't? I'll get you that, and leave him the box to play with still – which will be the harder o' the two – because I would gain your worships' good opinion of me. (III.v.213–15)

Edgworth's words pave the way to what will happen at the end of the play. Just as one might expect in a comedy, the licence was stolen by none other than the cutpurse. In fact, Edgworth used the word 'gelding' when he talks about his trade:

> Not yet, sir: except you would go with me and see't, it's not worth speaking on. The act is nothing without a witness. Yonder he is, your man with the box fall'n into the finest company, and so transported with vapours: they ha' got in a northern clothier and one Puppy, a western man that's come to wrestle before my Lord Mayor anon, and Captain Whit, and one Val Cutting that helps Captain Jordan to roar, a circling boy – with whom your Numps is so taken that you may strip him of his clothes, if you will. I'll undertake to geld him for you, if you had but a surgeon ready to sear him. (IV.iii.89–96)

After the puppet scene, the play goes back to the encounter between Quarlous, Littlewit, Cokes and Overdo. When Quarlous thanks Wasp for the licence to take Grace Wellborn as his ward, Wasp is totally surprised as he does not know the licence has been stolen all along. Wasp has been carrying the empty box without knowing it. The empty box signifies that the power has been long gone, only that man still holds it tight as if he is not aware of its meaninglessness. When the empty box is opened, Quarlous says to Overdo:

> Nay, sir, stand not you fixed here like a stake in Finsbury to be shot at, or the whipping-post i' the Fair, but get your wife out o' the air – it will make her worse else. And remember you are but Adam, flesh and blood! – you have your frailty. Forget your other name of Overdo, and invite us all to supper. There you and I will compare our 'discoveries', and drown the memory of all enormity in your bigg'st bowl at home. (V.vi.78–83)

I want to draw attention to the reaction of Overdo after the empty box is opened. The suggestion of him standing transfixed makes him sound like a figure that is haunted by the image of Medusa. Freud writes:

> To decapitate = to castrate. The terror of Medusa is thus a terror of castration that is linked to the sight of something. Numerous analyses have made us familiar with the occasion for this: it occurs when a boy, who has hitherto been unwilling to believe the threat of castration, catches sight of the female genitals, probably those of an adult, surrounded by hair, and essentially those of his mother.[33]

Moreover, Numps's reaction is equally interesting, as he says, 'I will never speak while I live again, for aught I know' (V.vi.86). He is another figure who is turned tongue-tied. The opening of the empty box should be read in parallel with the previous scene, in which the puppet Dionysus raises the garment and shows that there is nothing, neither male nor female, underneath. While the penultimate scene shows how the Puritan was converted after he sees the sight of nothingness, Quarlous, in the last scene, asks Overdo to forget his other name and invite everybody to supper. Both scenes use the unveiling to suggest the power of castration, which converts the power and makes them speechless. Quarlous asks Overdo to 'drown the memory of all enormity in your bigg'st bowl at home' (V.vi.82–3). The forgetting of his name frees Overdo, liberating him, which, perhaps, reminds us of another famous line in *Duck Soup*: 'Forget? You ask me to forget? A firefly never forgets.'[34] Firefly reduces himself to an object when he says that. Comedy exposes that 'firefly' can be a name and an object simultaneously. The forgetting of the symbolic and its power marks the ending of comedy; while the refusal to forget allows it to continue.

Notes

1. Levin, 'Jonson's Metempsychosis', p. 94.
2. See Jonson, *Cambridge Edition*, vol. 3, p. 659.
3. See Jonson, *Cambridge Edition*, vol. 4, p. 431.
4. Barton, *Ben Jonson, Dramatist*, p. 137. On alchemy, Katherine Eggert comments that '*The Alchemist*'s ambivalent treatment of alchemy and of other branches of the natural sciences establishes Jonson not simply as an advance man for the Scientific Revolution but rather as a writer profoundly engaged with scientific practice as it existed in his time, which was a long period of both transition and overlap between old and new.' See Eggert, '*The Alchemist* and Science', p. 201.
5. In a similar note, Richard Dutton writes that 'Jonson clearly exploits this "silly indulgence" in both *Volpone* and *The Alchemist*, but more fully in the latter play; the familiarity of the characters and their setting, compounded by the frank insight we are allowed "behind the scenes" is more conducive to our support than that decadent foreign splendour of Venice and its animal-type grandees.' See Dutton, *To the First Folio*, p. 117.
6. Haynes, 'Representing the Underworld', p. 36. Also, Bruce Boehrer suggests that 'Jonson may insist that the translation of base matter to precious metal is a hoax – what we would now call bullshit – but his comedy takes real delight in the opposite gesture: that of reducing gold to excrement.' See Boehrer, 'New Directions', p. 156.
7. On the relationship between Face and Subtle, Joyce Van Dyke comments that 'the play offers us no evidence that Face requires or receives coaching in acting from Subtle. In fact, the reverse is true.' See Van Dyke, 'Game of Wits in *The Alchemist*', p. 254. Commenting on this scene, Lynn S. Meskill suggests that 'the play begins with an argument as to whether the "shares" of each partner are equivalent to their work. The quarrel, it becomes clear, has been instigated by Face and continues throughout the play. However, these arguments between the conspirators, Subtle and Face, concerning shares are often couched in terms of who may claim paternity for their

alchemical swindling . . . From the outset, paternity and legitimacy are the freight of the play.' See Meskill, 'Jonson and the Alchemical Economy of Desire', p. 52.

8. McAdam and Sanders, 'New Directions', p. 147.
9. On the function of facial hair as prosthetic signifier, Mark Albert Johnston suggests that 'The smooth chin or face – no less artificial or culturally constructed than its hairy counterpart was – crucially signalled both the economic and gender status of its host.' See Johnston, 'Prosthetic Absence', p. 404. On Face's beard, Lois Potter writes that 'Face is not being shaved; he is merely taking off a false beard.' Comparing Face with Feste in *Twelfth Night*, she comments that the Clown [Feste] is 'separated from other characters not only by dress but also by the smooth face of someone who is not yet a man and will never be one. Face's beardlessness makes the point that a butler has no more autonomous existence than a woman.' See Potter, '"How quick was a quick change?"', pp. 203, 209.
10. Ross, 'Plague of *The Alchemist*', pp. 157–8.
11. Martin, *Between Theater and Philosophy*, p. 109.
12. Mardock, *Our Scene Is London*, p. 92.
13. Colin Burrow, in Jonson, *Cambridge Edition*, annotates that the 'grave sir' in the poem is unidentifiable. He writes: 'H&S suggest Camden, van den Berg suggests it is every reader, C. J. Summers argues for William Herbert, Earl of Pembroke; but "grave" suggests learning rather than rank. Cummings suggests that Camden or Sir Henry Savile are likely candidates, and would suit the concerns of the poem with reading history.' See Jonson, *Cambridge Edition*, vol. 5, p. 166.
14. Barton, *Ben Jonson, Dramatist*, p. 197.
15. Donaldson, *World Upside Down*, pp. 48–9.
16. McCanles, 'Festival in Jonsonian Comedy', p. 209.
17. Wells, 'Jacobean City Comedy and the Ideology of the City', pp. 38–9.
18. Martin, *Between Theater and Philosophy*, pp. 133–4.
19. Salingar, 'Crowd and Public in *Bartholomew Fair*', p. 142.
20. Levin, 'Jonson's Metempsychosis', p. 94.
21. Recent critics have also commented on the scene. For instance, Mark Thornton Burnett writes that the puppet show 'registers as an inherently "monstrous" type of entertainment: occupying the same site as Ursula's establishment, it even carries over, and rematerializes, her booth's "monstrous" subtexts'. See Burnett, *Constructing 'Monsters'*, p. 171. James D. Mardock argues that 'Littlewit and his puppet play are an inverted and failed version of the authorial relationship to the playhouse and the audience that Jonson posits in *Bartholomew Fair*. The clumsy and perfunctory Londonization of *Hero and Leander* in the puppet play serves to highlight Jonson's own tightly structured and successfully mimetic representation of urban space in the playhouse.' See Mardock, *Our Scene Is London*, p. 108.
22. In his discussion of carnival, Rocco Coronato suggests that 'In the world of carnival, judging is seeing. *Bartholomew Fair* enfolds different perspectives of the characters, putting the thief on the top of the hierarchy of gazers: the carnivalesque inversion of justice provides a way of seeing the grotesque.' See Coronato, *Jonson versus Bakhtin*, p. 114.
23. Adam Zucker writes that 'Dionysus' wooden strip-show might thus be

understood as a tiny burlesque of the ending of *Epicoene* . . . In both plays, social mastery is bestowed upon the character best able to manipulate those conventions of costume to craft a theatrical self in motion. Epicoene is Dauphine's puppet.' See Zucker, *Places of Wit*, p. 97.

24. Freud, 'Dissolution of the Oedipus Complex', pp. 175–6.
25. Freud, 'Dissolution of the Oedipus Complex', p. 177.
26. Žižek, *How to Read Lacan*, p. 34.
27. Žižek, *How to Read Lacan*, p. 34.
28. Linking vapour with humour, Gail Kern Paster writes that 'It is the congregation of vapors – of physical steam, of quarrelling language, of human moodiness – that reveals the production of emotion at the fair as a physical and social transaction between individuals rather than an experience within the body of the individual subject.' See Paster, '*Bartholomew Fair* and the Humoral Body', p. 267.
29. Lacan, 'Function and Field of Speech and Language', p. 230.
30. Easterling, *Parsing the City*, p. 111.
31. Easterling, *Parsing the City*, p. 121.
32. *Some Like It Hot*, directed by Billy Wilder.
33. Freud, 'Medusa's Head', p. 273.
34. *Duck Soup*, directed by Leo McCarey.

Chapter 7

Conclusion:
'Fools, they are the only nation':
Rereading the Interlude and Beyond

How, then, can these variations on Volpone's bastards enrich our understanding of the interlude in Act I scene ii? How can we see the interlude as the centre of the play? In this concluding chapter, I shall answer these questions through a rereading of the interlude. While the concept of metempsychosis relates to the debasement of souls, I will illustrate how it can be seen as a comedic metaphor, suggesting that the interlude develops from the importance of theatricality and emphasises its relationship to sex, language, coining and the diffusion of fixed identity. This diffusion suggests a logic of slippage, which is not unlike the power of epicene that we see in Chapter 4. The thinking of metempsychosis as demonstrated in *Volpone* is carnivalesque and full of deferral. The interlude and the transmigration described in it suggest how Jonson's comedy dissolves organic unity. Using Susan Sontag's concept of 'Camp', this chapter argues that Jonson's comedies represent a celebration of an epicene style. Moreover, this chapter uses the reading of Volpone's bastards to rethink some theories of comedy and modern film comedies. Finally, it suggests how some of the representations of the bastards can be seen in other early modern city comedies, such as those of Thomas Middleton. In sum, this chapter attempts to think about bastardy as a multivalent trope to discuss the city, capitalism, and comedy and jokes themselves as improper, bastard forms of utterance. Indeed, madness and folly are inseparable. There is only a very fine line between the two concepts.

A Rereading of the Interlude

NANO   Now room for fresh gamesters, who do will you to know
        They do bring you neither play nor university show;
        And therefore do entreat you that whatsoever they rehearse

May not fare a whit the worse for the false pace of the verse.
If you wonder at this, you will wonder more ere we pass,
    For know [*Pointing to Androgyno*], here is enclosed the soul of
        Pythagoras,
That juggler divine, as hereafter shall follow;
    Which soul (fast and loose, sir) came first from Apollo,
And was breathed into Aethalides, Mercurius his son,
    Where it had the gift to remember all that ever was done.
From thence it fled forth, and made quick transmigration
    To goldilocked Euphorbus, who was killed in good fashion
At the siege of old Troy by the Cuckold of Sparta.
    Hermotimus was next (I find it in my charta)
To whom it did pass, where no sooner it was missing
    But with one Pyrrhus of Delos it learned to go a-fishing;
And thence did it enter the sophist of Greece.
    From Pythagore, she went into a beautiful piece
Hight Aspasia, the *meretrix*; and the next toss of her
    Was again of a whore: she became a philosopher,
Crates the cynic (as itself doth relate it).
    Since, kings, knights, and beggars, knaves, lords, and fools gat it,
Besides ox and ass, camel, mule, goat, and brock,
    In all which it hath spoke, as in the cobbler's cock.

                                  (I.ii.1–24)

From the very beginning, the interlude establishes the relationship between theatre, sex and comedy. The first line of the interlude, 'Now room for fresh gamesters, who do will you to know', was the traditional cry of mummers when they began entertaining in a large household. Nano calls himself and his fellow bastards 'the fresh gamester'. In addition to meaning a player at games, the word 'gamester' also means an actor; a gambler; a merry, frolicsome person; and a promiscuous person (*OED*). Nano defines them as characters who relate to theatre and performance, who play the game of chance, and who are merry and sexually active. Indeed, it is important to see how the interlude upsets our 'usual' expectations. For example, while 'the false pace of the verse' relates to the styles that normally are used in morality plays, we do not necessarily need to see Nano's play as an 'immoral' production. Instead, the false pace of the verse can be read as a parody of morality plays. The use of such style in the interlude allows us to see the interlude as a reversal of morality, turning our 'normal' understanding upside down.

    The interlude challenges traditional morals by undermining Pythagorean philosophy. Nano points to Androgyno and says, 'For know, here is enclosed the soul of Pythagoras, / That juggler divine.' Pythagoras was famous for his belief in metempsychosis.[1] Among the implications of the attack against Pythagoras is a challenge to the idea of the 'philosopher', to someone who claims to see the 'truth' through rationality and reasoning, and to those who see the mind as superior to the body. The ridicule of 'philosopher' can be seen again, as Nano says:

> and the next toss of her [Aspasia]
> Was again of a whore: she became a philosopher,
> Crates the cynic (as itself doth relate it).
>
> (I.ii.19–21)

These lines confuse the distinction between a whore and a philosopher. By making fun of Pythagoras, who believed in the idea of the 'cosmos', the interlude demonstrates a distrust of the concept of an ordered whole. To read the universe as a 'beautiful and ordered whole' is an attempt to see the universe as an organised, well-structured object. The ridicule of Pythagoras's pious and ascetic conduct highlights the contrast between Pythagoras and Volpone. However, according to Nano, Pythagoras is enclosed in Androgyno's soul. If Androgyno is one of Volpone's bastards, the soul of Pythagoras should inhabit Volpone. The relationship between Pythagoras and Volpone remains ambiguous.

Some logic pertaining to Volpone's bastards can be read from the interlude. For instance, Pythagoras was reputed to have a golden thigh; however, if we associate his golden thigh with sexuality, it can be associated with the paralysed penis that Freud suggests.[2] The ridicule of the golden thigh turns Pythagoras's omnipotence into impotence, transforming the philosopher into Castrone. Such a suggestion recalls the joke on Morose in *Epicoene*. In other words, masculinity and patriarchy are challenged through the double meaning of the 'golden thigh'. This image also allows us to think of the representation of Nano: the gold can at the same time be seen as the *memento mori*. Something which is supposed to be magnificent on the surface can curiously cause a man to be an 'impotent'.

The relationship between language and identity is also established. Nano calls Pythagoras 'a juggler divine'. The words 'divine' and 'juggler' are contradictory in meaning, yet here they are put together. Such a play on words and meanings is another characteristic of the play. The interlude demonstrates the juggling of words. A juggler is a buffoon, a sorcerer and a conjurer. Juggling can refer to the interchanging of souls, meanings and identities. The image of a juggler is important as it relates to the concept of trickery and deception. In *A Midsummer Night's Dream*, Hermia says, 'O me, you juggler, you canker blossom, / You thief of love – what, have you come by night / And stol'n my love's heart from him?' (III.ii.283–5). Playing fast and loose corresponds with the soul of Pythagoras. If *Volpone* is about trickery and deception, such a meaning is implied in the interlude and in the soul of Pythagoras.

Moreover, the act of tossing can be associated with the tossing of coins, which is a game of chance and luck and recalls the beginning of the interlude when Nano says, 'Now, room for fresh gamesters.' Tossing relates to throwing Pythagoras's soul from Aspasia to another whore. The sexual meaning of 'toss' should not be overlooked: 'toss off', in modern sense, means an act of masturbation (*OED* 4).

Many references in the interlude allow us to associate with the themes in *Volpone* and other city comedies. The use of Lucian's Gallus in the interlude is related to *Volpone*. The soul of Pythagoras first comes from Apollo, whose own soul was 'breathed into Aethalides, Mercurius his son, / Where it had the gift to remember all that ever was done.' Aethalides was granted, by his father Mercury, a perfect and everlasting memory. The reference to memory is opposite to the notion of 'drowning the memory of all enormity' (V.vi.82–3) in *Bartholomew Fair*. The transmigration goes to the 'goldilocked Euphorbus, who was killed in good fashion, / At the siege of old Troy by the Cuckold of Sparta.' The notion of cuckoldry recalls *Volpone* and other early modern city comedies. The soul passes into a Greek philosopher, Hermotimus, who then becomes Pyrrhus of Delos, who could be one of several classical philosophers or one who is said, by Diogenes Laertius, without further explanation, to be a fisherman. The soul becomes 'the sophist of Greece', who is Pythagoras. Pythagoras is described by Lucian as a sophist. The power of reasoning and the power of speech can again be seen in Pythagoras.

The transmigration suggests the interchangeability of sexes and identity and that between philosopher and prostitute, which is carnivalesque. Pythagoras's soul becomes a woman. Nano says, 'From Pythagore, she went into a beautiful piece, / Hight Aspasia, the *meretrix*'. Two points should be noted here. First, the changing of sexes is in the interlude; and, second, *meretrix* is the Latin word for prostitute. In *A Chaste Maid in Cheapside* (1613), Middleton puns on *meretrix* and merry-tricks, turning a whore into an honest woman, showing the ambivalence between the two (V.iv.113). Aspasia was frequently attacked by Pericles's enemies as a prostitute and bawd because of her origins and her irregular union with Pericles. From Aspasia, the soul becomes Crates the cynic. After such transmigrations, the most carnivalesque part of the interlude appears, with Nano saying, 'Since, kings, knights, and beggars, knaves, lords, and fools gat it, / Besides ox and ass, camel, mule, goat, and brock, / In all which it hath spoke, as in the cobbler's cock'. Not only does the transmigration of souls confuse the difference between a philosopher and a prostitute, it blurs the distinction among kings, knights, beggars, knaves, lords and fools. Moreover, it disturbs the difference between humans and animals, as the soul becomes ox and ass, camel, mule, goat, and brock. The transmigration upsets the hierarchical order, crossing the boundary between human and animal, which is similar to, and may be even more radical than, the logic of castration that we see in *Epicoene*.

In fact, the transmigration does more than upset human identity, as it points to the power of language and fashioning. Nano says:

> But I come not here to discourse of that matter,
>   Or his one, two, or three, or his great oath, 'By *Quater*!'
> His musics, his *trigon*, his golden thigh,
>   Or his telling how elements shift; but I
> Would ask how of late thou hast suffered translation,
>   And shifted thy coat in these days of reformation?
>
> (I.ii.25–30)

The transmigration of souls is a 'translation'. The change of identity and that of language are interrelated; and they have a strong relation with the fashioning of clothes or that of plots. The transmigration is linked to being a turncoat. The change of identity is similar to that of clothes. Identity is on the surface and is superficial. There is no significant meaning underneath identity and language. The transmigration breaks down boundaries: it confuses the distinction between Volpone and Pythagoras, philosophers and prostitutes, kings and fools, and humans and animals. If Androgyno is in the 'house' of Volpone, these different identities and souls can be seen as part of Volpone. The identity of Volpone is doubled and redoubled because of the different transmigrations within Androgyno's soul. Therefore, not only is it difficult to distinguish clearly the differences between Volpone, Mosca and the three bastards, the deferral and slippage of identity is inherent in Androgyno.

Androgyno subsequently becomes a Puritan, a Carthusian, an obstreperous lawyer, a good and dull mule, an ass and, finally, an androgyne. While the metempsychosis relates to the debasement of souls, perhaps there is also another point for this process, namely, the soul of Androgyno incorporates 'everything': whether they are 'good' or 'bad', 'moral' or 'immoral', 'high' or 'low', they all inhabit Androgyno, and, thus, Volpone/*Volpone*. In the end, Androgyno says that s/he prefers the present state, namely, being an androgyne, not because of 'the delight of each sex thou canst vary' (I.ii.54), but because of his/her status as a fool. S/he says that being a fool is the 'one creature that I can call blessed; / For all other forms I have proved most distressèd' (I.ii.57–8). In other words, a fool treasures his/her state because s/he experiences what it means to be a puritan, whereas a puritan would not understand what it means to be a fool. In response, Nano says, 'Spoke true, as thou wert in Pythagoras still. This learnèd opinion we celebrate will' (I.ii.59–60). Understanding the value of being a fool makes Androgyno a philosopher. Therefore, the representation of the supposedly 'higher' figure, namely, philosopher, and the so-called lower one, namely, fool, are combined in Androgyno. Being a fool sums up the status of the bastards: it is an identity that is fluid and slippery. The nation of fools is a world of floating signifiers. It is a world of bastards that is full of slipping transformations.

The interlude concludes with *The Praise of Folly*:

> *Song*
> Fools, they are the only nation
> Worth men's envy or admiration;
> Free from care or sorrow-taking,
> Themselves and others merry making.
> All they speak or do is sterling.
> Your fool, he is your great man's dearling,
> And your lady's sport and pleasure;
> Tongue and bauble are his treasure.
> His very face begetteth laughter,
> And he speaks truth free from slaughter;
> He's the grace of every feast,
> And sometimes the chiefest guest;
> Hath his trencher and his stool
> When wit shall wait upon the fool.
>   Oh, who would not be
>   He, he, he?
>
>   (I.ii.66–81)

Volpone is about the nation of fools. Fools are what the transmigration of souls becomes. There is no fixed identity in this world of bastards. The fool is the androgyne: there is no determination of sexes in Jonson's fool. More importantly, this nation is connected with city comedy. According to the song, comedy is about money, as 'All they speak or do is sterling'. The word 'sterling' means both 'excellent' and money. In *Volpone*, behind most speeches of the characters lies only one motive, namely, chasing after money. The line suggests the importance of coining, which again relates to money, fashion and dissembling. A fool's relation with women is ambiguous. The fool is 'your lady's sport and pleasure' and the next line says 'Tongue and bauble are his treasure'. The bauble is slang for the male organ, which is the lady's sport and pleasure. However, his tongue has the same function, which can be seen as the substitution of the phallus. The relation between language and sex is important. Language can be used as a substitute to give women sexual pleasure (as in the case of Volpone in the face of Celia). The importance of sex and language should be seen in their relation to comedy, and, maybe, in particular, to city comedy. Freud argues that jokes are the substitutions of our sexual desire.[3] The sexual implication can again be seen from 'His very face begetteth laughter', as 'beget' means 'procreate'. The fool's face relates to the ugly face that Nano refers to in Act III scene iii:

> Admit your fool's face be the mother of laughter,
>   Yet, for his brain, it must always come after;
> And though that do feed him, it's a pitiful case
>   His body is beholding to such a bad face.

(III.iii.17–20)

This face is 'bad', yet, such a face is the mother (and interestingly, not the father) of laughter. And in the song in Act I scene ii, such a face 'begets' laughter as well. Such an ugly face has a sexual attraction for women. The reference to face recalls Face in *The Alchemist*. The changing of faces is similar to the shifting of coats. It is another reference to the fluidity of identities and meanings.

The song finishes with the ending 'When wit shall wait upon the fool. / Oh, who would not be / He, he, he?' Creaser annotates that the words 'he, he, he' are 'the only occasion in the earlier scenes of the play at least when both Q and F print the then alternative form "hee" for "he". This suggests that the song was meant to end on a punning giggle.'[4] 'He, he, he' can mean at the same time 'hee, hee, hee'. The line 'O, who would not be / He, he, he?' means that every 'he', namely, every man, is a fool. Nobody can escape from the nation of fools. The punning giggle demonstrates the ambiguity of laughter. No laughter is innocent of meaning. The seemingly pure 'he, he, he' refers to the audience, meaning 'you, you, you'. The ending of the song reveals that the joke is directed at the audience, reminding us once again of the title page of *Bartholomew Fair* in the 1640 folio.

Who should sing the 'Praise of Folly'? Critics tend to suggest that the song could be sung by Nano and Castrone, or that perhaps Volpone and Mosca could join the bastards to sing the song.[5] However, as A. K. Nardo rightly points out, these 'self-proclaimed "fools" are . . . the only characters in the play who neither gull others nor are themselves gulled'; they 'display a more active self-knowledge than any other character in the play'.[6] The fact that Jonson's bastards are the only characters who are set free at the end shows that the song could be sung by the three of them, and neither Volpone nor Mosca can join in. Moreover, the setting free of Jonson's bastards has one more important implication. Nardo writes:

Their Pythagorean interlude assures us that there has always been folly enough among kings, philosophers, and theologians, as well as whores, beggars, and beasts . . . Their joyous liberation assures us that there always will be folly; for, according to the learned Scoto, 'to be a fool born is a disease incurable' . . . Since Jonson sees this brand of transmigrating and proliferating foolery as all-pervasive and not vicious, the grotesques' freedom to 'go sport' softens the harshness of *Volpone*'s dark ending, presents a realistic but not despairing vision of the future folly of Venetian society, and points toward the broad tolerance Jonson will demonstrate in *The Alchemist* and *Bartholomew Fair*.[7]

The setting free of the bastards exhibits the carnivalesque quality of the play. Nardo rightly argues, 'It is not surprising that Jonson did not attempt to point toward a regeneration of Venetian society through a union between Celia and Bonario, for their virtue is impotent and forever imprisoned within themselves.'[8] Even though Jonson may be strongly influenced by Lucian, which enhances a moral reading of his plays, the setting free of Jonson's bastards and his treatment of Bonario and Celia are criticisms against moralism. There is no doubt that the Lucianic force is important in the reading of Jonson. However, it is also true that Jonson, perhaps in contrast to Shakespeare, does not focus on the idea of organic unity, thus, no 'heterosexual' sexual relationship is fulfilled. There is a power of the grotesque within *Volpone*, which challenges the concept of completeness, and, therefore, is carnivalesque in its own way. The freeing of the bastards becomes the excess of the play: they are the heterogeneous force that will be everywhere, running around in the city and in comedy.

The interlude starts with the concept of fashioning and develops into issues of sexuality, language, memory, cuckoldry, coining, identity, folly and the ambiguity of laughter. Within these ideas is the power of the grotesque, which challenges the concept of completeness and refuses the belief of a single reading and interpretation. The transmigration of souls suggests the deferral of a stable identity. Such deferral constructs and diffuses identity simultaneously. The process of debasement ends up with being a fool, which suggests the carnivalesque nature within this slippage, something that is essential to the understanding of Jonsonian comedies.

Ultimately, I want to associate Jonson's comedies with what Susan Sontag described as 'Camp', and to see Jonson as a 'proto-Camp' writer, especially if we read him from the perspective of the city and city comedy. Even though Sontag suggested that the starting point of what she defines as Camp is the late seventeenth and early eighteenth centuries, perhaps we can apply the concept to *Volpone* and see how Jonson's major comedies contain a certain sense of 'Camp'. Sontag writes: 'Camp is the triumph of the epicene style. (The convertibility of "man" and "woman," "person" and "thing.") But all style, that is, artifice, is, ultimately, epicene. Life is not stylish. Neither is nature.'[9] In her essay, Sontag suggests 'Camp' as a modern sensibility which has not been named and described.[10] She writes that 'the essence of Camp is its love of the unnatural: of artifice and exaggeration'.[11] While many critics focus on Jonson as a poet and use the words of Jonson the poet to comment on Jonson the dramatist, what we have seen in this book is that there is an internal force, a grotesque force, within Jonson's plays. While it is true that *Volpone* may have its serious implications for the early modern city and its emerging capitalism, what it celebrates is this 'nation of fools' which is epitomised by these three (or even four) bastards of Volpone. Jonson can be read as the master of epicene. If, according to Sontag, the epicene style means the convertibility of 'man' and 'woman', 'person' and 'thing', *Volpone* has definitely illustrated that. In the play, the dwarf can be read as the embodiment of phallic empowerment and death; Androgyno can be seen as Castrone, and vice versa. Mosca might think that he is different from the bastards, but what we see in the end may just be a servant living in his 'para-site'. *Volpone* demonstrates and celebrates the world of artifice. If Jonson in his poetry shows his love of nature and order, his drama might suggest otherwise. Sontag suggests:

> As a taste in persons, Camp responds particularly to the markedly attenuated and to the strongly exaggerated. The androgyne is certainly one of the great images of Camp sensibility. Examples: the swooning, slim, sinuous figures of pre-Raphaelite painting and poetry; the thin, flowing, sexless bodies in Art Nouveau prints and posters, presented in relief on lamps and ashtrays; the haunting androgynous vacancy behind the perfect beauty of Greta Garbo. Here, Camp taste draws on a mostly unacknowledged truth of taste: the most refined form of sexual attractiveness (as well as the most refined form of sexual pleasure) consists in going against the grain of one's sex. What is most beautiful in virile men is something feminine; what is most beautiful in feminine women is something masculine . . . Allied to the Camp taste for the androgynous is something that seems quite different but isn't: a relish for the exaggeration of sexual characteristics and personality mannerisms.[12]

Exaggeration and mannerisms are what we could think of when we remember Jonson: the beginning of the speech in *Volpone* Act I scene i, the parasite's soliloquy in Act III scene i, and the narrative of seduction in Act III scene vii are just a few examples which demonstrate this sense of flamboyant extravagance in Jonson's comedies. The main characters in *Epicoene*, perhaps, are really a troupe of 'swooning, slim, sinuous figures' who have 'thin, flowing, sexless bodies'. Indeed, Volpone can be seen as a figure that brings up the association of the Pardoner. He can only exist in the theatre, for his roles are his only identities. The same can be said about the parasite, as the idea of him living in his mirror stage suggests that he does not exist except when he is on his stage, performing. At the end of her essay, Sontag writes: 'the ultimate Camp statement: it's good because it's awful . . .'.[13] Perhaps we can say the same about Jonson: Volpone is appealing because he loves to exaggerate. Similar to the image of his gold, there is a glowing presence in him. Even though the audience would know that there is nothing behind his theatrical roles, it does not really matter. Contrary to what Jonson the poet would apparently want us to believe, we are not here to make moral judgements. While there are critiques of the nascent early modern capitalism in his play, there is another message in it: these theatrical roles are the only identities that a person can play. Volpone is attractive as a character because he is 'bad'. The play is enjoyable because it is cruel. It is cruel because underneath the surface of comedy lies the emptiness of tragedy; and beneath the sound of laughter is the echo of hollowness. *Volpone* is funny because it is violent. It allows us to see that pleasure and pain are inseparable. Sontag writes:

> The question isn't, 'Why travesty, impersonation, theatricality?' The question is, rather, 'When does travesty, impersonation, theatricality acquire the special flavour of Camp?' Why is the atmosphere of Shakespeare's comedies (*As You Like It*, etc.) not epicene, while that of *Der Rosenkavalier* is?[14]

The difference between Jonson and Shakespeare is that while the former shows the triumph of the epicene, the latter does not. Even though it is true that there is no marriage and comic resolutions in Jonson's plays, it should be counted as a merit, not the other way round, for the dramatist.

On Theory of Comedy

In Mel Brooks's *The Producers* (1967), an accountant and a producer realise they can make more money by producing a flop instead of a hit, so they choose a play called *Springtime for Hitler* in order to fail.[15] The play, which had been written by a Nazi fanatic, is supposed to be 'a love letter to Hitler'. However, by choosing the wrong play, the wrong director and the wrong cast, a popular comedy is produced instead. Seeing his love letter to 'The Führer' going down the drain, the Nazi fanatic writer becomes furious. Sitting among the hysterically laughing audience, he tells them to shut up; and says, 'I am the author, I outrank you.' His comments, of course, have no effect whatsoever on the audience, who are out of control. This episode questions whether we can set any limits to comedy, and whether the meaning of comedy and laughter can be controlled.

What can Volpone's bastards tell us about comedy? While this book has based many of its discussions on Alenka Zupančič's *The Odd One In*, I would like to illustrate how the characteristics of these bastards help us rethink some other theories of comedy. On laughter, Baudelaire argues that it 'is generally the apanage of madmen', and it always 'implies more or less of ignorance and weakness'.[16] On comedy and tragedy, Yeats writes that 'tragedy must always be a drowning and breaking of the dykes that separate man from man, and that it is upon these dykes comedy keeps house'.[17] Likewise, George Meredith suggests that 'comedy is the fountain of sound sense'.[18] Using Molière as an example, he argues, 'The source of his wit is clear reason; it is a fountain of that soil, and it springs to vindicate reason, common sense, rightness, and justice – for no vain purpose ever.'[19] While Meredith emphasises common sense in comedy, Bergson talks about the importance of being a human instead of a machine, writing: 'The first point to which attention should be called is that the comic does not exist outside the pale of what is strictly *human*.'[20] The function of comedy is to laugh at 'mechanical inelasticity', and 'the attitudes, gestures, and movements of the human body are laughable in exact proportion as that body reminds us of a mere machine'.[21]

On the other hand, Freud suggests the importance of the unconscious in jokes. For him, jokes can be divided into innocent jokes and tendentious jokes. The purpose of tendentious jokes can be hostility (serving the purposes of aggressiveness, satire and defence) or obscenity (serving the purposes of exposure).[22] Freud describes smut directed by men against women as an example of the mechanism of jokes, for it lifts inhibitions between the sexes. Freud suggests that our libido helps us to imagine or 'see' the peculiar organ of the other sex, which is a substitute for our original desire to touch that organ: 'Looking has replaced touching.'[23] Smut is the exposure of what is sexual about the other person:

> By the utterance of the obscene words it compels the person who is assailed to imagine the part of the body or the procedure in question and shows her that the assailant is himself imagining it. It cannot be doubted that the desire to see what is sexual exposed is the original motive of smut.[24]

Such joking comes into play because of inhibition and has the ability to diminish inhibition.

Bakhtin suggests the significance of the grotesque. He disagrees with the suggestion that the grotesque is purely the exaggeration and caricature of the negative.[25] He objects to the typical notion that the grotesque is necessarily satirical and, therefore, negative because, if the grotesque is just an exaggeration of the improper, it cannot explain the joyful lavishness that accompanies it.[26] By analysing an example of *Commedia dell'arte*, Bakhtin argues that the action of both the stutterer and Harlequin relates to the importance of rebirth.[27] By comparing the belfry to the image of the phallus, he shows how the grotesque relates to the bodily lower stratum and birth.[28]

George Bataille's comment on laughter illustrates that laughter breaks subjectivity. He suggests that laughter can be an erotic experience:

> On another level, to look at each other and laugh can be a type of erotic relation (in this case, rupture has been produced by the development of intimacy in lovemaking). In a general way, what comes into play in physical or psychological eroticism is the same feeling of 'magical subversion' associated with one person slipping into another.[29]

For two people to have contact with each other, there must be a certain level of resistance, and this resistance is the 'intensity of the contact'. When contact continues, the intensity lessens. This intensity of the contact shows that human contacts are heterogeneous. When there are comic elements, resistance will be violated.

From these examples, we can say that the views of Baudelaire, Yeats, Meredith and Bergson are closer to each other because they emphasise the importance of humanity and rationality in comedy. However, Freud, Bakhtin and Bataille relate comedy and laughter to something that challenges representation. Their suggestions show that comedy is beyond rational understanding and the control of humans. When I suggest that Volpone's bastards illustrate that it is difficult to assert a single identity, does it mean that Freud, Bakhtin and Bataille are right, and Baudelaire, Yeats, Meredith and Bergson are wrong?

Even though this book draws heavily on Freud's and Lacan's psychoanalytic theories to discuss comedy, the answer is 'No'. These bastards show that it is impossible to insist on any single meaning. Identity slips from one's control and is in itself a deferral. Volpone is funny and laughable because, while he seems to be a Venetian *Magnifico*, he could at the same time be a dwarf, an androgyne and a eunuch. Applying this concept to modern films, in *To Be, or Not to Be* (1942), Joseph Tura (Jack Benny) is funny because while he thinks he did a good job performing *Hamlet*, the fact is that what he did to *Hamlet* equals what Germany did to Poland.[30] Comedy is more than just self-ignorance. A person is laughable if he 'insists' that he is ignorant. The focus is on 'insistence' instead of on 'ignorance' because what is funny comes from the tension between insistence and deferral. And, in the case of Jonson, it would be the tension between madness and folly, between death (and castration, and nothingness) and the comic misrecognition of identities. The Marx Brothers are funnier because of the presence of Margaret Dumont. Groucho Marx once said that the secret to their chemistry was that she never understood what he said. Therefore, to insist on talking about the unconscious is exactly how someone may risk making himself laughable. These theories should be considered together. It is the insistence on being human that makes the unconscious slip out. It is the emphasis of the structure that forms the grotesque. Reflecting on Bergson's theory, it may be more correct to ask what it means to be a human and what it means to be a machine. To keep insisting on being a human can make someone a machine. To realise what is funny and to understand what comedy is, we need to think within and outside the structure simultaneously. Moreover, while emphasising the need to think outside the system, we have to be aware of the power of deferral, which would lead to a beyond that is beyond the structure. Comedy, then, is about simultaneously thinking and not thinking at a 'meta' level. While it is true that the presence of the dwarf, the androgyne and the eunuch allows us to read certain criticisms of Jonson on the early modern city, the play cannot simply be read from a moral perspective. At the same time, it cannot be seen as purely a celebration of the carnival either. The trace of Jonson the poet and Jonson the dramatist can equally be noticed in his comedy. While this book does not use Jonson the poet to read Jonson the dramatist, and in some cases it has even done the reverse, it does not mean that we only need to consider the persona of Jonson the dramatist. The more important point, perhaps, is that the presence of Jonson the poet makes us appreciate Jonson the dramatist a little bit more. The two forces go hand in hand; it would be wrong for us to glorify one and ignore the other.

On Modern Films

Perhaps we can also use the implications of Volpone's bastards to understand modern film comedy. The concept of fetishism can be seen in some of Mel Brooks's comedies. In *The Producers*, Leo Bloom (Gene Wilder) does not allow anyone to touch his blue blanket. In *Blazing Saddles* (1974), Hedley Lamarr loves to have his 'froggy' with him when he takes a bath. In one scene, while accidentally dropping froggy into his bathtub, Taggart (Slim Pickens) grabs the wrong 'froggy' when putting his hand into the tub to search for it.[31] Taggart's relation with Lamarr is not unlike the one between Mosca and Volpone. The fetishism raises questions of their sexuality, especially that of Leo Bloom, who shows a heavy dependence on Max Bialystock (Zero Mostel) in the film. After all, the performance that they finally produce may not just be seen as merely a mistake, it might reveal their unconscious, a certain kind of 'slip'. The fetishism is similar to the emphasis on body parts in *Young Frankenstein*, which at the end suggests that Frankenstein exchanges his brain with the monster's phallus.[32] It is important to ask why Frankenstein wants to produce a monster who has a huge 'schwanzs-tucker'. It might represent his 'lack' in some way and make him project his wishes onto the monster. However, I must emphasise that I do not want to put them in any definite category, for instance, homosexual or fetishist. After all, it is the ambiguity that makes them comic. The folly of Volpone's bastards tells us that no absolute category can be applied to anyone. If we are too definite about their identities and signification, we ruin the 'spirit', which is a non-spirit, perhaps, of comedy.

As discussed, the study of 'Volpone's bastards' can be applied to the comedy of the Marx Brothers as well. Adding to the discussions in previous chapters, I want to draw attention to Groucho Marx's cigar, which resembles the enormous 'schwanzstucker' in *Young Frankenstein*. It is alleged that Groucho once said, 'I like my cigar, too, but I take it out of my mouth once in a while', while interviewing a woman who had a large number of children. The image of Groucho is similar to a man who has an empowered phallus. However, the same omnipotent/ impotent ambiguity occurs if we recall his attitude towards Margaret Dumont in the films. For example, in *Duck Soup*, Firefly (Groucho) says to Mrs. Teasdale (Dumont), 'Will you marry me? Did he leave you any money? Answer the second question first . . . He left me his entire fortune . . . Is that so? Can't you see I'm trying to tell you I love you.'[33] Groucho's attitude towards Dumont is similar to Volpone's attraction towards Celia, who is described by Mosca as 'Bright as your gold, and lovely as your gold!' (I.v.114). Moreover, the logic of the question is in itself a kind of deferral. It drifts away from the first question and makes the primary become secondary, and vice versa.

Harpo Marx's image is equally interesting. His muteness allows us to associate him with the concepts of mutilation and deformity. The idea of 'castration' corresponds with his use of props, which can be seen as supplements to the phallus. His attitude towards women is equally ambiguous. Throughout their films, we often see him chasing women. One particular scene in *Duck Soup* shows him entering a woman's house and ends up with him sleeping with a horse instead of the woman. The ambiguity between innocence and perversity is demonstrated in Harpo.

Harpo's muteness draws discussion about the representation of death. Lacan writes:

> Is there anything that poses a question which is more present, more pressing, more absorbing, more disruptive, more nauseating, more calculated to thrust everything that takes place before us into the abyss or void than that face of Harpo Marx, that face with its smile which leaves us unclear as to whether it signifies the most extreme perversity or complete simplicity? This dumb man alone is sufficient to sustain the atmosphere of doubt and of radical annihilation which is the stuff of the Marx Brothers' extraordinary farce and the uninterrupted play of 'jokes' that makes their activity so valuable.[34]

Commenting on Lacan, Simon Critchley suggests:

> Harpo's face is a mute *mot*, a void that the subject cannot avoid, an abyss into which all attempts at comprehension or judgement are annihilated. Harpo stands over against the subject *als Ding*, his muteness blocks the subject's attempts at judgement and comprehension . . . At the heart of the laughter's complicity is hidden an ethical relation of *Fremdheit* that radically calls the subject into question.[35]

Critchley's argument demonstrates the ambiguity between comedy and tragedy. Harpo's muteness, like the figure of the deformed, is associated with the question of finitude. There might be a close connection between comedy and tragedy. After all, the most astonishingly shocking and funny scene in *Duck Soup* is the one when the brothers sing the song 'This Country's Going to War'. It blends the comic and tragic together as if they put the audience face to face with death, challenging their responses. Death laughs at you and makes you laugh. There is a similar effect in the last scene of Stanley Kubrick's *Dr. Strangelove or: How I Learned to Stop Worrying and Love the Bomb* (1964).[36] When the bomb finally explodes in the end, we hear the song 'We'll meet again, don't know where, don't know when . . .'. The same is equally true in Robert Altman's *M*A*S*H* (1970), of which the title song is 'Suicide Is Painless', drawing reference to *Hamlet*.[37] Another similar comparison would be Monty Python's *Life of Brian* (1979), a comedy also about misrecognition of identity, in which the characters sing 'Always Look on the Bright Side of Life' at the moment of crucifixion.[38] Near the end of the song, it says that 'You come from nothing, you're going back to nothing. What have you lost? Nothing!' Indeed, perhaps the lyrics should be rewritten as 'What have you got? Laughing!' as laughing may be built upon the feeling of void and emptiness. These films demonstrate that the climax of comedy can also be the height of tragedy. They mix the two together, making the meaning of laughter even more ambiguous.

On Early Modern City Comedy

Can Volpone's bastards help us understand other city comedies in the early modern period, such as those written by Thomas Middleton? The comedy of the bastards recalls Middleton's *A Mad World, My Masters* (1605). On the relationship between *Mad World* and city comedy, Laurie Maguire and Emma Smith argue that

> Although *Mad World* is representative of Middleton's dramaturgical skill, it is not representative of city comedy ... The play's main locus is not a city or a country but the theatre, and the plot concerns not the (im)morality of gulling (as one might expect from a city comedy) but its theatricality.[39]

Having said that, there are certain similarities between *Mad World* and the Jonsonian city comedies. For instance, the name Sir Bounteous Progress suggests the spirit of capitalism; the name Follywit points to the importance of folly, or, to be more precise, it raises the ambiguity between folly and wit, or seeing folly as a kind of wit.

The relationship between a disinherited nephew and his uncle reminds us of *Epicoene*. Follywit's appearance is worth noting. Sir Bounteous Progress suggests:

> And that's worth all indeed, my lord, for he's like to have all when I die. *Imberbis iuvenis* [beardless youth], his chin has no more prickles yet than a midwife's: there's great hope of his wit, his hair's so long a-coming. Shall I be bold with your honour, to prefer this aforesaid Ganymede to hold a plate under your lordship's cup? (II.i.137–42)[40]

There is an effeminate quality in the appearance of Follywit. He has the appearance of Ganymede, which seems to anticipate Dauphine's epicene characteristic. Again, there is a relation between disinheritance and gender ambivalence. It seems that Follywit may possess the quality of both Dauphine and Truewit.

Moreover, similar to *Epicoene*, there are many sexual jokes in Middleton's comedy that focus on body parts. For instance:

SIR BOUNTEOUS   My organist.
> *The organs play, and [servants with] covered dishes march over the stage.*

Come, my lord, how does your honour relish my organ?
FOLLYWIT   A very proud air, i'faith, sir.

(II.i.166–8)

Follywit says, 'Though guilt condemns, 'tis gilt must make us glad' (II.ii.31). Similar to *Volpone*, *A Mad World, My Masters* indicates the importance of gold. While in *Bartholomew Fair* we see the relation between castration and purse cutting, Middleton's play is linked with the concept of robbing. Sir Bounteous Progress is constantly robbed by his nephew in the play. In order to rob his uncle, Follywit dresses as a courtesan in Act IV scene iii. While this scene shows the importance of acting and imitation, the theme of sexual ambiguity is also suggested. Gunwater, the servant of Sir Bounteous Progress, is attracted to Follywit, who dresses as a courtesan. He says, 'Faith, you're too nice, lady, and as for my secrecy, you know I have vowed it often to you' (IV. iii.20–1). He kisses Follywit before he leaves. Later, in the same scene, we learn that Sir Bounteous has also kissed Follywit as a courtesan. He says:

> Ah sirrah, methink I feel myself well toasted, bumbasted, rubbed and refreshed. But i' faith, I cannot forget to think how soon sickness has altered her to my taste. I gave her a kiss at bottom o'th' stairs, and by th' mass, methought her breath had much ado to be sweet, like a thing compounded methought of wine, beer and tobacco. I smelt much pudding in't. (IV.iv.1–7)

This, of course, is a 'homosexual' joke about Sir Bounteous. However, the fact that he is excited by Follywit as a courtesan recalls how Morose is attracted by Epicene. The quality of the three bastards can be spotted in *A Mad World, My Masters*.

The final 'witty comedy' (V.i.74) that Follywit presents to Sir Bounteous is called *The Slip*.[41] The title suggests the importance of the unconscious in comedy. It reminds us of the deferral of identity by Nano, Androgyno, Castrone and Mosca.[42] 'Slip' is an important word in *A Mad World, My Masters*. For instance, referring to women's power of acting and deceiving, the courtesan says to Penitent, 'I thus translated, and yourself slipped into the form of a physician' (II.v.39–40). Here, 'slipping' is related to translation and transformation, meaning that it is relevant to the idea of shifting identity. Moreover, 'slipping' is the enemy of the cuckold. In Act III scene i, Harebrain, a man who is jealous of the ague that shakes all over his wife's body, says that he will 'observe her [his wife's] carriage and watch the slippery revolutions of her eye' (III.i.10–11). However, even though, as Mistress Harebrain says, 'jealousy is prick-eared, and will hear the wagging of a hair' (III. ii.186–7), Harebrain fails to realise the slippage and ends up enjoying the cuckoldry as he says to his wife, 'Never was hour spent better' (III. ii.258).[43] Commenting on this scene, Celia Daileader suggests that

> Middleton emphasizes the brevity of the offstage sex in *Women Beware Women*; contrastingly, in *Mad World*, the wily cover-up speech of the conspiring courtesan is notable for its duration, pointed up by the verbal filler she spins out so that the lovers may enjoy themselves.[44]

Harebrain's ear is indeed pricked by Penitent's wagging of his wife.
The prologue of *The Slip* suggests:

> We sing of wandering knights, what them betide
> Who nor in one place nor one shape abide.
> They're here now, and anon no scouts can reach 'em,
> Being every man well horsed like a bold Beacham.

(V.ii.18–21)

The importance of 'wandering' is suggested: to slip is to be wandering
from place to place and from shape to shape. This is the logic that we
witness in Volpone's bastards. At the end of the prologue, Follywit
says, 'The play being called *The Slip*, I vanish too' (V.ii.27). The slippage makes a subject shift from one identity to another, causing the
disappearance of 'I'. Indeed, one of the interesting points about *A Mad
World, My Masters* is that while Follywit seems to have gulled everyone, he is also fooled in the end. As Sir Bounteous says, 'Can you gull
us and let a quean gull you?' (V.ii.301). Therefore, 'when he has gulled
all, then is himself the last' (V.ii.316). In *A Mad World, My Masters*,
Middleton demonstrates an egalitarian attitude towards the city and
its logic of slippage. While the play shows how folly can be a source
of wit, the fact that even Follywit cannot exclude himself from the
slip illustrates that sometimes wit itself can also be regarded as a kind
of folly. The association of *A Mad World, My Masters* and *Volpone*
and *Epicoene* demonstrates that it is difficult to assert the status of
an author. The plays of Jonson, Shakespeare, Middleton and other
writers create a dialogue. Just as the War of the Theatres reflects the
conflict existing among Jonson, John Marston and Thomas Dekker,
there is a conflicting, yet complementary, relationship between these
playwrights.[45] Reading or watching a play is like a trip into the world
of bastards: the experience allows readers and audiences to 'slip' from
one play to another, which is a process of continuous re-creation.

How should we situate ourselves among Volpone's bastards? If we
can take any hint from Middleton, maybe the only way is to admit that
we all are part of them. Instead of attempting to safeguard ourselves
from being cuckolds, perhaps the better way is to be wittols. As Allwit
says in *A Chaste Maid in Cheapside*:

> I see these things, but like a happy man
> I pay for none at all; yet fools think 's mine;
> I have the name, and in his gold I shine;
> And where some merchants would in soul kiss hell
> To buy a paradise for their wives, and dye
> Their conscience in the bloods of prodigal heirs
> To deck their night-piece, yet all this being done,

Eaten with jealously to the inmost bone –
As what affliction nature more constrains
Than feed the wife plump for another's veins? –
These torments stand I freed of; I am as clear
From jealously of a wife as from the charge.
O' two miraculous blessings! 'Tis the knight
Hath took that labour all out of my hands.
I may sit still and play; he's jealous for me,
Watches her steps, sets spies. I live at ease;
He has both the cost and torment: when the strings
Of his heart frets, I feed, laugh, or sing:
[*Singing*] *La dildo, dildo la dildo, la dildo dildo de dildo.*

(I.ii.38–57)

On Allwit's name, Sylvia Adamson writes: 'how far is Allwit simply a "wit-all" [= "contented cuckold"], and how far made all-powerful by his wits?'[46] Gail Kern Paster says that

> As his name suggests, Allwit's role in the mercantile economy of Cheapside is to submit questions of emotional investment to a cost-benefit analysis – producing the satirical picture of a household organized entirely around the housekeeper's unconventional notion of self-interest and his desire to escape the dark emotions produced by possessiveness in the form of love.[47]

Perhaps a wittol indeed has all the wit: he sees both sides of the situation, yet he is content to be a Fool. He does not insist on the concept of property, and thus, has no need to keep a 'proper' wife.[48] The wittol is glad to only have the 'name' and shine because of other men's gold, meaning that he is willing to thrive on the signifier and appearance. As he would not insist on a connection between the signifier and the signified, he could 'sit still and play' and would not suffer from jealousy. The singing in the end is particularly interesting. While the singing is supposed to be meaningless, it refers to an artificial penis. Allwit is thriving on and highlighting the artificial nature of the phallic power. Indeed, perhaps he is exposing the fact that this 'fake' power is all the 'real' power that one can have, as to believe that there is any 'real' substance of this power is to be mad. Therefore, while the singing appears to be meaningless, it is all the meaning that one can have. The signifier and the patriarchal power coincide in the singing of *dildo*. The wittol plays with it and disregards the possible emptiness of it.

To be a wittol, one would need to keep a few bastards. In Act I scene ii, Allwit shouts to Wat and Nick, 'Peace, bastard! [*aside*] Should he hear 'em! [*Aloud*] These are two foolish children, they do not know the gentleman that sits there [referring to Sir Walter]' (I.ii.112–14). Indeed, keeping a bastard means having no property, as Allwit can disregard them whenever he wants. He says, 'No, by my troth, I'll swear / It's none of mine. Let him that got it keep it! / [*Aside*] Thus do I rid myself of fear, / Lie soft, sleep hard, drink wine, and eat good cheer' (I.ii.138–41). Having bastards does not seem to worry the characters in the play. For instance, even though Allwit tries to sabotage the marriage between Sir Walter and Moll in the hope that he can continue to be a wittol, Yellowhammer (Moll's father) says to himself after Allwit's exit, 'I have kept a whore myself, and had a bastard / By Mistress Anne' (IV.i.262–3). Therefore, for Yellowhammer, there is nothing wrong if Sir Walter has some bastards, because everybody has a few. According to the logic of city comedy, what is more important is that 'The knight is rich, he shall be my son-in-law' (IV.i.267). As long as he can 'have him [Sir Walter] sweat well ere they go to bed', he will have his daughter marrying Sir Walter (IV.i.269–70). While the line means that Yellowhammer wants Sir Walter to be treated in a steam tub for venereal disease, the portrayal makes the latter not unlike another piece of property: something that can be reused as long as it is washed and cleansed.

After the departure of Sir Walter and Davy, Allwit's wife suggests that she and her husband should let out their lodgings, and 'take a house in the Strand' (V.i.160–1). And at the end of the scene, Allwit says 'I have done, wench; And let this stand in every gallant's chamber: / "There's no gamester like a politic sinner, / For whoe'er games, the box is sure a winner"' (V.i.168–71). While the Oxford edition suggests that 'Allwit now sees himself as proprietor of a gaming house',[49] the box, following the suggestion of Bryan Loughrey and Neil Taylor, is a pun on coffin.[50] Therefore, the images of the gamester (recalling 'Now, room for fresh gamesters') and death are combined in the wittol. Different from a 'possessed' city subject, a wittol understands the emptiness of the box. Being the ultimate gamester, the wittol holds and epitomises the box. Even though the box is empty, it has the power to collect them all. There may be nothing wrong in being a wittol and a bastard. The fact that the bastards of Volpone are the only characters who are set free may suggest that the only way is to admit that we are all bastards, and thus, we are all born to be Fools.

Conclusion

Are we not all Volpone's bastards? The indication that we are all living in the nation of fools echoes the words of the Fool in *King Lear*:

> That sir which serves and seeks for gain,
>   And follows but for form,
> Will pack when it begins to rain,

And leave thee in the storm.
But I will tarry; the fool will stay,
    And let the wise man fly.
The knave turns fool that runs away;
    The fool no knave, perdy.

(II.iv.72–9)

The Fool's words suggest that we are either fools or knaves in this world, which is also the theme of *King Lear*, a play performed at court on 26 December 1606, probably around the same time as *Volpone*. Commenting on their differences, Lacan writes that 'The "fool" is an innocent, a simpleton, but truths issue from his mouth that are not simply tolerated but adopted, by virtue of the fact that this "fool" is sometimes clothed in the insignia of the jester', whereas a knave 'doesn't retreat from the consequences of what is called realism; that is, when required, he admits he's a crook'.[51] He compares fools and knaves to left-wing and right-wing intellectuals. However, he also says, 'But what is not sufficiently noted is that by a curious chiasma, the "foolery" which constitutes the individual style of the left-wing intellectual gives rise to a collective "knavery"', namely, 'that innocent chicanery, not to say calm impudence, which allows them to express so many heroic truths without wanting to pay the price'.[52] Using again an example from modern film comedy as a parallel to this point, in *Life of Brian*, after Brian learns that his father is actually a centurion in the Roman army, we have the following conversation between him and his mother:

BRIAN   You mean . . . you were raped?
MANDY   Well, at first, yes.
BRIAN   Who was it?
MANDY   Heh. Naughtius Maximus his name was. Hmm. Promised
    me the known world he did. I was to be taken to Rome. House by
    the Forum. Slaves. Asses' milk. As much gold as I could eat. Then, he,
    having his way with me had . . . voom! Like a rat out of an aqueduct.
BRIAN   The bastard![53]

Is he referring to his father, or himself? Both, I suppose. Thinking of comedy, maybe we can put the idea of madness in the above conversation, asking, 'Is he mad?' And the answer to it would be, 'Well, at first, yes'. As Truewit says, 'he that thinks himself the master wit is the master fool' (*Epicoene* III.vi.42–3), to which Lacan would probably respond, '*Les non-dupes errent* (Those in the know are in error)'.[54] *Volpone* was written and performed at the beginning of the seventeenth century, a century which, according to L. C. Knights, 'has long been recognized as marking in some ways the beginning of "the modern world"'.[55] Alluding to the famous thesis of T. S. Eliot, he suggests that a 'dissociation of sensibility' was starting to happen in that period, pointing to Francis Bacon as the crucial figure of this development.[56] Knights writes:

> The modern reassessment of the seventeenth century is largely a recognition of what was lost as well as gained by the transition to the modern world – a transition that took place not only in the spheres of practical achievement and conscious intellect but in those more subtle and more profound modes of perceiving and feeling that underlie men's conscious philosophies and explicit attitudes, and that have become so ingrained and habitual that it is only by a deliberate effort of the intelligence that we can recognize them as *not* inevitable, absolute, and unchanging, the permanent *données* of 'human nature': that is why they are best studied in our literature.[57]

If *Volpone*, or comedy, has taught us anything, it is the lesson that madness can be easily slipped into folly, and vice versa.

Notes

1. On metempsychosis, see Skutsch, 'Notes on Metempsychosis'; Marcovich, 'Pythagoras as Cock'.
2. Freud, 'Dissolution of the Oedipus Complex', p. 177.
3. Freud, *Jokes and Their Relation to the Unconscious*, pp. 90–116.
4. Creaser (ed.), *Volpone, or, The Fox*, p. 219.
5. See Creaser (ed.), *Volpone, or, The Fox*, p. 219; Parker (ed.), *Volpone, or The Fox*, p. 108; Kernan (ed.), *Ben Jonson: Volpone*, p. 45.
6. Nardo, 'Transmigration of Folly', p. 106.
7. Nardo, 'Transmigration of Folly', p. 109.
8. Nardo, 'Transmigration of Folly', p. 108.
9. Sontag, 'Notes on Camp', p. 280.
10. Sontag, 'Notes on Camp', p. 275.
11. Sontag, 'Notes on Camp', p. 275.
12. Sontag, 'Notes on Camp', p. 279.
13. Sontag, 'Notes on Camp', p. 292.
14. Sontag, 'Notes on Camp', p. 280.
15. *The Producers*, directed by Mel Brooks.
16. Baudelaire, 'On the Essence of Laughter', p. 149.
17. Yeats, 'Tragic Theatre', p. 241.
18. Meredith, 'Essay on Comedy', p. 14. On Meredith, see Meredith, *The Egoist*.
19. Meredith, 'Essay on Comedy', p. 17.
20. Bergson, *Laughter*, p. 9.
21. Bergson, *Laughter*, pp. 15, 32.
22. Freud, *Jokes and Their Relation to the Unconscious*, p. 97. See also Freud, 'Humour'. On analysis of 'Humour', see Critchley, 'Comedy and Finitude'. On the use of Bergson and Freud in the discussion of comedy, see Douglas, 'Social Control of Cognition'; Weber, 'Laughing in the Meanwhile'.

23. Freud, *Jokes and Their Relation to the Unconscious*, p. 98.
24. Freud, *Jokes and Their Relation to the Unconscious*, p. 98.
25. Bakhtin, *Rabelais and His World*, pp. 306, 307.
26. Bakhtin, *Rabelais and His World*, pp. 306, 307.
27. Bakhtin, *Rabelais and His World*, p. 308.
28. Bakhtin, *Rabelais and His World*, p. 312.
29. Bataille, 'Laughter', p. 61. For a discussion of Bataille's theory on laughter, see Parvulescu, *Laughter*.
30. *To Be or Not to Be*, directed by Ernst Lubitsch.
31. *Blazing Saddles*, directed by Mel Brooks.
32. *Young Frankenstein*, directed by Mel Brooks.
33. *Duck Soup*, directed by Leo McCarey.
34. Lacan, *Ethics of Psychoanalysis*, pp. 66–7.
35. Critchley, 'Comedy and Finitude', pp. 232–3.
36. *Dr. Strangelove or: How I Learned to Stop Worrying and Love the Bomb*, directed by Stanley Kubrick.
37. *M*A*S*H*, directed by Robert Altman.
38. *Life of Brian*, directed by Terry Jones.
39. Maguire and Smith, '"Time's comic sparks"', pp. 187–8.
40. All the quotations of Middleton are from Middleton, *Thomas Middleton*.
41. Michelle O'Callaghan writes that 'The "Trick", as *The Slip* foregrounds, is part of the structure of the traditional comic plot. It is a device that characterises the New Comedy plot in which a trick must be devised by the protagonist in order to overcome the patriarchal blocking figure.' See O'Callaghan, *Thomas Middleton*, p. 36.
42. In *Every Man in His Humour*, Brainworm says, 'Let the world think me a bad counterfeit if I cannot give him the slip at an instant' (II.v.134–5).
43. Or, as Biron says in *Love's Labour's Lost*, 'A lover's ear will hear the lowest sound / When the suspicious head of theft is stopped' (IV.iii.309–10).
44. Daileader, *Eroticism on the Renaissance Stage*, p. 32.
45. On this subject, see Cathcart, *Marston, Rivalry, Rapprochement, and Jonson*.
46. Adamson et al., 'Middleton and "Modern Use"', p. 204.
47. Paster, 'Ecology of the Passions', p. 154.
48. Different from Allwit, Ford, in *The Merry Wives of Windsor*, refuses to be a wittol. In Act II scene ii, he first says, 'But "cuckold", "wittol"! "Cuckold" – the devil himself hath not such a name' (II.ii.262–4). And at the end of his speech, as if he is substituting 'cuckold' for 'wittol', he says 'God's my life: cuckold, cuckold, cuckold!' (II.ii.274).
49. Middleton, *Thomas Middleton*, p. 951.
50. Middleton, *Five Plays*, p. 228.
51. Lacan, *Ethics of Psychoanalysis*, pp. 224–5.
52. Lacan, *Ethics of Psychoanalysis*, p. 225.
53. *Life of Brian*, directed by Terry Jones.
54. Žižek, *How to Read Lacan*, p. 33.
55. Knights, *Explorations*, p. 102.
56. Knights, *Explorations*, p. 102.
57. Knights, *Explorations*, p. 102.

Bibliography

Adamson, Sylvia (with Hannah Kirby, Laurence Peacock and Elizabeth Pearl), 'Middleton and "Modern Use": Case Studies in the Language of *A Chaste Maid in Cheapside*', in Suzanne Gossett (ed.), *Thomas Middleton in Context* (Cambridge: Cambridge University Press, 2011), pp. 197–210.

Adelman, Janet, *Blood Relations: Christian and Jew in The Merchant of Venice* (Chicago: University of Chicago Press, 2008).

Adorno, Theodor, 'Commitment', in Theodor Adorno, Walter Benjamin, Ernst Bloch, Bertolt Brecht and Georg Lukács, *Aesthetics and Politics* (New York: Verso, 2007), pp. 177–95.

Almansi, Guido, *The Writer as Liar: Narrative Technique in the Decameron* (London: Routledge & Kegan Paul, 1975).

Arnott, Geoffrey W., 'Studies in Comedy, I: Alexis and the Parasite's Name', *Greek, Roman and Byzantine Studies* 9:2 (Summer 1968), pp. 161–8.

Bacon, Francis, 'Essay XLIV – Of Deformity' (c. 1625), in *Essays* (London: Dent 1972), pp. 131–2.

Bakhtin, Mikhail, *Rabelais and His World*, trans. Hélène Iswolsky (Cambridge, MA: MIT Press, 1968).

Barber, C. L., 'Testing Courtesy and Humanity in *Twelfth Night*', in *Shakespeare's Festive Comedy: A Study of Dramatic Form and Its Relation to Social Custom* (Princeton: Princeton University Press, 1959), pp. 240–61.

Barbour, Richmond, '"When I acted young Antinous": Boy Actors and the Erotics of Jonsonian Theater', *PMLA* 110:4–6 (1995), pp. 1006–22.

Barish, Jonas A., 'The Double Plot in *Volpone*', in Jonas A. Barish (ed.), *Jonson: Volpone: A Casebook* (London: Macmillan, 1972), pp. 100–17.

— (ed.), *Jonson: Volpone: A Casebook* (London: Macmillan, 1972).

Barton, Anne, *Ben Jonson, Dramatist* (Cambridge: Cambridge University Press, 1984).

Bataille, Georges, 'Laughter', in Fred Botting and Scott Wilson (eds), *The Bataille Reader* (Oxford: Blackwell, 1997), pp. 59–63.

Baudelaire, Charles, 'On the Essence of Laughter', in Jonathan Mayne (trans. and ed.), *The Painter of Modern Life and Other Essays* (London: Phaidon Press, 1964), pp. 147–65.

Belsey, Catherine, 'Disrupting Sexual Difference: Meaning and Gender in the Comedies', in John Drakakis (ed.), *Alternative Shakespeares* (London: Methuen, 1985), pp. 166–90.

Benjamin, Walter, 'Theses on the Philosophy of History', in Hannah Arendt (ed.), *Illuminations*, trans. Harry Zohn (New York: Schocken Books, 1969), pp. 253–64.

—, *The Origin of German Tragic Drama*, trans. John Osborne (London: Verso, 1998).

Berger, Thomas L., William C. Bradford and Sidney L. Sondergard, *An Index of Characters in Early Modern English Drama Printed Plays, 1500–1660* (Cambridge: Cambridge University Press, 1998).

Bergson, Henri, *Laughter: An Essay on the Meaning of the Comic*, trans. Cloudesley Brereton and Fred Rothwell (Los Angeles: Green Integer, 1999).

Blamires, Alcuin, *Chaucer, Ethics, and Gender* (Oxford: Oxford University Press, 2006).

Blazing Saddles, film, directed by Mel Brooks. USA: Crossbow Productions, 1974. DVD, USA: Warner Home Video, 2006.

Bloch, Howard, *The Scandal of the Fabliaux* (Chicago: University of Chicago Press, 1986).

Boccaccio, Giovanni, *The Decameron*, trans. G. H. McWilliam (London: Penguin Books, 1995).

Boehrer, Bruce Thomas, *The Fury of Men's Gullets: Ben Jonson and the Digestive Canal* (Philadelphia: University of Pennsylvania Press, 1997).

—, 'New Directions: *The Alchemist* and the Lower Bodily Stratum', in Erin Julian and Helen Ostovich (eds), *The Alchemist: A Critical Reader* (London: Arden Shakespeare, 2013), pp. 150–70.

Bosman, Anston, '"Best play with Mardian": Eunuch and Blackamoor as Imperial Culturegram', *Shakespeare Studies* (2006), pp. 123–57.

Bowers, Rick, *Radical Comedy in Early Modern England: Contexts, Cultures, Performances* (Burlington, VT: Ashgate, 2008).

Brady, Jennifer and W. H. Herendeen (eds), *Ben Jonson's 1616 Folio* (Newark: University of Delaware Press, 1991).

Bray, Alan, *Homosexuality in Renaissance England* (London: Gay Men's Press, 1988).

Brisson, Luc, *Sexual Ambivalence: Androgyny and Hermaphroditism in Graeco-Roman Antiquity*, trans. Janet Lloyd (Berkeley: University of California Press, 2002).

Brown, Steve, 'The Boyhood of Shakespeare's Heroines: Notes on Gender Ambiguity in the Sixteenth Century', *Studies in English Literature, 1500–1900* 30:2, Elizabethan and Jacobean Drama (Spring 1990), pp. 243–63.

Bullets Over Broadway, film, directed by Woody Allen. USA: Miramax, 1994. DVD, USA: Miramax, 1999.

Burnett, Mark Thornton, *Constructing 'Monsters' in Shakespearean Drama and Early Modern Culture* (New York: Palgrave, 2002).

Burton, Jonathan, 'English Anxiety and the Muslim Power of Conversion: Five Perspectives on "Turning Turk" in Early Modern Texts', *JEMCS* 2:1 (Spring/Summer 2002), pp. 35–67.

Carr, Carol A., 'Volpone and Mosca: Two Styles of Roguery', *College Literature* 8:2 (Spring 1981), pp. 144–57.

Cathcart, Charles, *Marston, Rivalry, Rapprochement, and Jonson* (Aldershot: Ashgate, 2008).

Cave, Richard Allen, *Ben Jonson* (Basingstoke: Macmillan Education, 1991).

Cave, Richard Allen, Elizabeth Shafer and Brian Woolland (eds), *Ben Jonson and Theatre: Performance, Practice and Theory* (London: Routledge, 1999).

Chaucer, Geoffrey, *The Riverside Chaucer*, gen. ed. Larry D. Benson (Boston: Houghton Mifflin, 1987).

Coronato, Rocco, *Jonson versus Bakhtin: Carnival and the Grotesque* (Amsterdam: Rodopi, 2003).

Cousins, A. D. and Alison V. Scott (eds), *Ben Jonson and the Politics of Genre* (Cambridge: Cambridge University Press, 2009).

Cox, Catherine, *Gender and Language in Chaucer* (Gainesville: University Press of Florida, 1997).

Critchley, Simon, 'Comedy and Finitude: Displacing the Tragic-Heroic Paradigm in Philosophy and Psychoanalysis', in *Ethics, Politics, Subjectivity: Essays on Derrida, Levinas and Contemporary French Thought* (New York: Verso, 1999), pp. 217–38.

Daileader, Celia R., *Eroticism on the Renaissance Stage: Transcendence, Desire, and the Limits of the Visible* (Cambridge: Cambridge University Press, 1998).

Danby, John F., *Shakespeare's Doctrine of Nature* (London: Faber, 1961).

Danson, Lawrence, *The Harmonies of The Merchant of Venice* (New Haven: Yale University Press, 1978).

Davis, Lennard J. (ed.), 'Constructing Normalcy', in *The Disability Studies Reader* (New York: Routledge, 2010), pp. 3–19.

Davis, Norman, *A Chaucer Glossary* (Oxford: Clarendon Press, 1979).

De Man, Paul, 'Autobiography as De-facement', *MLN* 94:5, Comparative Literature (1979), pp. 919–30.

Derrida, Jacques, 'Structure, Sign and Play in the Discourse of the Human Sciences', in *Writing and Difference*, trans. Alan Bass (London: Routledge Classics, 2001), pp. 351–70.

DiGangi, Mario, 'Asses and Wits: The Homoerotics of Mastery in Satiric Comedy', *English Literary Renaissance* 25 (1995), pp. 179–208.

Dinshaw, Carolyn, *Chaucer's Sexual Poetics* (Madison: University of Wisconsin Press, 1989).

Dolar, Mladen, 'To Be or Not to Be? No, Thank You', in Ivana Novak, Jela Krečič and Mladen Dolar (eds), *Lubitsch Can't Wait: A Theoretical Examination* (Ljubljana: Slovenian Cinematheque, 2014), pp. 111–31.

Dollimore, Jonathan, *Sexual Dissidence: Augustine to Wilde, Freud to Foucault* (Oxford: Clarendon Press, 1991).

Donaldson, Ian, *The World Upside Down: Comedy from Jonson to Fielding* (Oxford: Clarendon Press, 1970).

—, 'Volpone: Quick and Dead', *Essays in Criticism* 21 (1971), pp. 121–34.

—, *Jonson's Magic Houses: Essays in Interpretation* (Oxford: Clarendon Press, 1997).

—, 'Unknown Ends: *Volpone*', in *Jonson's Magic Houses: Essays in Interpretation* (Oxford: Clarendon Press, 1997), pp. 106–24.

Douglas, Mary, 'The Social Control of Cognition: Some Factors in Joke Perception', *Man*, New Series 3:3 (September 1968), pp. 361–76.

Dr. Strangelove or: How I Learned to Stop Worrying and Love the Bomb, film, directed by Stanley Kubrick. USA: Columbia Pictures, 1964. DVD, USA: Sony Pictures Home Entertainment, 2002.

Duck Soup, film, directed by Leo McCarey. USA: Paramount Pictures, 1933. DVD, USA: Universal Studios Home Entertainment, 2011.

Dutton, Richard, *Ben Jonson: To the First Folio* (Cambridge: Cambridge University Press, 1983).

— (ed.), *Ben Jonson* (Harlow: Longman, 2000).

—, *Ben Jonson, Volpone and the Gunpowder Plot* (Cambridge: Cambridge University Press, 2008).

Easterling, Heather C., *Parsing the City: Jonson, Middleton, Dekker, and City Comedy's London as Language* (New York: Routledge, 2006).

Eggert, Katherine, 'The Alchemist and Science', in Garrett A. Sullivan, Jr., Patrick Cheney and Andrew Hadfield (eds), *Early Modern English Drama: A Critical Companion* (New York: Oxford University Press, 2006), pp. 200–12.

Eliot, T. S., 'Ben Jonson', in *The Sacred Wood: Essays on Poetry and Criticism* (London: Methuen, 1960), pp. 104–22.

Empson, William, *Seven Types of Ambiguity* (New York: New Directions, 1947).

Fiedler, Leslie, *Freaks: Myths and Images of the Secret Self* (New York: Anchor Books, 1993).

Findlay, Alison, *Illegitimate Power: Bastards in Renaissance Drama* (Manchester: Manchester University Press, 1994).

Fineman, Joel, 'Fratricide and Cuckoldry: Shakespeare's Doubles', in Murray M. Schwartz and Coppélia Kahn (eds), *Representing Shakespeare: New Psychoanalytic Essays* (Baltimore: Johns Hopkins University Press, 1980), pp. 70–109.

Fizdale, Tay, 'Jonson's Volpone and the "Real" Antinous', *Renaissance Quarterly* 26:4 (Winter 1973), pp. 454–9.

Flaig, Paul, 'Lacan's Harpo', *Cinema Journal* 50:4 (Summer 2011), pp. 98–116.

Fortin, Rene E., 'Launcelot and the Uses of Allegory in *The Merchant of Venice*', *Studies in English Literature, 1500–1900* 14:2, Elizabethan and Jacobean Drama (Spring 1974), pp. 259–70.

Foucault, Michel, *Madness and Civilization: A History of Insanity in the Age of Reason*, trans. Richard Howard (London: Tavistock, 1967).

—, *The History of Sexuality: I*, trans. Robert Hurley (London: Penguin Books, 1978).

—, *The Order of Things: An Archaeology of the Human Sciences* (New York: Vintage Books, 1994).

France, Peter (ed.), *The New Oxford Companion to Literature in French* (Oxford: Clarendon Press, 1995).

Freud, Sigmund, *Jokes and Their Relation to the Unconscious* (1905), *The Standard Edition of the Complete Psychological Works of Sigmund Freud*, vol. 8, trans. James Strachey, Anna Freud, Alix Strachey and Alan Tyson (London: Hogarth Press, 1953–74).

—, 'On Narcissism: An Introduction' (1914), in *The Standard Edition of the Complete Psychological Works of Sigmund Freud*, vol. 14, trans. James Strachey, Anna Freud, Alix Strachey and Alan Tyson (London: Hogarth Press, 1953–74), pp. 67–102.

—, 'Some Character-Types Met with in Psycho-analytic Work' (1916), in *The Standard Edition of the Complete Psychological Works of Sigmund Freud*, vol. 14, trans. James Strachey, Anna Freud, Alix Strachey and Alan Tyson (London: Hogarth Press, 1953–74), pp. 309–36.

—, 'The Uncanny' (1919), in *The Standard Edition of the Complete Psychological Works of Sigmund Freud*, vol. 17, trans. James Strachey, Anna Freud, Alix Strachey and Alan Tyson (London: Hogarth Press, 1953–74), pp. 217–56.

—, 'Beyond the Pleasure Principle' (1920), in *The Standard Edition of the Complete Psychological Works of Sigmund Freud*, vol. 18, trans. James Strachey, Anna Freud, Alix Strachey and Alan Tyson (London: Hogarth Press, 1953–74), pp. 7–64.

—, 'Medusa's Head' ([1922] 1940), in *The Standard Edition of the Complete Psychological Works of Sigmund Freud*, vol. 18, trans. James Strachey, Anna Freud, Alix Strachey and Alan Tyson (London: Hogarth Press, 1953–74), pp. 273–374.

—, 'The Dissolution of the Oedipus Complex' (1924), in *The Standard Edition of the Complete Psychological Works of Sigmund Freud*, vol. 19, trans. James Strachey, Anna Freud, Alix Strachey and Alan Tyson (London: Hogarth Press, 1953–74), pp. 173–9.

—, 'Fetishism' (1927), in *The Standard Edition of the Complete Psychological Works of Sigmund Freud*, vol. 21, trans. James Strachey, Anna Freud, Alix Strachey and Alan Tyson (London: Hogarth Press, 1953–74), pp. 152–7.

—, 'Humour' (1927), in *The Standard Edition of the Complete Psychological Works of Sigmund Freud*, vol. 21, trans. James Strachey, Anna Freud, Alix Strachey and Alan Tyson (London: Hogarth Press, 1953–74), pp. 159–66.

Fuchs, Barbara, 'Faithless Empires: Pirates, Renegadoes, and the English Nation', *ELH* 67:1 (Spring 2000), pp. 45–69.

Fudge, Erica, Ruth Gilbert and Susan Wiseman (eds), *At the Borders of the Human: Beasts, Bodies and Natural Philosophy in the Early Modern Period* (Basingstoke: Macmillan, 1999).

Garber, Marjorie, 'Descanting on Deformity: Richard III and the Shape of History', in *Shakespeare's Ghost Writers: Literature as Uncanny Causality* (New York: Methuen, 1987), pp. 28–51.

—, *Vested Interests: Cross-Dressing & Cultural Anxiety* (New York: Routledge, 1992).

—, *Vice Versa: Bisexuality and the Eroticism of Everyday Life* (New York: Simon & Schuster, 1995).

Garland, Robert, 'Disfigurement World', *History Today* 42:11 (1992), pp. 38–44.

Gherovici, Patricia, *Please Select Your Gender: From the Invention of Hysteria to the Democratizing of Transgenderism* (New York: Routledge, 2010).

Ghose, Indira, 'Licence to Laugh: Festive Laughter in *Twelfth Night*', in Manfred Pfister (ed.), *A History of English Laughter: Laughter from Beowulf to Beckett and Beyond* (Amsterdam: Rodopi, 2002), pp. 35–46.

Gibbons, Brian, *Jacobean City Comedy: A Study of Satiric Plays by Jonson, Marston, and Middleton* (Cambridge, MA: Harvard University Press, 1968).

Goldberg, Jonathan, *Sodometries: Renaissance Texts, Modern Sexualities* (Stanford: Stanford University Press, 1992).

Greenblatt, Stephen, 'The False Ending in *Volpone*', *Journal of English and Germanic Philology* 75 (1976), pp. 90–104.

—, 'Fiction and Friction', in Thomas C. Heller, Morton Sosna and David

E. Wellbery with Arnold I. Davidson, Ann Swidler and Ian Watt (eds), *Reconstructing Individualism: Autonomy, Individuality, and the Self in Western Thought* (Stanford: Stanford University Press, 1986), pp. 30–52.

—, *Shakespearean Negotiations: The Circulation of Social Energy in Renaissance England* (Berkeley: University of California Press, 1988).

Greiner, Norbert, 'Scenic Laughter in Ben Jonson's Plays', in Bernhard Reitz and Sigrid Rieuwerts (eds), *Anglistentag 1999 Mainz: Proceedings* (Postfach: Wissenschaftlicher Verlag Trier, 2000), pp. 161–70.

Halperin, David, 'Why Is Diotima a Woman?', in *One Hundred Years of Homosexuality: And Other Essays on Greek Love* (New York: Routledge, 1990), pp. 113–52.

Happé, Peter, 'The Vice and the Folk-Drama', *Folklore* 75 (1964), pp. 161–93.

—, 'The Vice: A Checklist and an Annotated Bibliography', *Research Opportunities in Renaissance Drama* 22 (1979), pp. 17–35.

—, '"The Vice" and Popular Theatre', in Antony Coleman and Antony Hammond (eds), *Poetry and Drama, 1570–1700: Essays in Honour of Harold F. Brooks* (London: Methuen, 1981), pp. 13–31.

—, 'Theatricality in Devils, Sinnekins, and the *Vice*', *Cahiers élisabéthains* 53 (Spring 1998), pp. 1–12.

Harris, Jonathan Gil, '"I am sailing to my port, uh! uh! uh! uh!": The Pathologies of Transmigration in *Volpone*', *Literature and Medicine* 20:2 (Fall 2001), pp. 109–32.

Hawkins, Harriet, 'Folly, Incurable Disease, and *Volpone*', *Studies in English Literature, 1500–1900* 8:2, Elizabethan and Jacobean Drama (Spring 1968), pp. 335–48.

Haynes, Jonathan, 'Representing the Underworld: *The Alchemist*', *Studies in Philology* 86:1 (Winter 1989), pp. 18–41.

Hennessey, Oliver, 'Jonson's Joyless Economy: Theorizing Motivation and Pleasure in *Volpone*', *English Literary Renaissance* 38:1 (2008), pp. 83–105.

Hinchliffe, Arnold P., *'Volpone': Text and Performance* (London: Macmillan, 1985).

Hockey, Dorothy C., 'The Patch Is Kind Enough', *Shakespeare Quarterly* 10:3 (Summer 1959), pp. 448–50.

Homer, *The Odyssey*, trans. A. T. Murray, rev. George E. Dimock (Cambridge, MA: Harvard University Press, 1998).

Howard, Jean E., 'Crossdressing, the Theatre, and Gender Struggle in Early Modern England', *Shakespeare Quarterly* 39:4 (Winter 1988), pp. 418–40.

Hui, Isaac, '"To what base uses we may return, Horatio!" – *Hamlet*, Comedy and Class Struggle', *Comedy Studies* 4:2 (September 2013), pp. 155–65.

Hutson, Lorna, 'Liking Men: Ben Jonson's Closet Opened', *ELH* 71 (2004), pp. 1065–96.

Jackson, Gabriele Bernhard, 'The Protesting Imagination' (1969), in R. V. Holdsworth (ed.), *Jonson: Every Man in His Humour and The Alchemist, a Casebook* (London: Macmillan Press, 1978) , pp. 92–113.

Jensen, Ejner J., *Ben Jonson's Comedies on the Modern Stage* (Ann Arbor: UMI Research Press, 1985).

Johnston, Mark Albert, 'Prosthetic Absence in Ben Jonson's *Epicoene, The Alchemist*, and *Bartholomew Fair*', *English Literary Renaissance* 37:3 (2007), pp. 401–28.

Jones, Robert, *Engagement with Knavery: Point of View in 'Richard III', 'The Jew of Malta', 'Volpone' and 'The Revenger's Tragedy'* (Durham, NC: Duke University Press, 1986).

—, 'Volpone: The Chimera of Fox and Fool', in *Engagement with Knavery: Point of View in 'Richard III', 'The Jew of Malta', 'Volpone' and 'The Revenger's Tragedy'* (Durham, NC: Duke University Press, 1986), pp. 99–121.

Jonson, Ben, *Ben Jonson*, 11 vols, ed. C. H. Herford and Percy Simpson (Oxford: Clarendon Press, 1925–52).

—, *Ben Jonson: Volpone*, ed. Alvin B. Kernan (London: Yale University Press, 1962).

—, *Volpone, or, The Fox*, ed. John W. Creaser (London: Hodder and Stoughton, 1978).

—, *Epicoene, or, The Silent Woman*, ed. Roger Holdsworth (London: Ernest Benn, 1979).

—, *Volpone, or The Fox*, ed. Brian Parker (Manchester: Manchester University Press, 1983).

—, *The Cambridge Edition of the Works of Ben Jonson*, 7 vols, gen. eds David Bevington, Martin Butler and Ian Donaldson (Cambridge: Cambridge University Press, 2012).

Julian, Erin and Helen Ostovich (eds), *The Alchemist: A Critical Reader* (London: Arden Shakespeare, 2013).

Kahn, Coppélia, 'The Providential Tempest and the Shakespearean Family', in Murray M. Schwartz and Coppélia Kahn (eds), *Representing Shakespeare: New Psychoanalytic Essays* (Baltimore: Johns Hopkins University Press, 1980), pp. 217–43.

Kay, W. David, '*Epicoene*, Lady Compton, and the Gendering of Jonsonian Satire on Extravagance', *Ben Jonson Journal: Literary Contexts in the Age of Elizabeth, James and Charles* 6 (1999), pp. 1–33.

Kimbrough, Robert, 'Androgyny Seen through Shakespeare's Disguise', *Shakespeare Quarterly* 33:1 (Spring 1982), pp. 17–33.

Knights, L. C., *Drama and Society in the Age of Jonson* (London: Chatto & Windus, 1937).

—, 'Jonson and the Anti-Acquisitive Attitude', in *Drama and Society in the Age of Jonson* (London: Chatto & Windus, 1937), pp. 200–27.

—, *Explorations: Essays in Criticism, Mainly on the Literature of the Seventeenth Century* (Harmondsworth: Penguin Books, 1964).

Knowles, Ronald (ed.), *Shakespeare and Carnival: After Bakhtin* (New York: St. Martin's Press, 1998).

Krell, David Farrell, *The Purest of Bastards: Works of Mourning, Art, and Affirmation in the Thought of Jacques Derrida* (University Park: Pennsylvania State University Press, 2000).

Kristeva, Julia, 'Manic Eros, Sublime Eros: On Male Sexuality', in *Tales of Love*, trans. Leon S. Roudiez (New York: Columbia University Press, 1987), pp. 59–82.

Kruger, Steven, 'Claiming the Pardoner: Toward a Gay Reading of Chaucer's Pardoner's Tale', *Exemplaria* 6:1 (1994), pp. 115–39.

Lacan, Jacques, *The Four Fundamental Concepts of Psychoanalysis*, ed. Jacques-Alain Miller, trans. Alain Sheridan (New York: Norton, 1981).

—, 'Desire and the Interpretation of Desire in *Hamlet*', in Shoshana Felman (ed.), *Literature and Psychoanalysis: The Question of Reading: Otherwise* (Baltimore: Johns Hopkins University Press, 1982), pp. 11–52.

—, *The Ethics of Psychoanalysis, 1959–1960*, trans. Dennis Porter (London: Routledge, 1992).

—, *On Feminine Sexuality: The Limits of Love and Knowledge*, trans. Bruce Fink (London: W. W. Norton, 1998).

—, *Écrits: The First Complete Edition in English*, trans. Bruce Fink with Héloïse Fink and Russell Grigg (New York: W. W. Norton, 2006).

—, 'The Function and Field of Speech and Language in Psychoanalysis', in *Écrits: The First Complete Edition in English*, trans. Bruce Fink with Héloïse Fink and Russell Grigg (New York: W. W. Norton, 2006), pp. 197–268.

—, 'Mirror Stage as Formative of the *I* Function as Revealed in Psychoanalytic Experience', in *Écrits: The First Complete Edition in English*, trans. Bruce Fink with Héloïse Fink and Russell Grigg (New York: W. W. Norton, 2006), pp. 75–81.

Laqueur, Thomas, *Making Sex: Body and Gender from the Greeks to Freud* (Cambridge, MA: Harvard University Press, 1990).

Leggatt, Alexander, *Citizen Comedy in the Age of Shakespeare* (Toronto: University of Toronto Press, 1973).

Leicester, Marshall, Jr., *The Disenchanted Self: Representing the Subject in the Canterbury Tales* (Berkeley: University of California Press, 1990).

Levin, Harry, *The Myth of the Golden Age in the Renaissance* (London: Faber, 1970).

—, 'Jonson's Metempsychosis' (1943), in Jonas A. Barish (ed.), *Jonson: Volpone: A Casebook* (London: Macmillan, 1972), pp. 88–99.

Levin, Kate, 'Unmasquing *Epicoene*: Jonson's Dramaturgy for the Commercial Theater and Court', in James Hirsh (ed.), *New Perspectives on Ben Jonson* (Madison, NJ: Fairleigh Dickinson University Press, 1997), pp. 128–53.

Life of Brian, film, directed by Terry Jones. UK: HandMade Films, 1979. DVD, USA: Criterion Collection, 1999.

Loxley, James and Mark Robson, *Shakespeare, Jonson, and the Claims of the Performative* (London: Routledge, 2013).

Lucian, *Lucian*, 8 vols, trans. A. M. Harmon (Cambridge, MA: Harvard University Press, 1913–67).

McAdam, Ian and Julie Sanders, 'New Directions: Staging Gender', in Erin Julian and Helen Ostovich (eds), *The Alchemist: A Critical Reader* (London: Arden Shakespeare, 2013), pp. 127–49.

McAlpine, Monica, 'The Pardoner's Homosexuality and How It Matters', *PMLA* 95.1 (January 1980), pp. 8–22.

McCanles, Michael, 'Festival in Jonsonian Comedy', *Renaissance Drama* 8 (1977), pp. 203–19.

McPherson, David C., *Shakespeare, Jonson, and the Myth of Venice* (Plainsboro, NJ: Associated University Presses, 1990).

Maguire, Laurie and Emma Smith, '"Time's comic sparks": The Dramaturgy of *A Mad World, My Masters* and *Timon of Athens*', in Gary Taylor and Trish Thomas Henley (eds), *The Oxford Handbook of Thomas Middleton* (New York: Oxford University Press, 2012), pp. 181–95.

Mahood, M. M., *Shakespeare's Wordplay* (London: Routledge, 2001).

Malieckal, Bindu, '"Wanton irreligious madness": Conversion and Castration in Massinger's *The Renegado*', *Essays in Arts in Sciences* 31 (October 2002), pp. 25–43.

Mann, Jill, *Chaucer and Medieval Estate Satire: The Literature of Social Classes and the General Prologue to the Canterbury Tales* (Cambridge: Cambridge University Press, 1973).

Marchitell, Howard, 'Desire and Domination in *Volpone*', *Studies in English Literature, 1500–1900* 31:2, Elizabethan and Jacobean Drama (Spring 1991), pp. 287–308.

Marcovich, Miroslav, 'Pythagoras as Cock', *The American Journal of Philology* 97:4 (Winter 1976), pp. 331–5.

Mardock, James D., *Our Scene Is London: Ben Jonson's City and the Space of the Author* (New York: Routledge, 2008).

Martin, Mathew R., *Between Theater and Philosophy: Skepticism in the Major City Comedies of Ben Jonson and Thomas Middleton* (London: Associated University Presses, 2001).

M*A*S*H, film, directed by Robert Altman. USA: Aspen Productions, 1970. DVD, USA: Twentieth Century Fox, 2003.

Masi, Michael, *Chaucer and Gender* (New York: Lang, 2005).

Massinger, Philip, *The Renegado, or, The Gentleman of Venice*, ed. Michael Neill (London: Arden Shakespeare, 2010).

Meredith, George, 'An Essay on Comedy', in *Essay on Comedy* (New York: Doubleday Anchor, 1956), pp. 3–57.

—, *The Egoist: An Annotated Text, Backgrounds, Criticism*, ed. Robert M. Adams (New York: W. W. Norton, 1979).

Meskill, Lynn S., 'Jonson and the Alchemical Economy of Desire: Creation, Defacement and Castration in *The Alchemist*', *Cahiers élisabéthains* 62:1 (October 2002), pp. 47–63.

—, *Ben Jonson and Envy* (Cambridge: Cambridge University Press, 2009).

Middleton, Thomas, *Five Plays*, ed. Bryan Loughrey and Neil Taylor (Harmondsworth: Penguin Books, 1988).

—, *Thomas Middleton: The Collected Works*, ed. Gary Taylor and John Lavagnino (Oxford: Clarendon Press, 2007).

Montaigne, Michel de, 'Of the Lame or Crippel', in *The Essayes of Michael, Lord of Montaigne*, Vol. III, Ch. XI, trans. John Florio (London: J. M. Dent & Sons Ltd, 1921–23), pp. 277–89.

Nardo, A. K., 'The Transmigration of Folly: Volpone's Innocent Grotesques', *English Studies: A Journal of English Language and Literature* 58 (1977), pp. 105–9.

Neely, Carol Thomas, *Distracted Subjects: Madness and Gender in Shakespeare and Early Modern Culture* (Ithaca: Cornell University Press, 2004).

Neill, Michael, '"In everything illegitimate": Imagining the Bastard in English Renaissance Drama', in *Putting History to the Question: Power, Politics, and Society in English Renaissance Drama* (New York: Columbia University Press, 2000), pp. 127–48.

Noyes, R. G., *Ben Jonson on the English Stage, 1660–1776* (New York: Blom, 1966).

O'Callaghan, Michelle, *Thomas Middleton, Renaissance Dramatist* (Edinburgh: Edinburgh University Press, 2009).

O'Connor, John J., 'Physical Deformity and Chivalric Laughter in Renaissance England', *New York Literary Forum* 1 (1978), pp. 59–71.

Orton, Joe, *The Complete Plays of Joe Orton* (London: Methuen Drama, 1976).

Ovid, *Ovid's Metamorphoses: The Arthur Golding Translation, 1567*, ed. John Frederick Nims (New York: Macmillan, 1965).

—, *Metamorphoses, Volume I: Books 1–8*, trans. Frank Justus Miller, rev. G. P. Gould, 3rd edn (Cambridge, MA: Harvard University Press, 1977).

—, *Metamorphoses*, trans. A. D. Melville (Oxford: Oxford University Press, 1986).

Oxford English Dictionary (OED) Online, Oxford: Oxford University Press, <http://www.oed.com/> (last accessed 19 October 2017).

Partridge, Edward B., 'The Allusiveness of *Epicoene*', *Journal of English Literary History* 22 (1955), pp. 93–107.

Partridge, Eric, *Shakespeare's Bawdy: A Literary & Psychological Essay and a Comprehensive Glossary* (London: Routledge & Kegan Paul, 1968).

Parvulescu, Anca, *Laughter: Notes on a Passion* (Cambridge, MA: MIT Press, 2010).

Paster, Gail Kern, '*Bartholomew Fair* and the Humoral Body', in Garrett A. Sullivan, Jr., Patrick Cheney and Andrew Hadfield (eds), *Early Modern English Drama: A Critical Companion* (New York: Oxford University Press, 2006), pp. 260–71.

—, 'The Ecology of the Passions in *A Chaste Maid in Cheapside* and *The Changeling*', in Gary Taylor and Trish Thomas Henley (eds), *The Oxford Handbook of Thomas Middleton* (New York: Oxford University Press, 2012), pp. 148–63.

Peacock, Alan J., 'Ben Jonson, Celia, and Ovid', *Notes and Queries* (September 1986), pp. 381–4.

Pequigney, Joseph, 'The Two Antonios and Same-Sex Love in *Twelfth Night* and *The Merchant of Venice*', *English Literary Renaissance* 22:2 (Spring 1992), pp. 201–21.

Plato, *Lysis; Symposium; Gorgias*, trans. W. R. M. Lamb (Cambridge, MA: Harvard University Press, 2001).

Potter, Lois, '"How quick was a quick change?": *The Alchemist* and Blackfriars Staging', in Peter Kanelos and Matt Kozusko (eds), *Thunder at a Playhouse: Essays on Shakespeare and the Early Modern Stage* (Selinsgrove: Susquahanna University Press, 2010), pp. 200–11.

Pushkin, Alexander, 'A Journey to Arzrum at the Time of the 1829 Campaign', in *Tales of Belkin and Other Prose Writings*, trans. Ronald Wilks (London: Penguin Books, 1998), pp. 129–79.

Rackin, Phyllis, 'Androgyny, Mimesis, and the Marriage of the Boy Heroine on the English Renaissance Stage', in Stephen Orgel and Sean Keilen (eds), *Shakespeare and Gender* (New York: Garland, 1999), pp. 53–66.

Richard III, film, directed by Laurence Olivier. UK: London Film Productions, 1955. DVD, USA: Criterion Collection, 2004.

Ross, Cheryl Lynn, 'The Plague of *The Alchemist*', in Richard Dutton (ed.), *Ben Jonson* (Harlow: Longman, 2000), pp. 149–66.

Rossiter, A. P., 'Angel with Horns: The Unity of Richard III', in Graham Storey (ed.), *Angel with Horns: Fifteen Lectures on Shakespeare* (London: Longman, 1989), pp. 1–22.

Said, Edward, *Orientalism* (London: Penguin Books, 1991).

Salingar, Leo, 'Crowd and Public in *Bartholomew Fair*', *Renaissance Drama* 10 (1979), pp. 141–60.

—, 'The Idea of Venice in Shakespeare and Ben Jonson', in *Shakespeare's Italy: Functions of Italian Locations in Renaissance Drama* (Manchester: Manchester University Press, 1993), pp. 171–84.

Sanders, Julie, *Ben Jonson in Context* (Cambridge: Cambridge University Press, 2010).

—, Kate Chedgzoy and Susan Wiseman (eds), *Refashioning Ben Jonson: Gender, Politics, and the Jonsonian Canon* (New York: St. Martin's Press, 1998).

Schwartz, Murray M. and Coppélia Kahn (eds), *Representing Shakespeare: New Psychoanalytic Essays* (Baltimore: Johns Hopkins University Press, 1980).

Shakespeare, William, *Twelfth Night*, ed. J. M. Lothian and T. W. Craik (London: Methuen, 1975).

—, *Othello, The Moor of Venice*, ed. Michael Neill (Oxford: Clarendon Press, 2006).

—, *The Norton Shakespeare*, ed. Stephen Greenblatt, Walter Cohen, Jean E. Howard and Katharine Eisaman Maus (New York: W. W. Norton, 2008).

Shapiro, Gary, *Archaeologies of Vision: Foucault and Nietzsche on Seeing and Saying* (Chicago: University of Chicago Press, 2003).

Shapiro, H. A., 'Notes on Greek Dwarfs', *American Journal of Archaeology* 88:3 (July 1984), pp. 391–2.

Shapiro, James, *Shakespeare and the Jews* (New York: Columbia University Press, 1996).

Siebers, Tobin, *Disability Theory* (Ann Arbor: University of Michigan Press, 2008).

—, *Disability Aesthetics* (Ann Arbor: University of Michigan Press, 2010).

Skutsch, O., 'Notes on Metempsychosis', *Classical Philology* 54:2 (April 1959), pp. 114–16.

Some Like It Hot, film, directed by Billy Wilder. USA: Ashton Productions, 1959. DVD, USA: Twentieth Century Fox, 2001.

Sontag, Susan 'Notes on Camp', in *Against Interpretation and Other Essays* (New York: Farrar, Straus and Giroux, 1967), pp. 275–92.

Spenser, Edmund, *The Faerie Queene*, ed. Thomas R. Roche, Jr. and C. Patrick O'Donnell, Jr. (London: Penguin Books, 1978).

Spivack, Bernard, *Shakespeare and the Allegory of Evil: The History of a Metaphor in Relation to His Major Villains* (New York: Columbia University Press, 1958).

Stallybrass, Peter and Allon White, *The Politics and Poetics of Transgression* (Ithaca: Cornell University Press, 1986).

Steggle, Matthew (ed.), *Volpone: A Critical Guide* (London: Continuum, 2011).

Sullivan, Garrett A., Jr., Patrick Cheney and Andrew Hadfield (eds), *Early Modern English Drama: A Critical Companion* (New York: Oxford University Press, 2006).

Tambling, Jeremy, '*Richard III*, Mourning and Memory', in *Allegory and the Work of Melancholy: The Late Medieval and Shakespeare* (New York: Rodopi, 2004), pp. 194–204.

Tanner, Tony, *Venice Desired* (Oxford: Blackwell, 1992).

Taylor, Gary, *Castration: An Abbreviated History of Western Manhood* (New York: Routledge, 2000).

— and Trish Thomas Henley (eds), *The Oxford Handbook of Thomas Middleton* (New York: Oxford University Press, 2012).

The Producers, film, directed by Mel Brooks. USA: Crossbow Productions, 1967. DVD, USA: MGM, 2003.

Tiffany, Grace, *Erotic Beasts and Social Monsters: Shakespeare, Jonson, and Comic Androgyny* (Newark: University of Delaware Press, 1995).

To Be or Not to Be, film, directed by Alan Johnson. USA: Brooksfilms, 1983. DVD, USA: Twentieth Century Fox, 2006.

To Be or Not to Be, film, directed by Ernst Lubitsch. USA: Romaine Film Corporation, 1942. DVD, USA: Criterion Collection, 2013.

Traub, Valerie, 'The Homoerotics of Shakespearean Comedy', in Kate Chedgzoy (ed.), *Shakespeare, Feminism and Gender* (New York: Palgrave, 2001), pp. 135–60.

Vandiver, E. P., Jr., 'The Elizabethan Dramatic Parasite', *Studies in Philology* 32:3 (July 1935), pp. 411–27.

Van Dyke, Joyce, 'The Game of Wits in *The Alchemist*', *Studies in English Literature, 1500–1900* 19:2, Elizabethan and Jacobean Drama (Spring 1979), pp. 253–69.

Vaught, Jennifer C., *Carnival and Literature in Early Modern England* (Burlington, VT: Ashgate, 2012).

Vitkus, Daniel, 'Turning Turk in *Othello*: The Conversion and Damnation of the Moor', *Shakespeare Quarterly* 48:2 (Summer 1997), pp. 145–76.

— (ed.), *Three Turk Plays from Early Modern England: Selimus, A Christian Turned Turk and The Renegado* (New York: Columbia University Press, 2000).

Weber, Samuel, 'Laughing in the Meanwhile', *MLN* 102:4, French Issue (September 1987), pp. 691–706.

—, *The Legend of Freud* (Stanford: Stanford University Press, 2000).

Weimann, Robert, *Shakespeare and the Popular Tradition in the Theatre: Studies in the Social Dimension of Dramatic Form and Function*, ed. Robert Schwartz (Baltimore: Johns Hopkins University Press, 1978).

Wells, Stanley, Gary Taylor, John Jowett and William Montgomery, *William Shakespeare: A Textual Companion* (Oxford: Clarendon Press, 1987).

Wells, Susan, 'Jacobean City Comedy and the Ideology of the City', *ELH* 48:1 (Spring 1981), pp. 37–60.

Welsford, Enid, *The Fool: His Social and Literary History* (Gloucester, MA: P. Smith, 1966).

Wilson, Edmund, 'Morose Ben Jonson', in Jonas Barish (ed.), *Ben Jonson: A Collection of Critical Essays* (Upper Saddle River, NJ: Prentice Hall, 1963), pp. 60–74.

Withington, Robert, '"Vice" and "Parasite": A Note on the Evolution of the Elizabethan Villain', *PMLA* 49:3 (September 1934), pp. 743–51.

Womack, Peter, *Ben Jonson* (Oxford: Blackwell, 1986).

Yeats, W. B., 'The Tragic Theatre', in *Essays and Introductions* (London: Macmillan, 1961), pp. 238–45.

Young Frankenstein, film, directed by Mel Brooks. USA: Gruskoff/Venture Films, 1974. DVD, USA: Twentieth Century Fox, 1998.

Zelig, film, directed by Woody Allen. USA: Orion Pictures, 1983. DVD, USA: MGM, 2006.

Žižek, Slavoj, *How to Read Lacan* (New York: W. W. Norton, 2007).

—, *The Sublime Object of Ideology* (London: Verso, 2008).

—, *Living in the End Times* (New York: Verso, 2010).

Zucker, Adam, 'The Social Logic of Ben Jonson's *Epicoene*', *Renaissance Drama* 33 (2004), pp. 37–62.

—, *The Places of Wit in Early Modern English Comedy* (Cambridge: Cambridge University Press, 2011).

Zupančič, Alenka, *The Odd One In: On Comedy* (Cambridge, MA: MIT Press, 2008).

Index

References to notes are indicated by n.